THE
BUILDINGS
OF
ARMAGH

Prepared by
Robert McKinstry
Richard Oram
Roger Weatherup
Primrose Wilson

Monuments & Buildings Record
Waterman House
5-33 Hill Street
Belfast BT1 2LA

Published by the Ulster Architectural Heritage Society
181a Stranmillis Road, Belfast BT9 5DU.

© Ulster Architectural Heritage Society
Published 1992
Typesetting and Printing - Nicholson & Bass Ltd.
ISBN 0 900 457 42 2

The Authors:
Robert McKinstry is an architect.
Richard Oram is an Investigator of Historic Buildings for D.O.E.(N.I).
Roger Weatherup is Curator of Armagh County Museum.
Primrose Wilson is Chairman of the Ulster Architectural Heritage Society.

Front Cover: *Engraving of the Archbishop's Palace from Stuart 1819.*

Back Cover: *Armagh Cathedral, Design for Mosaic Decoration.*
Elevation of one bay of aisle by G.C.Ashlin R.H.A. August 1901.

Title Page: *The Seal of the Borough of Armagh.*
This Seal was in use from c.1690 until 1840 when the Corporation was dissolved by an Act of Parliament. It is inscribed 'THE : SEAL : OF : THE : BURR : OF : ARMAGH'. Corporation records state that the earlier Seal, in use from 1613, was removed by the adherents of James II in 1688. This Seal was smaller than the example illustrated and bore the same device and wording; in addition it had a castle in the margin, the symbol of a fortified town.
The Seal in present use is inscribed 'THE SEAL OF THE CITY OF ARMAGH' and bears a larger harp. New armorial bearings were matriculated in 1958 and the present Seal incorporates them.
(Armagh County Museum 454-35)

THE
BUILDINGS
OF
ARMAGH

Monuments & Buildings Record
Waterman House
5-33 Hill Street
Belfast BT1 2LA

ULSTER ARCHITECTURAL HERITAGE SOCIETY

CONTENTS

ACKNOWLEDGEMENTS

The Ulster Architectural Heritage Society gratefully acknowledges the generous financial assistance towards the publication of this book of the following

ARMAGH DISTRICT COUNCIL
IAN DONALDSON
J.B.KINGSTON & PARTNERS
NORTHERN IRELAND TOURIST BOARD
TRUSTEE SAVINGS BANK
MR & MRS E.B.WILSON

The authors wish to convey particular thanks to John Butler, Hugh Dixon, Philip Doughty, the late Dr G.O.Simms and Damien Wood for contributing essays which give an additional dimension to the book. The authors are most grateful to Colin Hatrick who supplied the text on stained glass with the assistance of Jack Calderwood and Roger Weatherup. The authors acknowledge permission for the use of W.R. Rodger's poem, 'Armagh', to Lucy Rodgers Cohen. The Ordnance Survey map was reproduced with the sanction of the Controller of H.M. Stationery Office. Particular thanks go to Karen Latimer who proof read the text.

The authors acknowledge the help of the following in researching historical facts, providing information on buildings, or assisting in any other way:
The staff of Armagh County Museum and in particular Mrs E. Graham; the Chief Executive, Armagh District Council; the Deputy Keeper, Armagh Public Library; Dr J. Butler of the Armagh Observatory Library; R. Bell; C.W.L. Bennett; Rev. Fr.J. Clyne and Rev. Fr.R. Murray: I. Donaldson; F. Hamond; S. Hartley; the staff of the Irish Architectural Archive; the staff of the Linenhall Library; D. Mansbridge; H. Millar, Armagh Royal School; the Office of Public Works; Mrs A. Paisley; H.D.McC. Reid; R. Scott; the staff of the Headquarters Library of the Southern Education and Library Board; the Director of the Ulster Museum. Also all those citizens of Armagh who took so much interest in this survey and answered our enquiries so patiently.

We are grateful to have been allowed access to the interior of the following buildings:
St Patrick's Church of Ireland Cathedral; The Diocesan Hall; St Mark's Church; St Patrick's Roman Catholic Cathedral; St Malachy's Church; Abbey Street Methodist Church; First Armagh Presbyterian; The Mall Presbyterian; The Gospel Hall; Gough Barracks; The Gaol; The Palace and Chapel; The City Hospital; The former Unionist Club.

The text was typed by Primrose Wilson with assistance from Lydia and Demelza.

ARMAGH
W.R. Rodgers.

There is a through-otherness about Armagh
Of tower and steeple,
Up on the hill are the arguing graves of the kings,
And below are the people.

Through-other as the rooks that swoop and swop
Over the sober hill
Go the people gallivanting from shop to shop
Guffawing their fill.

And the little houses run through the market-town
Slap up against the great,
Like the farmers all clabber and muck walking arm by arm
With the men of estate.

Raised at a time when Reason was all the rage,
Of grey and equal stone,
This bland face of Armagh covers an age
Of clay and feather and bone.

Through-other is its history, of Celt and Dane,
Norman and Saxon,
Who ruled the place and sounded the gamut of fame
From cow-horn to klaxon.

There is a through-otherness about Armagh
Delightful to me,
Up on the hill are the graves of the garrulous kings
Who at last can agree.

EDITORIAL
Primrose Wilson

The Ulster Architectural Heritage Society exists to promote the appreciation and enjoyment of good architecture of all periods. In Armagh there is a great deal to be enjoyed and appreciated. The centre of the city has the greatest concentration of listed buildings anywhere in Ulster which means that Armagh has the highest survival rate of quality historic fabric in the Province. It is also worth noting that the most distinguished Irish architects have left their mark on Armagh. Gavin Stamp, the architectural historian, in an article entitled 'The Optimism of Armagh' in The Independent in August 1989 commented that Armagh 'remains one of the finest Georgian cities in Ireland'. He concluded the article by saying that 'Armagh is not just one of the best towns in Ulster, but potentially, one of the most interesting Georgian towns anywhere in the British Isles'.

The authors of this List take particular pleasure in visiting or working in Armagh. We welcome the increased appreciation of its architectural heritage, the enhancement schemes which are currently under way and the more enlightened attitudes of the roads engineers. It is to be hoped that the damage wrought to the city of Armagh by the roads programme in the Sixties will not be repeated. It is a matter of concern to us that sometimes re-generation can lead to a change in the character of the environment it seeks to enhance. Our anxiety that this should not happen to Armagh was the motivation for the compilation of this List.

Armagh has many advantages for those who attempt to record its buildings. It has a very positive compact shape, a visually distinctive character and a readily recognisable collection of buildings of different periods. In many towns and cities, though happily in only a few cases in Armagh, the advent of plastic windows and doors, the rendering of brickwork, the ribbon pointing of masonry and removal of chimneys and natural slate from roofs have despoiled good traditional buildings. Fashion plays its role in alterations too and the current trend of stripping and revealing stonework and joinery which was originally rendered is prevalent. Another is installing 'off the peg' doors with integral fanlights. Plastic windows and doors are inappropriate in older buildings and should never be used; neither should sash windows be replaced by those which are top hung. The removal of chimneys which are architectural features of a building alters its appearance and proportions. The impact on a street or terrace of such alterations is that it brings about a change of character; the neighbourhood is no longer an harmonious whole but a collection of individual buildings. In this List we have drawn particular attention to streets and buildings which have remained true to their traditional origins. We hope that by doing so the value of these original features to the architectural heritage of Armagh will be appreciated and their owners will endeavour to maintain their buildings with a minimum of alteration.

In this List the authors have attempted to record all buildings within their defined limits - the excellent, the good, the indifferent and the bad (we have adopted an A and B grading for the better buildings). The boundary of the survey embraces the conservation area and goes beyond it to include buildings of interest or importance to Armagh. We had great difficulty in establishing correct street numbers as these seem to change through time. In most cases we have used the O.S. data base map founded on survey material collected between 1961-4 with revisions up to 1976 and where building has taken place since then used the new street numbering.

Our survey records the situation up to July 1991 but, because a great deal of work is taking place at present, some changes will have occurred prior to publication. Therefore, this Armagh List, like a photograph of a moment in time, records one year out of a life span of some fifteen hundred years and more. It is also a token of our admiration for a splendid place.

THE CITY OF ARMAGH
D.R.M. Weatherup

Approach Armagh by any road and its architectural heritage is immediately apparent for the twin spires of one cathedral and the tree embowered tower of the other are to be seen silhouetted against the sky. As the city is entered the Royal School or the Observatory, the Palace Demesne or St. Malachy's Church, the windmill stump or the Callan Bridge testify to the accuracy of first impressions as do the Mall, the Market House, the City Hospital, the Public Library and the stone built houses of its streets.

Armagh has been a place of human habitation for over two thousand years having been founded, according to legend, by a pagan queen named Macha and from her the city takes its name. Its focus is the hill on which the Church of Ireland Cathedral stands where Macha, conscious of its steep sided security, built her palace which was then named Ard Mhacha or Macha's Height.

After about three hundred years the hill was abandoned in favour of the townland of Navan three miles to the west where a later Queen Macha constructed a new fortress called Emain Macha. For about six hundred years it was the centre of power in the region and the setting for the epic tales of the Ulster Cycle. These relate stories of mythical figures like Cuchullain and Deirdre of the Sorrows and kings and queens like Conor MacNessa and Maeve of Connaught.

In the fourth century the King of Ulster was defeated and driven with his followers from the area. The great fortress of Emain was destroyed and the victors returned to occupy the hill of Armagh. Thus it was to Armagh at the end of his mission to convert the Irish to Christianity that St.Patrick came in 444 A.D. A year later, having persuaded Daire the local chieftain to grant him the hilltop site, he built the first church there. Around it were founded other churches, colleges and schools as it developed into one of those great centres of religion and learning that gave Ireland the name of 'The Isle of Saints and Scholars' in the Europe of the Dark Ages.

In the ninth century the Vikings from Scandinavia came, at first to plunder but later to settle in the richer countries that lay to the south of their own harsh lands. Armagh was amongst the Irish monastic foundations which attracted the attention of these pirates. They frequently put the city to the sword, sacked the monasteries, stole the treasures of the churches and abbeys and slew or carried off into slavery both clergy and scholars. In 1014 Brian Boru, High King of

Ireland, broke the Vikings' power at the Battle of Clontarf. Brian Boru, his son and nephew were killed on the battlefield and their bodies brought to Armagh and buried on the north side of the Great Stone Church which the High King had visited ten years earlier.

After the defeat of the Norsemen there followed years of internecine warfare as the O'Neills established their dominance over the area. The invasion of Ulster by the Anglo-Normans brought further troubles to Armagh. John de Courcy burned the city on two occasions, as did his successor Hugh de Lacy. In the fourteenth century Armagh suffered in the campaign of Edward Bruce and in the Elizabethan wars it became a strategic position between the English strongholds of Dundalk and Newry and the Irish forces under the O'Neill chieftains in County Tyrone. At that period it was again as important a military fortress as it was a centre of religion.

The Reformation caused further dissension and the dissolution of the monasteries in 1537 led to the dispersal of the last of the learned monks from the city. The County was shired by the Lord Deputy, Sir John Perrott, in 1586 although the English hold on the Province of Ulster was very insecure. In 1598 the Irish won a major victory at the battle of the Yellow Ford on the River Callan close to Armagh when the English commander, Marshall Bagenal, was killed and his army routed. Three years later, using a new strategy, Lord Mountjoy, overthrew the O'Neills and following the Flight of the Earls in 1607, when Hugh O'Neill and Rory O'Donnell left for Europe, King James I commenced the Plantation of Ulster.

Under this scheme English and Scottish settlers were given grants of land on which to establish manors, construct fortified houses and settle loyal tenants. Undertakers, as these settlers were called, were issued with patents for markets and fairs which concentrated traders and craftsmen in selected market towns. Armagh received a charter in 1613, although as an archiepiscopal endowment there had been earlier patents. An entry in the church registers referred to a re-grant in 1467, and in 1558 there was an attestation of this patent. When in 1641 the Irish under Sir Phelim O'Neill attempted to regain their lost lands the war brought disaster to the planters. Most fled while many lands were despoiled and numbers killed but after the campaigns of the Cromwellian forces they returned to start again. It was not until the end of the century after the Williamite wars that a measure of peace came to the county.

The more settled conditions of the eighteenth and early nineteenth centuries enabled farming and thus trade and commerce to revive. It was during this period under the patronage of the Primates of the Established Church, notably Archbishops Robinson (1765-94) and Lord John George Beresford (1822-62), that the present architectural distinction of Armagh was achieved. Outstanding Irish architects like Thomas Cooley, Francis Johnston, George Ensor and William Murray employed their talents in the city. For example in Primate Robinson's time there were built the Palace, Prison, Observatory, Royal School and Public Library.

To many of these structures Lord John George Beresford made additions, notably to the Palace, the Library and the Royal School. It was under this Primate that the Church of Ireland Cathedral was extensively restored between 1834 and 1839 when the medieval church, built by Archbishop O'Scannail in 1268, was largely refashioned. The foundation stone of the Catholic Cathedral was laid by the Most Rev. Dr. Crolly in 1840 but the potato famine delayed the work and it was not dedicated until 1873. The break in the work and the death of the original architect, T.J.Duff, led to the appointment of J.J.McCarthy who revised the design. The projected great central tower was omitted and the two at the western end were given their distinctive tall spires.

Great hardship was caused by the famine although Armagh, like other linen producing counties, did not suffer so severely. However, by the end of the century changing conditions had led to a diminution in Armagh's eminence. The coming of the railway in 1848, the transfer of Major General Sir Thomas Pearson and the District Staff to new army headquarters in Belfast eight years earlier and the foundation of the Queen's College in that town in 1845 contributed to a decline in Armagh's social importance. Furthermore the Act of Disestablishment of 1869 reduced the wealth and influence of the Church of Ireland Archbishops who had, for over a hundred years, advanced the city's architectural quality.

The patrons were now to be the wealthy merchants and commercial companies employing a new generation of architects such as W.J. Barre, Charles Lanyon and J.J.Phillips. The railway enabled manufacturers to import coal and raw materials in bulk and thus build large mills and factories to the detriment of local small industries. Merchants could bring in mass produced cheap goods but the railway also facilitated the introduction of new and better building materials and furnishings. So as well as a legacy of rows of mill workers' houses (now mostly gone) there are still many fine suburban brick terraces and villas erected for the more prosperous citizens. The comparatively small scale of nineteenth century industrialisation and the town's expansion into the surrounding fields meant that many of the earlier buildings were not pulled down.

In the present century Armagh remains a county and assizes town and is still Ireland's primatial city. It also functions as a commercial, administrative, market and minor industrial centre. It still retains some of the grace and distinction of its great past although much has been lost. Housing estates now sprawl over the drumlins around it and many of the characteristic stone buildings have been allowed to deteriorate. Many have been demolished and rebuilt to the drab and soulless designs, and in the colourless materials, of the nineteen sixties and seventies. Yet there is now a growing awareness in the city of the value of its unique architectural heritage. This is demonstrated by, for example, the new houses on Barrack Hill and in Castle Street and the refurbishment of properties in Scotch Street and on the Mall. With Armagh District Council, the Armagh Regeneration Trust and various divisions of the Department of the Environment and other government agencies collaborating with local architects and property owners it is to be hoped that future developments will continue to be sympathetic, with retention and restoration the order of the day.

SOURCES OF INFORMATION

Armagh Cathedral Guide, Derby, 1991.

Armagh Civic Week Guide, Armagh 1968.

Ashe, T. A View of the Archbishopric of Armagh,1703.

Bassett, G.H. The Book of County Armagh, Dublin, Sealy, Bryers and Walker, 1888.

Bell, G.P., Cairns W.J. Armagh Central Area Study, D.O.E(NI), 1976.

Bieler, L. The Patrician Texts in the Book of Armagh, Dublin, Dublin Institute of Advanced Studies , 1979.

Brett, C.E.B. Court Houses and Market Houses of the Province of Ulster, Belfast, UAHS, 1973.

Clarkson, L.A. and E.M. Crawford. Ways to Wealth, The Cust Family of eighteenth century Armagh, Belfast, Ulster Society for Irish Historical Studies, 1985.

Coleman, Reverend A. Historical Memoirs of the City of Armagh, New Edition, Dublin, Browne and Nolan, 1900.

Coote, Sir Charles, Statistical Survey of the County of Armagh, Dublin, Graisberry and Campbell, 1804.

Craig, M. The Architecture of Ireland from the earliest times to 1880, London, Batsford, 1982.

Cruickshank, D. A Guide to the Georgian Buildings of Britain and Ireland, London, Weidenfeld & Nicolson, 1985.

Curl, J.S. Classical Churches in Ulster, Belfast, UAHS, 1980.

Davidson, J. Notes Historical and Topographical on St. Patrick's Cathedral.

Dixon, H. (1) An Introduction to Ulster Architecture, Belfast, UAHS, 1975.

Dixon, H. (2) Ulster Architecture 1800-1900, Belfast, UAHS, 1972.

Dixon, H. (3) manuscript notes for D.O.E./H.M.B.B. Archaeological Survey (unpublished)

Gallogly, Reverend J. The History of St. Patrick's Cathedral Armagh, Dublin, Gill, 1880.

Gazeteer of Irish Stained Glass, Dublin, 1988.

Gould, M.H. The Workhouses of Ulster, Belfast, UAHS, 1983.

Griffith's Valuation Books 1834, 1839, 1864.

Hall, S.C. Ireland - its Scenery and Character, Vol.2. (London, How and Parsons)1842

Hamlin, A. (Ed) Historic Monuments of Northern Ireland, Belfast, HMSO, 1983.

Hicks, J.F. A History of the Cathedral.

History of Armagh Girls' High School

Leslie, J.B. Armagh Clergy and Parishes, Dundalk, Tempest, 1911.

Lewis, S.L. A Topographical Dictionary of Ireland, Second Edition, 1847.

Lindsay, E.M. The Story of the Armagh Planetarium. c.1965-7.

Lock, M. The City of Armagh, a list of buildings of architectural and historic importance, 1964.

Lockington, J.W. A History of the Mall Presbyterian Church, Armagh 1837-1987, Belfast, 1987.

Lundie, G.T. First Armagh Presbyterian Church Tercentenary 1673-1973, Armagh, Trimble, 1973.

Lynn, J.M. A Short History of Wesleyan Methodism on the Armagh Circuit, Belfast, 1887.

Malins, E., The Knight of Glin. Lost Demesnes: Irish Landscape Gardening, 1660-1845, London, Barrie and Jenkins, 1976.

Maps -

- Bartlett's 1601.

- Griffith's Valuation Map of Armagh 1839.

- Livingston, Robert. for the Lord Primate 1766; copied by Noble, J.T. 1855. (Armagh County Museum No.167-62)

- O'Hagan, J. Map of Armagh 1851 (Armagh County Museum No.46-36)

- O.S. 1835 and 1864.

- Noble,J.T. for Lee McKinstry, 1831.(Armagh County Museum no.93/84)

- Rocque, J. A Topographical Map of County Armagh, 1760.

McCourt, E. The Poor Law and the Workhouse, Armagh, Dungannon Multi-purpose Centre, 1981.

McCutcheon, W.A. The Industrial Archeology of Northern Ireland, Belfast, HMSO, 1980.

Moore, P. Armagh Observatory 1790-1967, Armagh, Armagh Observatory, 1967.

Myles, J. The Church Furnishings of L.N.Cottingham 1787-1847, Victorian Society Annual 1990 pp.23-41.

o Fiaich, T. St. Patrick's Cathedral Armagh. (The Irish Heritage Series: 58), Dublin, Easons, 1987.

O'Muiri, R. St.Malachy's Church, Armagh, Golden Jubilee, 1938-88, 1988.

de Paor, Maire and Liam, Early Christian Ireland, London, Thames and Hudson, 1958.

Paterson, T.G.F.(A) Armachiana Vols. 1-18 and 20-25.

Paterson, T.G.F.(B) The Bulletin of the Ulster Place-Name Society, Vol.1 part 3.

Paterson, T.G.F. (HH) Harvest Home, Armagh, 1975.

Patton, M. Historic Buildings, Groups of Buildings, Areas of Architectural Importance in Bangor and Groomsport, UAHS, 1964.

Pierce, R. Coey, A. Oram, R., Taken for Granted, Belfast, RSUA/HBC, 1984.

Potterton, H. Irish Church Monuments 1570-1880, Belfast, UAHS, 1975.

Public Works, The Architecture of the Office of Public Works 1831-1987.

Reeves, Wm. The Ancient Churches of Armagh, Dublin, Lusk, 1860.

Reeves, Wm. The Primacy of Ireland, Armagh 1886.

Rogers, E. (1) Memoir of Armagh Cathedral with an account of the Ancient City, Belfast, Baird, 1876.

Rogers,E.(2) Record of the City of Armagh, Armagh, Armagh Guardian, Ryan D'Arcy, M., The Saints of Ireland, Dublin, 1974.

Sheehy, J.J.J.McCarthy and the Gothic Revival in Ireland, Belfast, UAHS, Sotheby's Sale Catalogue, 23-24 Sept. 1987.

Stalley, R.(Ed) Daniel Grose (c.1766-1838) The Antiquities of Ireland.
A Supplement to Francis Grose, Dublin, Irish Architectural Archive, 1991.
Stuart, J. Historical Memoirs of the City of Armagh, Newry, 1819.
Taylor and Skinner, Maps of the Roads of Ireland, London and Dublin, 1778.
Trimble, C.D. The City of Armagh, 1964.
Weatherup, D.R.M. (1) Armagh Historic Photographs of the Primatial City, Belfast, The Friar's Bush Press, 1990.
Weatherup, D.R.M.(2) A Short Historical Guide to St. Patrick's Cathedral.
Young, A., A Tour in Ireland, 1776, 1777 and 1778, reprint Cambridge, 1925.

ARCHIVES CONSULTED
Armagh County Museum
Armagh Public Library
H.M.B.B.
Irish Architectural Archive
Irish Military Archives
Office of Public Works
Police Authority Archives
R.U.C. Museum
St. Patrick's Roman Catholic Cathedral

NEWPAPERS AND JOURNALS
Armagh Guardian
Belfast Telegraph
Church of Ireland Gazette
Irish Builder (I.B.)
Irish Times
Journal of Irish Archaeology (J.I.A.)
Seanchas Ardmaca (S.A.)
Specify
Ulster Architect
Ulster Gazette
Ulster Journal of Archaeology (U.J.A.)

Journal of Irish Archaeology
-Lynn, C. Methodist Old Meeting House, Abbey Street. Early Christian and Medieval Occupation. Excavations at No.16 Scotch Street and No.39 Scotch Street. Vol 4 1987-88 pp. 68-9.

Seanchas Ard Mhacha, Journal of the Armagh Diocesan Historical Society
- Duffy, S.S. Armagh Mechanics' Institute 1825-31, Vol.13. No.1 1988. pp.122-172.
- Glancy, M. The incidence of the Plantation on the City ofArmagh, Vol.1.No.2. 1955. pp.115-160.
- Glancy, M. The Primates and the Church Lands of Armagh,Vol.5. 1970. pp.370-396.

- Kilroy, P. The Society of the Sacred Heart in Armagh 1851-59.Vol.9. No.2. 1979. pp.350-361.
- Mohan, C. Archbishop Richardson Robinson, Vol.6. No.1. 1971. pp.94-130.
- Paterson, T.G.F. Old St. Malachy's. Vol.1. No.2. 1955 pp.169-191.
- Williamson, A.P. Armagh District Lunatic Asylum, Vol.8. No.1975. pp.111-120.

Ulster Journal of Archaeology - Third Series -
- Brown, C.J. Harper, A.E. Account of Excavations on the Cathedral Hill in 1968, Vol.47. 1984. pp.109-161.
- Lynn, C. Account of Excavations at the Friary, Vol.38. 1975.pp.61-80.
- Lynn, C. Excavations at Nos.46-48 Scotch Street, Armagh. 1979-80. Vol.51. 1988. pp.69-84.

ILLUSTRATIONS

The authors are grateful to the Armagh County Museum for permission to use the photograph of a watercolour of the Court House and photographs of Armagh Gas Works, Macan Asylum for the Blind, Vicar's Hill, The Royal Hotel, Dobbin Street, Charlemont Place stable block, Armagh Railway Station, St Mark's Rectory in Cathedral Close, Woodford Terrace Newry Road, Drelincourt School, Hartford Place and The Manager's House, Belfast Bank. Dr Maurice Craig kindly permitted the use of his photographs of Barrack Street, Castle Street, The Butter and Egg Market from Dobbin Street, Upper Irish Street and The Shambles Grain Market and Mr P.J.Hamill that of St. Malachy's Church. The Department of the Environment (N.I.) agreed to the reproduction of a photograph of the Savings Bank and Barrack Hill. The Irish Architectural Archive granted permission to reproduce photographs of the interior of St Patrick's Cathedral (R.C.), the proposed tower for St. Patrick's (C.of I.), elevations of Armagh Gaol, Ground Plan of Armagh Lunatic Asylum, The Court House, Bank of Ireland Scotch Street and the inner porch door of the Archbishop's Palace. The National Library of Ireland graciously gave permission to use photographs from the Lawrence Collection of The Pavilion, Beresford Arms Hotel, English Street c.1895 and the interior of St Patrick's Cathedral (C.of I.). The Public Record Office of Northern Ireland agreed to the use from the Allison Collection of a ground plan of St Malachy's Church and a photograph of Market Street.
All other reproductions were taken by M.Campbell of the Mall Studio, Armagh in 1991/2.

ARMAGH'S OLD CATHEDRAL

Dr G.O.Simms.
Archbishop of Armagh and Primate of All Ireland 1969-80.

'Cathedrals are great: they speak of the Infinite.
They are lovely: they speak of the source of all beauty.
They are historic: they speak of the Eternal.'
(Gilbert Thurlow, Cathedrals at work, 1968)

If the old site on the hill of Armagh could tell its story, what tales of destruction, pillaging and many burnings would we hear. Above the noise of battles, however, a brave spirit of courage and conviction can be traced through many centuries. The present building, crowning the height of Queen Macha (Ard-Macha), symbolises a stalwart continuity of faith and witness, battered but unbowed, from the first days of worship and learning inspired by St. Patrick's leadership and sustained by a glorious tradition of early Irish Christianity.

This site for a Christian sanctuary presented by the local chieftain Daire for the building of 'a great stone church (Daimh-liag, Duleek)' laid the foundations of a greater tradition. The opening quotation puts this local story in a wide perspective.

In the history of the cathedral, from fifth century beginnings, many developments in church architecture and in the building of libraries and schools took place. The archaeologists at work today, together with the annalists of a thousand years ago, have helped us to trace the long story from the mists of history until these later times of well documented records. Three names of note are gratefully remembered by all who love the ancient cathedral. Many others could be included among the benefactors of a building in constant need of restoration and repair, yet the thirteenth century Archbishop O Scannail, Primate Richard Robinson in the eighteenth century, and Lord John George Beresford, for forty years archbishop in the nineteenth century, undertook restorations of special significance to ensure that the continuing life of worship and witness should be ordered with reverance and dignity.

Moelpatrick O Scannail was a Dominican friar and Bishop of Raphoe who was postulated Archbishop of Armagh in February 1261 and the appointment was ratified by Pope Urban IV in November. (It is said that it was Urban IV who ordered a bull confirming the dignity of the Primacy of All Ireland to the See of Armagh in 1263). On coming from Raphoe the archbishop faced a formidable task for there had been

1

extensive destruction of churches in 1189 and apparently the Daimh-liag 'the great stone church' had suffered sorely. At an earlier date, the annals have this entry: 'on the fifth of the Ides of January 1125, which fell on Friday, the roof was raised on the great Daimh-liag of Ard-Macha, after having been fully covered with shingles by Celsus, successor to Patrick, one hundred and twenty years since it had a complete roof'. Repair work never lasted very long in those days.

With the O Scannail restoration, the cathedral was given the shape of the early English style of cathedral which is still the plan and outline of the present-day structure. Enlarging the simpler design of the old stone church, its nave connected with choir and sanctuary by the familiar and traditional semi-circular arch, O Scannail added aisles, transepts and the under croft or crypt. In fact, with the enlarging of the cathedral there was a comprehensive rebuilding programme which continued over a considerable period after O Scannail's death in 1270. To him we are indebted for a building which sits firmly on its site, centrally placed in the city of seven hills. Stephen Gwynn, including Armagh in his book 'The Fair Hills of Ireland', calls the cathedral hill, Armagh's Janiculum, so well placed is this height for the surrounding view of spires, domes, turrets and the distant obelisk on Knox's Hill. The O Scannail design brought a sense of solidity in turbulent days. The tower, with its modest height and calm serenity, exudes a sense of enduring strength and peace.

In the later days of the eighteenth century, Richard Robinson, during a remarkable primacy of building and restoring, included the cathedral in his vast programme of adorning Armagh with dignified and serviceable public buildings. Robinson, who succeeded his brother William in the baronetcy in 1785 and had himself become Baron Rokeby of Armagh in 1777, was the sixth son of William and Anne Robinson of Rokeby in Yorkshire and Merton Abbey in Surrey. He was educated at Westminster School and matriculated at Christ Church, Oxford, in 1726 at the age of seventeen. Graduating B.A. in 1730 and M.A. in 1733 he then became chaplain to the Archbishop of York and in 1738 rector of Elton in the East Riding and a Prebendary of York, moving to Hutton as rector in 1742. In 1751 he accompanied the Duke of Dorset, the newly re-appointed Lord Lieutenant, to Ireland as one of his chaplains, and later that year was consecrated Bishop of Killala before moving in 1759 to Ferns and Leighlin and in 1761 was translated to Kildare. In 1765 he was appointed Archbishop of Armagh and Primate of All Ireland.

The Archbishop, like his brother Sir Thomas Robinson, had a flair for impressive landscaping and architectural design. Sir Thomas name is associated with Castle Howard and Sir John Vanbrugh in Yorkshire, while Primate Robinson employed the distinguished Thomas Cooley for the restoring and improving of the Armagh cathedral. Cooley's pupil, Armagh's own architect, Francis Johnston, continued the work, which had encountered considerable difficulties. In a letter dated January 2nd 1823, Francis Johnston looks back on the problem which caused Primate Robinson much trouble. Johnston wrote 'Having spent I may say some years in and out of the old Fabrick, I am almost acquainted with every stone of it, and am very sorry to add that it is a dangerous subject to attempt any considerable improvement upon. The Lord Primate Robinson fitted up the west aisle for the morning service about fifty years ago and made other repairs and improvements to the Church and no alteration, no, not even a brush of paint has, I believe, been used (at least in the west aisle) since that time, even the hangings of the Throne were the same when I saw it about three years ago. A very superb steeple was designed by Mr Cooley from that of Magdalen College, Oxford, and was carried up under by superintendence about seventy feet above the roof of the Church, when the piers and arches supporting it were perceived to be giving way and the Primate immediately ordered it to be taken down. His Grace's intention at that time was to have had the tower and steeple erected at the west end of the Church, but Mr Cooley's death and other circumstances occurred to prevent H.Grace's intention being carried out.' This was in the year 1783.

Reading between the lines of this revealing letter, written by an architect of such great repute as Francis Johnston, it is no surprise to find that Primate Lord John George Beresford was determined to undertake a restoration of even greater thoroughness. Born in Tyrone House, Dublin, in November 1773, Lord John George Beresford was the third son of the first Marquis of Waterford and was educated at Eton and Oxford, gaining a Doctorate in Divinity in 1805 and in the same year was raised to the Episcopate as Bishop of Cork and Ross. He became Archbishop of Dublin in 1820 by way of Raphoe and Clogher and two years later was translated to Armagh. In 1834 Beresford began the work, engaging the services of the architect L.Cottingham who had been responsible for strengthening and rebuilding the piers which supported Hereford cathedral's tower.

The spire of Armagh, the shape of which can be seen in the 1661 seal of the Dean and Chapter, was removed. Nearly all the traces of antiquity have been obliterated in the course of this reconstruction. Vast sums of money were needed for Cottingham's plans. Primate Beresford gave all but the subscribers' ten thousand pounds to foot the formidable bill of thirty four thousand for the completed work. He also presented a fine Walker organ to replace the instrument which Primate Robinson had given. Beresford's munificence was proverbial, although there was sadness for the lovers of the old architecture when the beautiful west doorway with its richly moulded and cusped arch, its canopied niches and pinnacles could not be preserved.

ARCHBISHOPS INVOLVED IN BUILDING WORKS ON ST PATRICK'S ROMAN CATHOLIC CATHEDRAL

Damian Wood
Vice-Principal St. Patrick's College

With the advent of Catholic Emancipation in 1829, the Roman Catholic Archbishops, after an absence of centuries, resumed residence in Armagh. It was Archbishop Crolly who set about the construction of St Patrick's Roman Catholic Cathedral. Dr William Crolly was Bishop of Down and Conor from 1825-35; during his episcopacy he had churches built in many parishes and was also responsible for the building of St Malachy's Seminary. He was transferred to the primatial See in 1835 and took up residence in Armagh. Dr Crolly's first task was to build a seminary for the education of ecclesiastical students, a task successfully accomplished with the opening of St Patrick's Seminary in 1838.

Primate Crolly had also determined to give Armagh a cathedral and on 17th March 1840 the foundation stone was laid on a site adjacent to the seminary. The plan of the building by the Newry architect Thomas J.Duff was for a cruciform perpendicular Gothic Church with a large square central tower and two smaller ones on the south front flanking the great doorway. The Cathedral was to be built of Armagh limestone and Dungannon freestone was to be used internally for the arches and pillars.

By 1847 the Great Famine was at its height and Cathedral funds were diverted to the work of relief, causing the building work to halt, with the walls built to a height of 34 feet. In 1849 Primate Crolly died of cholera and was buried under the sanctuary of the unfinished Cathedral.

In 1852 Dr Joseph Dixon succeeded Dr Cullen as Archbishop of Armagh and work was resumed on the Cathedral in 1854. By then the original architect had died and his chosen successor was J.J.McCarthy who was destined to become the most famous of Irish Gothic Revival architects of the nineteenth century. McCarthy favoured a style in French Gothic. The three-towers were abandoned for two slender spires of 210 feet each surmounted by massive 10 feet crosses. The unusual thickness of the pillars supporting the arches over the sanctuary are a relic of the old plan.

In 1865 Dr Dixon organised the Great Bazaar for the 'National Cathedral' the proceeds of which realised in excess of £7,000. He died in 1866 with the building still incomplete. It was the appointment of Dr Daniel McGettigan as Primate in 1870 which gave the final impetus to the building work. On 24th August 1873 the ceremony of solemn dedication, attended by some 20,000 people, took place. McGettigan's finished building has an external roof height of 100 feet, is 212 feet in length and is 120 feet broad across the transepts. The principal entrance is on the southern side, approached by the seven-terraced flight of steps leading from the Cathedral gates to the piazza. The large central doorway is flanked by two smaller doorways. There are also auxiliary doorways in the transepts.

In the years following the ceremony Dr McGettigan continued to make additions. The Telford organ was dedicated in 1875 and a stained glass window was erected in the Cathedral in memorial to Dr Crolly and Dr Dixon. Also completed were the Archbishop's house in 1876-7, the sexton's lodge in 1884-6, to a classic design by Hague, and in 1886 the sacristan's lodge. Primate McGettigan died on 3rd December 1887 and was buried in the new Catholic Cemetery in Armagh.

When Dr Michael Logue came to the See of Armagh in 1887 the exterior work had been completed but the interior was poor and bare. Dr Logue was responsible for the splendid interior decoration of the Cathedral and, with the exceptions of the Stations of the Cross and some features in the Lady Chapel, everything in the way of ornament in the inside dates from his primacy. The work of interior decoration was carried out mainly between 1900 and 1904, to the designs of Ashlin and Coleman. Dr Logue was also responsible for the purchase of the site on which the Cathedral stands and for the erection of the Sacristy, Synod Hall and Muniment Room for the preservation of documents of the diocese. These are housed in the two-storied block to the north of the main building and joined to the Cathedral by a semi-circular covered cloister. In 1900 Dr Logue organised the National Cathedral Bazaar which realised a sum of £30,000. On 24th July the Cathedral was consecrated. Cardinal Logue died in 1924 and was interred in the Catholic cemetery in the central burial plot reserved for the Primates of Armagh.

Dr Tomas O'Fiach, who succeeded Dr Conway in 1977, was the first Armagh man to hold the primacy since St Malachy in 1139. He was responsible for the redesigning of the sanctuary area of the Cathedral as a result of the Second Vatican Council's decree on Sacred Liturgy in the 1960s. In order to afford the congregation greater visibility the sanctuary area was raised, enlarged and opened to designs by Liam McCormick. This involved the removal of the 1904 marble screens, the magnificent Gothic high altar, the altars in the Chapels of Our Lady, St

The Sanctuary of the Catholic Cathedral of St. Patrick before the reconstruction of 1982. This illustration shows the magnificent marble screens, pulpit, high altar and communion rails all removed at that time. (Irish Architectural Archive).

Joseph and St Brigid and the pulpit. On 13th June 1982 the new sanctuary containing relics of St Malachy and St Oliver Plunkett in the altar was dedicated. Cardinal O'Fiach died while on pilgrimage to Lourdes on 8th May 1990. On 17th March he had presided over the celebrations for the 150th anniversary of the foundation of the Cathedral.

(Coleman.
Gallogly.
Hicks.
O.Fiaich.
Sotheby's sale catalogue 23/24 September 1987)

ARCHITECTS IN ARMAGH BEFORE 1900

Hugh Dixon
An Historic Buildings Adviser to the National Trust

After most of the medieval glories of the city had been smashed before or during the O'Neill wars, Armagh was hardly architectural at all until the later eighteenth century. Few references to the designing of buildings occur. Successive Primates attempted to patch up the Cathedral, but only occasionally do the names of their architectural advisors occur. The most distinguished of these was Sir Thomas Robinson, Surveyor of the Royal Works, who was brought in by Primate Bramhall in 1662 to advise on the stability of the Cathedral, but it is not clear how much work was actually done. More obviously, architectural activity occurred under Primate Boulter, whose works included the first four houses of Vicar's Hill facing the west front of the Cathedral in the 1720s. The designer's name is not known but the terrace is so self-consciously and neatly detailed that it is more comfortable to believe that the builder was using at least a sketch from an architectural office where the principles of Palladianism were understood. The obvious candidates in Ireland at this stage are either Sir Edward Lovett Pearce or his assistant and successor as the principal Irish architect of his generation, Richard Castle.

While the addition of these houses to the oeuvre of either would do nothing to enhance their reputations, the terrace has some importance in being a very early example of the grouping of street houses into a single, formal composition. As with so many aspects of the development of Armagh, it is the arrival of Richard Robinson in 1760 which marks a change. As well as enjoying good architecture in itself, Robinson understood its social and political importance, just as he understood what a boost it would be if the Primate established a proper seat at Armagh rather than using a patched-up town house on very occasional visits. Robinson patronised several architects and set an example for others to do the same.

John Carr from Robinson's family county of Yorkshire provided the designs for an obelisk in the Archbishop's demesne. But it is doubtful whether he supervised the construction and, as the project was financed by Robinson's friend, the Duke of Northumberland, Robinson may not have commissioned Carr. His early, and most productive association, was with Thomas Cooley (1740-84) a young English architect who had risen to prominence in Dublin. His designs for Robinson brought an unexampled classical sophistication to Armagh. Happily some of his exquisite drawings are preserved in a building which owes its origin to one of them. This is Robinson's library, set close by Vicar's Hill at the top of Abbey Street, as part of a small classical campus through which visitors pass on their way to the Cathedral. The library, originally a neat cube, was extended and refaced in the 1840s by Mr. Monserrat, of whom nothing else is known.

On a grander scale, Cooley designed the great classical barrack-like block to the south of Gaol Square, a commission which though obviously not directly from Robinson was almost certainly influenced by him.

Decidedly closer to Robinson's interest was the building of the Royal School. Here Cooley set aside his pure classicism in favour of battlemented blocks around a quadrangle. This provides a curious foretaste of the early Victorian liking for adapting appropriate historic styles to modern usage. Even so, Cooley's school can barely be described as Tudor Revival; the regimented organisation of the elevation and the rigid symmetry of the whole composition place the building firmly within the classical tradition. Cooley's early death, one of the minor calamities of Irish architectural history, might have been more regretted had it not brought into prominence a young Armagh man who was to become the greatest Irish architect of his generation.

Francis Johnston (1760-1829) having been partly trained with Robinson's encouragement in Cooley's Dublin office, succeeded as Robinson's principal designer in Armagh. So closely has Johnston been associated with the development of Armagh, that there has been a tendency to ascribe too many buildings to him. Nevertheless, he was responsible for several of the city's major buildings, and the examples he set proved to be an example and an inspiration to others. For Robinson, Johnston completed those works which Cooley had left unfinished. He tried to patch up the Cathedral and even added a spire, but this very soon had to be removed because its weight started crushing the ancient fabric of the tower below.

More successfully, he completed the Archbishop's Palace and its exquisite classical chapel. He also designed the Observatory to fulfil another of Robinson's enthusiasms. What Johnston achieved under Robinson's patronage, he was able to consolidate through his own official advancement. In 1805, he was appointed Architect to the Board of Works, with responsibilities for a wide range of public buildings. His office would have been responsible for works at Armagh Gaol and possibly at the Market House which was financed by Robinson's successor, Primate Stuart. Johnston himself took the responsibility for designing the Court House. This fine architectural set piece, set a seal of classical authority on the Mall which was to last half a century. Until the 1860s, all the buildings round the Mall displayed a neat classicism, entirely untouched by the seductive opportunities of the Early Victorian fancy dress party.

This continuing tradition of Armagh limestone, cut with archaeological attention to pattern book studies of antiquity, though obviously derived from the example of Cooley and Johnston, no doubt owes as much to families of largely unidentified local masons. Not only in the city, but also in the surrounding market towns and villages, is this apparent and its vigour is one of the hallmarks of the county's historical building stock.

Johnston's nephew and assistant, William Murray, eventually succeeded him as architect to the Board of Works. Their combined signatures appear on the designs for Armagh Lunatic Asylum just before Johnston's death in 1829. The Asylum, now St Luke's Hospital, though in a more remote situation, continued the classical tradition. More centrally placed was Murray's Charlemont Place, of the 1830s and sufficiently important in Murray's eyes to have the designs exhibited at the Royal Highbernian Academy. By this time he had been replaced at the Office of Public Works by Jacob Owen who brought a new professionalism to the practice of architecture in Ireland and in particular to public works through the offices of the County Surveyors. The Surveyor for Armagh, Henry Lindsay, was more of an engineer than an architect and his influence on local building styles seems to have been minimal.

As with most county towns, the major building of the mid-nineteenth century derived chiefly from national institutions rather than from local enterprise. George Wilkinson, architect to the Poor Law Commissioners, produced one of his neat stripped-Tudor workhouses for Tower Hill. For the Belfast Bank, Charles Lanyon produced one of his best Mannerist-revival essays, and his firm was later responsible for the rather more florid stucco Italianate house for the Northern Bank. Occasionally an official architect would produce a design for a local patron, as with William Farrell, area architect to the Ecclesiastical Commissioners, who seems to have had a hand in the neat classicism of the Macan Blind Asylum (now demolished).

Apart from their involvement in the design of the churches, of which more presently, Ulster's main High Victorian architects are barely represented. The very conservative First Presbyterian Church Lecture

Hall, near the foot of College Street, is most interesting as an early work by W.J.Barre.

There is little hint in its unadorned facade which would suggest that within a few years this architect would be designing the Ulster Hall, the Provincial Bank and the Albert Memorial Clock, all in Belfast. Of Charles Lanyon's younger partners, W.H.Lynn and John Lanyon, both distinguished individual practitioners elsewhere, there is at Armagh only the comfortable planning and eclectic historicism of the Charles Shiel's Institute. Curiously, there was a late polychrome flourish and by a local man. This was John Henry Fullerton, whose houses at Umgola and on the Portadown Road stand out immediately from the general mood of Armagh limestone or dull red brick.

It is with its nineteenth century churches, however, that Armagh excels. In a broad progress from archaeological classicism to the triumphant uplands of the Gothic Revival, Armagh may be regarded as typical; in quality it is outstanding. Pure classicism is minimal. The anonymous Mall Presbyterian Church of 1837 is good enough to be the work of either Thomas Duff or William Smyth.

Much later and less distinguished is the Methodist Church in Abbey Street where James Phillips, normally a Goth, tried to be sympathetic with classical neighbours. Classical in feeling though not in garb, are the early parts of St. Mark's C. of I. Church to the east of the Mall. Indeed, this church is in itself a concise statement of the progress of the Gothic Revival. The centrally placed tower and one western bay are all that remain of Francis Johnston's toy Gothick Church of 1811. William Farrell's nave of the 1830s is more spikey and exciting but still not based on the medieval originals. The chancel and eastern parts by contrast definitely are, as might be expected, from the major partnership of English Gothic Revivalists, William Slater and Richard Herbert Carpenter. Similar, though earlier progress, can be seen at the two cathedrals both, of course, dedicated to St. Patrick. The old cathedral (Church of Ireland) was given a thorough overhaul under Primate J.G.Beresford by another English architect, L.N.Cottingham. His work in the 1830s is not without archaeological observation, but its main importance was to give stability, even though this meant the replacement or masking of much historic fabric. In the light of later and more sophisticated revival work, it is easy to criticise Cottingham, but it is not fair to bracket him with the destroyers of the eighteenth century. On the contrary, his late Georgian work is satisfying, undemonstrative and now of a rarity which deserves the kind of

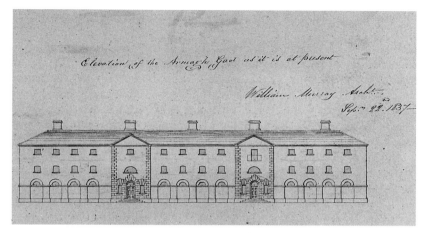

An elevation of ARMAGH GOAL as surveyed by William Murray on 22nd September, 1837. (Irish Architectural Archive).

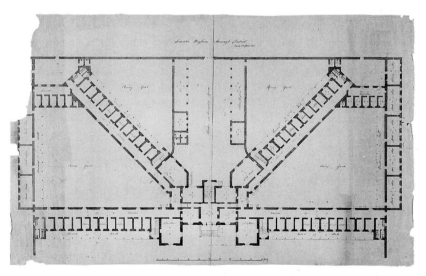

Ground plan of ARMAGH LUNATIC ASYLUM by Francis Johnston dated 1825. (Irish Architectural Archive).

respect it received from Sir Thomas Drew, who was called in at the end of the century to repair the piers supporting the central tower. His work, which gave cathedral scale to the crossing arches in the chancel, is a sanction rather than a rebuke to Cottingham's nave.

Significantly more dramatic was the erection of a Catholic Cathedral from 1840. This began in the capable hands of Thomas Duff, who designed a great church in Collegiate Perpendicular with a single central style, somewhat like the old cathedral. Work halted during the Great Famine when the nave walls had reached eaves level. Duff died in 1848 and his successor as architect from 1854 was James Joseph McCarthy, 'The Irish Pugin', whose revivalism was altogether more abrasively serious. Abandoning Duff's central tower, he confronted Armagh instead with a twin-towered-and-spired western front in the most approved 'Middle Pointed' style. Structural work was largely complete by 1873, but towards the end of the century there was a major programme of embellishment with mosaic and painting and sculpture, resulting in one of the great monuments of Ireland's Gothic Revival.

Such was the impact of all this medieval revival work, that everybody wanted to join in. Happenings on the west side of the Mall were particularly remarkable with the arrival of Young and Mackenzie's First Presbyterian Church, fully Gothic, and its even more strident neighbour, J.H. Fullerton's Masonic Hall at the foot of Jenny's Row. Not for another century was the classicism of Armagh to be so thoroughly shaken to its roots.

'FIFTY YEARS AGO'

The Market House - now the Technical School

Henry McAvinchey

(This is the text of a talk given to the Local Study Group of the Armagh Diocesan
Historical Society by Mr McAvinchey in 1956)

The Market House situated in Market Street in front of the old Cathedral, was erected by Archbishop Stuart in the year 1815. It was a two-storied building, built of dressed limestone in large ashlar blocks, each stone having a 1" chisel draft around it, the rest is finished in what is known in the building trade as sparrow picked, that is, it is finished with a punch, dressed with a wooden mallet.

There is some fine stone work in the bottom storey, and it was finished with a grand ornamental cornice dressed in local limestone with stone balustrades and coping. It was surmounted on the front with a clock which struck the hours. The bottom storey was used for the buying and selling of corn, grain and potatoes and was fitted with several large scales for weighing these goods, and had some space for short time storage.

The upper storey was used for public meetings, lectures, concerts, etc. and it was in common use as a good dancing hall, as it had a good pitch pine floor. This was supported on several pitch pine beams, about 18" x 18" and gave a great spring to the floor. It was used on several occasions to hold political meetings and at election times as a polling booth. At the back were several small buildings like stalls, in which different goods were sold on market days.

I remember my grandmother telling me that workmen used to assemble here each morning 'before the bells on the Cathedral began to ring', to offer themselves for work to anyone who would require their services. They turned up with their own tools, a spade, a shovel, or perhaps a barrow. If it was the harvest time, they carried pitchforks, rakes, sycles or at a later date scythes. Many women would turn up also, to work at gathering potatoes, lifting corn, gathering stones off land, milking and butter making. The wages offered were a few shillings a week.

The Market House was controlled by a body known as the Tolls Committee who also controlled the Tontine Rooms and the flax market, pork market, fowl market, butter and eggs market, which were situated in different parts of the town, and at all of which they collected tolls. The Committee continued to exist until the end of the last century, when shortly after the Local Government Act was passed for Ireland, the Armagh Urban District Council came into existence and they had a Bill moved in the Westminster House of Commons and supported by the then Irish party 'to have the Tolls Committee abolished and the Tontine Rooms, the Market House and markets given to the Urban Council with the right to run markets and collect tolls'.

The Market House continued to be used for the purposes for which it was built up to 1913, when the Urban Council who were responsible at the time for Technical Education and who held a school in one of the houses called 'The Seven Houses' (later the Labour Exchange) instructed the Principal of the Technical School to draw plans for the converting of the Market House into the Armagh Technical School. So Mr John Caffery, who a couple of years before reconstructed the Tontine Rooms into the City Hall, became the architect of the new Technical School. Mr Robert Cullen of Portadown secured the contract - he, also, built the City Hall. Mr Frank Donaghy, a mason, was foreman, and Edward McAvinchey was clerk of works.

In the reconstructed work, the bottom of the old Market House was not disturbed and this portion was left as it had been. The top storey was taken down with the heavy stone cornices and clock house. The wooden floors were taken up and replaced with reinforced concrete floors. These extended over the back wall to a new reinforced concrete beam which carried the new walls of the new school. This is a splendid job.

The second floor and the roof were also of reinforced concrete, making a flat roof on the new building. Reinforced concrete was new to this district at the time. The flat roof was covered with two layers of Trinidad asphalt, but some alarm took place a couple of years after the school was finished - "that it was too heavy" and it was taken off and replaced with felt. This worried the inhabitants so much that the Urban Council had the striker of the clock silenced!

The stone work for the new work was made to match the old stone work and a very good job was made of it, as an observer at the present time could not tell which is the old and which is the new. Time has made the whole building tone to the same colour. A new doorway was added with columns and ornamental lintel and is a very good job in my opinion. The stone dressers were the last of families who had carried on this trade from father to son for generations. (Stone-dressing is almost a thing of the past)

During the building of the wall a dispute arose with the Contractor and the Clerk of Works on the construction of the new walls. Specified in the contract the walls were to be 14" wide, backed with brick work. The bricks were sand and lime made in Newry by a Mr Redmond. They broke easily in working and the Contractor was not leaving enough room behind the stonework to take at least a $4\frac{1}{2}$" brick. He did not want to dress large stones down to $8\frac{1}{2}$" or 9" as he maintained he was not being paid for this work. The Clerk of Works stopped the job and he was backed by the Architect and the dispute had to go to Arbitration. The case was heard in the City Hall by Mr. Patrick Lavery, Solicitor, and Mr. James Lennon represented the Council. The Architect gave evidence with the Clerk of Works. The Contractor was represented by a Mr. Cullen, Solicitor, Portadown (a son of the Contractor's). The foreman and the Contractor gave evidence. A local Government Inspector was arbitrator.

After a prolonged hearing it was eventually settled that the Contractor was not interpreting the specifications right. The result was that he had to dress the stones to take a full brick and insert Bond Stones where required.

When finished, the old Market House had been converted from a two-storied building to a three-storied one; considerably enlarged, with many class-rooms, wood block floors, and fulfilled its purpose at the time as the Armagh Technical School and up to the present. The lower portion continued to be used as a grain market, up to the time of the Second World War when it was taken over and after some reconstruction became the Local Food Office. The large gates remained but windows were fixed behind them and the gates not disturbed. When the Food Office was closed the Technical Authorities turned this portion into a wood-working class and an engineering classroom by making a concrete stair at the ground floor.

The Market House turned Technical School may soon have to change its name again, as there seems to be a demand for a much larger and more commodious building, more in keeping with modern requirements in education. It is still a very sound and good building and has a splendid appearance and does lend some dignity to our ancient city with the Cathedral in the background. We all hope that our city fathers will see to it, when the time comes that it is turned to some useful purpose in keeping with its past.

Note on the author by his friend P.J.Hamill.

Harry McAvinchey (born 09.06.1890) was a master stone-mason who came of a line of craftsmen. His grandfather, the first of the family to reside in the City of Armagh, came from the Ballymacnab area to work on the building of the new Cathedral and it was he who put the final stone in place on top of the spires. Harry took great pride in his trade and was a veritable storehouse of information on its many aspects. He was one of the last of the master craftsmen to have a smattering of 'Bearlagar na Saor', the secret language of the masons which had been used since the Middle Ages to protect the secrets of the trade. Harry's quick and active mind found delight in researching local history. He was a founder-member of Cumann Seanchais Ard Macha, The Armagh Diocesan Historical Association, and often with his friends, George Paterson and Fely Hughes, he entertained fellow members with talks on local topics. One of these was on 'Bearlagar na Saor'. Unfortunately, no record of the talk exists and Harry's own notes on the subject has long since disappeared. Harry died on December 21st 1962.

THE ARCHITECTURE OF ARMAGH OBSERVATORY

John Butler

Armagh Observatory

To the casual observer, the small, picturesque Observatory at Armagh looks not dissimilar to many other country houses in Ireland of the late eighteenth century. It has a square, rather sparsely ornamented Georgian residence connected by a low wing to an eastern tower. However, on closer inspection, one becomes aware of a building with a number of rare, if not unique, features and one that tells us not only something of its architect, Francis Johnston, but also something of the history of astronomy over the past two hundred years. To understand and appreciate its architectural features it is necessary to know something of the types of building constructed for making astronomical observations in the eighteenth century in other parts of Europe.

Early observatories in western Europe were often towers surmounted by a platform and simply served to raise the astronomer above the noise, smoke and turmoil of the narrow streets. The two great public observatories of the preceding century, Paris and Greenwich, were scarcely more advanced and for both it seems the requirements of aesthetics took precedence over those of practical astronomy. It was remarked by Sir Christopher Wren of his design for the Royal Greenwich Observatory 'it was for the observator's habitation and a little for pomp.' The inconvenience to the astronomers at Paris of making their observations through tall windows, and the obstruction caused by ornamental features of the building is well documented. Indeed it was concluded by some astronomers and architects that it was just not possible to create a building which was both pleasing to look at and suitable for practical astronomy. While the founding of observatories remained a prestigious preoccupation, only to be undertaken by rich patrons, this dominance of aesthetics over practicality tended to prevail.

The conflict is well illustrated by the necessity for solid and substantial foundations, a point that should have been plainly evident to an architect, but which was neglected in parts of the Greenwich Observatory to the extent that the subsoil below some of the buildings moved and threatened their collapse. A gradual awareness of the great importance of the stability of foundations for instruments, which began in Scandinavia, early in the 18th century, reached its ultimate fruition in the Observatory of Trinity College, Dublin, built at Dunsink in 1785.

A remarkable account was written by its first Director, H. Ussher, on why Dunsink was built as it was. It is a model of clarity and simplicity and it laid the ground rules for successful observatories of the future. Ussher explained the importance of the Observatory site and the geology of the surrounding area. He insisted that instruments for measuring the position of stars should rest on bed-rock and that buildings which housed them should be close to the ground and not on high towers. He also specified that the foundations of the instruments should be independent of the building so that vibrations were not transmitted to the delicate apparatus. Only instruments which were intended to view the whole sky were to be placed on high towers to give them a clear view of the horizon. Though Dunsink was the first building to be entirely conceived and built along these lines, some aspects of its design did appear in the earlier observatories at Oxford (Radcliffe 1771), at Kew (King's Observatory 1769) and the 'New Observatory Buildings' at Greenwich (1749-50). It seems likely that some of Ussher's ideas derive from the experience of English astronomers he met on his visit to England prior to the building of Dunsink and in particular, Maskelyne, the Astronomer Royal at Greenwich. Unfortunately, although Dunsink was built in 1785, the delay in delivery of its major instrument for over twenty years, meant that its superior design could not be tested until many years later. Indeed, Armagh Observatory which was built in 1789-91 received its principal instrument, the Troughton Equatorial Telescope, in 1795, a decade earlier than Dunsink.

For the Observatory at Armagh, several of Ussher's principles were not heeded, in particular his criteria for selecting a suitable site. At Armagh the site chosen was a drumlin hill of compacted boulder clay on the edge of the then city of Armagh. It has been reported that Archbishop Richard Robinson had a town plan for his primatial city and that he wished to place his new buildings in prominent positions so that they could be seen from his palace, set against a background of natural woodland. This is in fact the case with the Observatory and it illustrates, once again, the conflicting interests of benefactors wishing to erect an aesthetic building and astronomers wanting to found a practical observatory. Later, in the nineteenth century, this point is unlikely to have escaped the attention of the third director, Thomas Romney Robinson, when he announced that he had detected a seasonal movement of the entire Observatory which he attributed to the percolation of water into the underlying boulder clay.

Another crucial factor in Ussher's account which was ignored by Francis Johnston, and which later came to haunt Armagh observers, was the siting of the main instruments to the east of the residence. The hot air from the chimneys of the residence was carried by the prevailing west wind over the astronomical instruments where it caused the star images to quiver in the telescopes. This undoubtedly limited the accuracy of some measurements of star positions.

For Ussher, in his description of Dunsink, there could be no compromise of the practical requirements of an observatory for the sake of architectural elegance. However, at Armagh, Francis Johnston achieved a fair degree of compromise and as a result produced a building of great charm. As one of his earliest commissions it includes his first attempts to use features that were often to recur in later, much grander, buildings. For instance, in place of the usual rectangular features, he frequently used curves notably the rounded corners for some rooms, the curved chimney breasts, and the curved architraves around the ground floor windows. Another example is the unique cupola dome over the staircase which serves the double purpose of enabling the astronomer to check the sky before opening the dome and illuminating the first floor landing.

No more pertinent example of the difference in approach between the design of Dunsink and Armagh Observatories could be found than the comparison of the well-proportioned and well-lit spiral stairwell around the central telescope pillar at Armagh, which rises from the foundations through the ground and first floors to the base of the dome. At Dunsink, a much more substantial central pillar was used, which left space for only a narrowly confined and ill-lit staircase between the pillar and outer wall. At Armagh, Francis Johnston was forced by the lack of rigidity of the clay substrate, to abandon another of Ussher's principles, namely the independent support of the telescope. Apparently, he tried to mitigate this shortcoming of his design, by placing a wooden staircase on top of the stone staircase, thereby reducing the transmission of vibrations from the stairs to the instruments above.

Francis Johnston is well known for the minimal decoration of the exterior of his buildings. In contrast, in his interiors, his use of decoration, though restrained, incorporated much fine detail. Both of these characteristics are evident at Armagh Observatory, particularly in the fine beaded woodwork in the ground floor apartments.

The original dome on the south side of the building is one of the earliest astronomical domes to survive in the British Isles, if not in Europe. Moveable domes were less common in eighteenth century observatories than in those of the nineteenth century, when, mainly because of the rise in popularity of equatorial instruments, they became ubiquitous. Many of the early domes that were built have been removed or replaced over the intervening years, including those at Greenwich and Dunsink. The Armagh dome remains in its original state. It is particularly interesting to see how Francis Johnston has attempted to strengthen what is inevitably a weak and flexible type of structure; namely a hemisphere with a slice taken out of it. A hemispherical dome, if supported evenly, would be a relatively strong structure. However, when a segment is removed to allow the enclosed telescope to view the sky, it becomes flexible and liable to warp. Domes are notoriously difficult to design and, to this day, many observatory domes, even new ones, function badly. One of the points Ussher raised with respect to astronomical domes was the necessity of good thermal insulation so that the instrument was not heated unduly by the sun. This would give rise to different flexure and expansion of the instrument as its various parts cooled at different rates during the following night. To overcome this problem and also to improve the rigidity of the dome, Francis Johnston lined the outer copper dome with light horizontal reeded lathes. The copper segments of the outer dome do not radiate from the centre, but from an off centre point; presumably also for rigidity purposes.

To the east of the main building lies a low, single storey, building which, though now connected by a passage way, was possibly originally separate. This building housed the transit instrument and the Observatory's famous Earnshaw clocks. It appears to have been built along the lines suggested by Ussher, with independent stone piers for the clocks and instruments. About halfway along this building is a two storey tower, known as the Sector Tower, which was built in 1841, probably over the existing building. This is a rather late date for such a tower as by then sectors had been superseded for measuring zenith distances of stars by a type of instrument which Armagh already possessed, namely a mural circle. Thomas Romney Robinson built the Sector Tower to house the Sisson Zenith Sector, one of the instruments from the King's Observatory at Kew, which had been presented to Armagh Observatory by Queen Victoria. Possibly Robinson was embarrassed by the gift of valuable, but outdated instruments, and wished to make some conspicuous sign that he could put them to use. In fact he was quickly defeated by an antiquated design and rejected the Sisson Zenith Sector for accurate measurements. The tower now supports an anemometer by Munroe (1870) which was erected at Armagh as part of an automatically recording weather station set up by the Board of Trade. The Cup Anemometer, of which this is an early example was developed and first put to use at Armagh Observatory by Robinson, its inventor.

Between the East Tower and the Sector Tower lies the Mural Circle Room, which was built to house a very fine, large instrument for measuring star positions. The Mural Circle was mounted on a stone wall of massive construction, which unfortunately is no longer in place. Nevertheless, a wooden replica of the wall has been made and now serves to support the partly restored instrument. It was with this instrument that the bulk of the observations associated with the Armagh Catalogue of Stars, published in 1859, were made.

At the eastern extremity of the Observatory rises a round tower, shorter than, but nevertheless rather reminiscent of, those enigmatic bell towers of medieval Irish monasteries. However, instead of a conical roof, it carries a second copper dome, very similar to the earlier dome on the south side of the residence. The tower was built in 1827 and may possibly also be the work of Francis Johnston who died in Dublin two years later. It belonged to the second main phase of building at the Observatory which followed the appointment of John George Beresford as Archbishop of Armagh. This second dome, though it was originally built to house a Herschel reflector, became in 1834-35 the home of one of the most original and interesting telescopes that has been built in the British Isles. It was the first telescope to be commissioned from Thomas Grubb, founder of the Dublin Telescope Manufacturing Company, and can justly claim to have been the forerunner of many subsequent reflecting telescopes. It had an aperture of 15 inch and included amongst its several innovative features were an equatorial mounting and a clockwork drive.

To the south of the East Dome, at some distance from the main Observatory building, are two low-lying domes, one of which houses the Robinson Memorial Telescope, built in 1885 by Grubb and the other an 18 inch Calver telescope that was later converted into a Schmidt telescope for celestial photography.

The Robinson Memorial Telescope was widely used by Dreyer, the fourth director, to check his earlier observations of nebulae made with Lord Rosse's great six-foot telescope at Birr. Ultimately these observations were compiled in his famous New General Catalogue of Nebulae and Clusters of Stars, first published in 1888 and still in print to-day. It is the order in which they occur in this catalogue which gives the nebulae their well-known NGC number. This world famous book is probably the most important contribution to astronomy to have come from Armagh Observatory. The Robinson Memorial Telescope, or 'Ten-Inch', as it is widely known, was also used more recently (1967), by Dr A.D. Andrews and colleagues in a remarkable observation of a huge flare (explosion) on a star, which was seen simultaneously from Armagh and, with the giant two hundred and fifty foot, radio telescope at Jodrell Bank. This type of work, now largely done by satellites, has provided a fruitful line of research for Armagh astronomers over the past two decades.

Beyond the immediate precincts of the Observatory, there are several buildings of architectural interest. The small gate lodge at the entrance with its pointed windows is an early example by Francis Johnston of the Gothick style which featured in many of his more famous later buildings. These included the Chapel Royal, Dublin Castle, Glanmore Castle, County Wicklow and Charleville Castle, County Offaly. Francis Johnston is known as one of the pioneers in Ireland of the Gothick style.

Further afield are the meridian marks, which were built to provide a stable reference point on the horizon with which the instruments could be checked for any disturbance. It was from observations of one of these that T.R. Robinson detected an earthquake in 1846. The earlier meridian marks were built of stone. One, the northern mark, at Tullyards, just off the Armagh-Loughgall Road, is an arch-shaped structure surmounted by two pinnacles. These served to provide the initial alignment of the transit instrument, with finer adjustment provided by a small copper disk with a triangular hole in its centre. Another meridian mark of similar design was built to the south of the Observatory at Corkley but was destroyed in the nineteenth century. Both of these marks were built in or around the early 1790s and were almost certainly the work of Francis Johnston. A second, southern meridian mark, which still survives, was built at Ballyheridan just beyond the southern extremity of the Palace Wall. It is a square neo-classical column and is probably also the work of Francis Johnston. Adjacent to the northern stone mark stands a cast iron obelisk in the

ARMAGH OBSERVATORY. Founded by Archbishop Richard Robinson in 1791 and designed by Francis Johnston. The main block constituted the Director's house and observatory dome. The easterly extension and dome were added by John George Beresford in 1835. (M. Campbell).

Egyptian style. It is the work of Gardner's foundry at Armagh and was erected in 1864 when the Jones Mural Circle was converted by Robinson to serve as a meridian circle. With his modified instrument, Robinson was able to measure both coordinates of stars (right ascension and declination) with the one instrument and a single observer, where previously he had required two. The fine adjustment of the instrument relied on an adjustable pointer which is hidden in the apex of the obelisk so that it was visible from the Observatory, but not to the vandals that so frequently tried Robinson's patience. Both of the northern markers have been recently restored by the Department of the Environment and may be visited by making a short excursion from the city.

Though a number of such meridian marks were erected at observatories from the eighteenth century up until the mid-nineteenth century, when they were superseded by instrumental developments, those at Armagh are the only ones known to survive in Ireland. In Great Britain about a dozen examples have been recorded, most of them associated with observatories in Scotland which have themselves, long since, disappeared.

THE STONES OF ARMAGH

Philip S. Doughty
Keeper of Geology, Ulster Museum

There is a pleasant intimacy about the old streets of Armagh which is one of the city's delights. The street patterns are irregular, some narrow, but many with opening vistas to grander structures and long views over hummocky roofscapes to the two cathedrals and the open drumlin country beyond. No other northern city shares this charm which derives partly from the hilly site, imaginatively used, but also from the human scale, the nature of its architecture, and a very particular use of local building materials. These rocks give a character, sometimes craggy, often noble, which seems entirely suited to this ancient ecclesiastical market town and its people. This brief note describes the dominant building materials, their appearance, their working and something of their origins with some examples of prominent buildings in which they can be seen.

It might help to commence with a little simple geology to assist in the practical examination of building materials, and to give a grasp of how the three major groups of rocks are formed.

IGNEOUS ROCKS are formed directly from a moulten state by cooling from a very high temperature, usually 1000 C or more. They can cool within the earth forming coarse grained rocks such as granites, or they may emerge violently at the surface where they cool quickly to form glassy or fine grained rocks such as basalts. Igneous rocks are used largely as facings on modern commercial premises in Armagh as well as in the street and are incorporated in other monuments.

When particles of minerals or rocks settle through water or air they form blankets on sea beds and land surfaces which in cross section appear as layers. These are the beds or strata of SEDIMENTARY ROCKS. Some of these rocks contain the remains of animals or plants in the form of fossils. Limestones, sandstones and shales are typical sedimentary rocks and the first two are important local building materials.

The third group of rocks are those which have been changed by the effects of heat, or pressure, or both, usually deep in the earth. These are the METAMORPHIC ROCKS and are formed from igneous, sedimentary or even earlier metamorphic rocks. Slates and marbles are typical examples of this group and both are common, but less prominent, in Armagh.

One of the earliest building materials is manifested as rubblestone walling in many of the early buildings of the city. Good examples can be seen in the crudely truncated terrace, known locally as the Seven Houses, in Upper English Street, built in 1768-70, and in St. Mark's Place, 1834, on the Mall, adjacent to the Armagh County Museum. St. Mark's Place exhibits random rubble masonry which harmonises surprisingly well with its dressings of red brick and limestone quoins. The Seven Houses show the same material random coursed. On close examination it can be seen that the rock consists of angular fragments of a pale grey limestone suspended in a pinkish brown sandstone. It represents a land deposit formed around two hundred and fifty million years ago when desert sands inundated a scree or desert gravels. The rock is named the Drumarg Conglomerate Formation on the geological map. It can now be seen only in the sides of an old quarry in Drumarg Downs townland. It is well developed in a band about two hundred metres wide around the city. It was formerly extensively worked for building, most probably because it was soft and readily yielded to the hammer.

The dominant rock, the single material which determines the essential character of most major buildings, is the local carboniferous limestone. It has been used in noble and mean structures and in a wide variety of finishes from smoothest ashlar, with finely carved detail, to the roughest rock-faced dressing. To the geologist, or anyone else with an eye for materials, it is the nature of its best use in Armagh that is surprising. It was treated by the local masons as a freestone, which means that it was cut freely in any direction with a variety of tools without regard to its original orientation in the quarry. Most sedimentary building stones are not used in this way and cut blocks are normally presented with the bedding horizontal, as in the quarry. If this is not done, weather tends to penetrate inclined bedding planes and eventually pieces spall off or water penetration accelerates weathering and loss of surface and detail.

The famous freestones in wide use are Portland Stone, from the Portland Bill area south of Weymouth, and Bath Stone. Both are limestones that occur in thick beds without minor bedding planes and, freshly quarried, they are soft, described as "green" by quarrymen, and readily worked. They contain remnant mineralised groundwater, "quarry sap", which slowly migrates to the cut surface and there evaporates leaving the minerals in the surface layer as a kind of case-hardening. It is the ease of working in all directions and subsequent hardening that made these stones so popular. In contrast the Armagh limestones are extremely hard and well consolidated leaving little room for groundwater and requiring no case-hardening. This means that the rock is homogenous and consequently predictable under the pitcher and mallet, very desirable qualities, but its great hardness presented problems not confronted by the masons working the English freestones. This should have led to buildings with plain cornices, simple mouldings, and rough tooled finishes, dictated by the economics of the time required to work the stone. In fact the refined buildings of the city show all the elaborations of the finest West Country eighteenth and nineteenth century architecture, reminiscent of Pultney Street and the other principal terraces of Bath. There are elaborate plinths, mouldings, cornices, pilasters, pillars and shafts and finishes ranging from rough pitched, through plain ashlars to rustications, with faces boasted, furrowed, broached and pick panelled. The classic proportions may be missing from Armagh's vernacular Georgian buildings but the quality of the masonry certainly equals the standard elsewhere.

Examples of carboniferous limestone buildings survive in all parts of the old city. The bold use of very basic rock-faced masonry can be well appreciated on the newly restored Bell's Store on the Mall, in sharp contrast to the clean, plain ashlar of the Scotch Church, 1837-40, next door. On the east side of the Mall Armagh County Museum facade and Charlemont Place are in fine dense stone, the former with a pediment supported on columns obviously cut with their long axes along the bedding plane. The crispness of Charlemont Place, with its rich detailing and extensive reeding, shows the extreme resistance of this stone to weathering. The Market House of 1815, with its later additions, is another striking structure showing the adaptability and resilience of this medium. The much mauled facade of the old County Infirmary of 1774, on Abbey Street, is an interesting combination of rubblestone walling of Drumarg Conglomerate with one of the earliest extensive uses of limestone dressings. The Public Library, a little further up the street (1771) is a building of great distinction and amongst the earliest examples of a highly finished structure in the city. It shows that outstanding workmanship was achieved by local masons within a few years of the start of quality building. The dominant limestone edifice of the city is undoubtedly St. Patrick's Roman Catholic Cathedral, a towering twin-spired edifice completed in 1870.

Despite its exposed position the stonework is still extremely sharp and detailed with even the delicate toolwork surviving one hundred and twenty years of exposure. Only the mortar shows signs of weathering and reaction in a few places.

There is no high quality limestone building construction now, and the mason's craft has largely died out, but it is interesting to see the retention of random rubble walling in limestone to the present time, the small terrace on Castle Street being a good example. It is without pretention but retains the general character of the area because it has used the local limestone.

The source of the limestone in Armagh's buildings presents an interesting problem. Armagh city sits firmly astride an outcrop of carboniferous limestones about three miles wide extending six miles E.N.E and around eight miles W.N.W. In 1844 George Wilkinson mentions the light coloured limestone of excellent quality used extensively in the buildings of the city and lists only one source named as Gribbon's Quarry 'near the town'. George Kinahan, writing in 1889, repeats this description with the note that 'formerly these quarries were very extensively worked'. Navan Quarry is mentioned separately and described as producing a dark limestone. The latter reference suggests that the quarries close to Armagh were used for the bulk of building with Navan as an inferior, and possibly later, source. Navan stone was certainly used for St. Patrick's Roman Catholic Cathedral around 1840 and is a dense pale weathering stone of highest quality. Many other important early structures are known to have used pale limestones from Navan. Clearly much research is still needed into both limestone sources and to discover more about the masons who produced such excellent work but about whom almost nothing is known.

Sandstone of building quality is not available close to Armagh and consequently it is little used. There are two notable exceptions. St. Patrick's Church of Ireland Cathedral is faced in a sandstone which has also been used in the precinct walls and gateposts. It is a purple-streaked warm brown in colour pitted where clay galls (small clots of soft clay minerals) have been weathered out. It has a slight sparkle. It was raised from a specially opened pit near Wilson's Bridge, about one mile north of the city, between 1840 and 1845. In the mass it is not an attractive rock and has not weathered uniformly. The thirteenth century cathedral was originally of Drumarg Conglomerate but so severely weathered that the sandstone facing was deemed essential.

The iron ties fixing the sandstone to the underlying fabric now appear to be rusting and some spalling is evident. The carved heads of the cathedral were replaced in the same nineteenth century period but the stones used were 'English reds', probably the St. Bees Sandstone, or Penrith, both easily traded to the County Down coast. The second significant sandstone building is the old Belfast Bank of 1851 in Upper English Street, now a tourist information centre. This richly ornamented frontage, with its adjacent arch, is built in a golden sandstone with thin rust-brown lines and stains. Its heavy rustication and carving is in sharp contrast to its neighbours and adds some lively variety to the street. The rock is not local and although it could be an example of one of the Dungannon Sandstones, which take carving detail without severe weathering, it seems more likely to be a Scottish sandstone, perhaps Gifnock from just outside Glasgow and much favoured in Belfast in the nineteenth century.

There are a few surviving examples of limestone paving in the city, one of the best being outside Charlemont Place, where slabs polished by generations of pedestrians show the bold circles of sections through fossil brachiopods and cushions of fossil corals giving a tantalising glimpse of the tropical seabeds of three hundred and thirty million years ago. Limestone is not a good paving material because it smooths so readily and becomes greasy in the rain, but its use is so rare and its appearance so striking, that a few examples should be preserved.

No account of Armagh stones is complete without reference to Armagh Red Marble. This was the commercial name applied to a series of red-stained limestones which took a good polish. They were found beneath the Drumarg Conglomerate at a famous, now lost, site called Red Barn Quarry. The best example of its use was in the magnificent screen in St. Patrick's Roman Catholic Cathedral, ablaze with rich marbles but now removed and replaced by the blander, more austere, Leinster Granite altar. The small chapel altar on the east side survives as a reminder of the former glory. A fine memorial rail in the Protestant Cathedral is probably also a local example. It was widely used in church interior work in Belfast although the best example surviving in original form is in St. John's College Chapel, Cambridge, where it is used in columns.

Bricks are rare but there are a few cases where they dominate, as in Russell Street. Early in the nineteenth century bricks were made from local clays but after the advent of the railway the local industry died in the face of imported brick. This came mainly from Scotland and England and it is from this later period that most of the brick built buildings of Armagh date. The local bricks were hand-made, burnt in clamps, rather than kilns, employing coal from the only local source, Coalisland, County Tyrone. The clamps were often constructed in a way that deliberately created colour variations. In some instances these variations were intensified by the use of salt glazes and used to form patterns in the finished brickwork. They exhibit a rich series of variations around a basic red colour.

The major uses of igneous rock tend to be as facing slabs on modern commercial premises and here there is a hybrid international mosaic. There are extreme contrasts from the Swedish Bonaccord Blood Red Granite (City Meat Centre) to the almost black, with metallic flecks, of the Rustenberg Gabbro from South Africa (Woolworth's) and increasing use of the Baltic Brown Granite from Finland, with its strangely rounded crystals of feldspar. Monuments are another source; for example the South African War Memorial in the Mall shows two varieties of Newry granodiorite, a darker and lighter grey, and the figure stands on the only block of Shap granite, from the east Cumbrian fells, so far discovered in the city.

Throughout the nineteenth century the architect builders of Armagh were confident of their materials and knew exactly the range of mason's skills available to them, the finishes they could use and the final effect, including the ultimate patination of weathering. There are signs of a welcome and intelligent revival of interest in materials which should be encouraged at all levels, not simply to restore and maintain existing fabrics but to enliven new developments. It should never be forgotten that when the finest buildings were constructed on the local pastures in the eighteenth and nineteenth centuries, they were very much of their time.

The Buildings of Armagh

ABBEY LANE

This lane is the last remaining fragment of the original Abbey Lanes. They formed links between the Franciscan friary and other religious sites in the city.

A quaint little shopping lane with two-storey buildings of considerable potential on one side. On the other side there are blank walls, the back areas of Thomas Street shops, and a car park which destroys the sense of enclosure of the lane. The views of the backs of shops overpower the lane particularly at the junction with Thomas Street where the black asbestos slate hanging is a very dominant vertical feature.

Some of the cosy little shops have lively paintwork and good hand-painted signs; there are several brackets for hanging signs but only one is in use.

ABBEY STREET

An ancient way down from the cathedral to English Street and so called because it ran down past the Abbey of St. Peter and St. Paul and that of St. Columba. To-day the old houses fronting the footpath, as they mount the steep curving hill suggest a medieval origin. Abbey Street's distinctly Continental air is, perhaps, explained by old historical links.

AIB Manager's House: B+. (1896) Architects Watt and Tulloch. A five-bay, two-storey red brick building with sandstone copings, string courses and window surrounds, the continuation of the bank building in English Street. Fine chimneys with stone cornices. Ornamental overdoors with name panel and small finials. A parapet wall with a gable capped by a small segmental pediment links the two buildings. A brick screen wall with service entrance (impressive piers caps with balls on stems but bare functional gates) linked to a stone outbuilding (brick-faced on the street side) continues the bank's design theme up the street and concludes this unified composition of varied parts. The building has been well cleaned recently.

3 Abbey Street: Three-bay, two-storey substantial painted brick building. Sash windows, glazing bars missing from ground floor. Remains of timber exterior architrave to front door is probably not original; fine stone steps. Low service door with recessed panel above continues line of head of ground floor window.

5-9 Abbey Street: Three two-bay, two-storey roughcast colour-washed houses. No.5 has an ugly sheeted dormer window. All windows have been renewed; replacement by replica of the original design would be beneficial. Good stone steps and cills. Gable wall of no.9 is of coursed conglomerate and limestone.

11-13 Abbey Street: (c.1830) Latterly a Unionist Club but originally a Primitive Methodist Meeting House, with later additions. A three-storey, four-bay smooth rendered building set at an angle to the street to form a little entrance court. This leads up to a quietly imposing church entrance door with cut stone architrave and bracketed cornice (now painted). The house and church offices have been converted into three flats entered by the original church door. Above the carriage arch there is a recessed panel reading 'Unionist Club' in good painted lettering.

The meeting house at the rear is a two-storey, five-bay building of coursed random rubble limestone with brick dressings around the windows. The original and very attractive tall cast-iron four-centred arch-headed windows are divided into small panels by thin cast-iron glazing bars that terminate in simple tracery. On the first floor the timber sash windows with glazing bars are domestic in scale and in appearance quite unlike those on the ground floor. Inside, the ground floor hall has heavy exposed timber beams with diagonal bracing resting on stone corbelled brackets. At the entrance end there is a curious balcony cut off from the hall by a screen of fixed and hinged panelled shutters.

The meeting house was occupied until recently, but is now lying empty and dilapidated. It is good to know that it may be restored and put to public use.

15 Abbey Street: A substantial four-bay, two-storey dwelling with dry dash finish and cement quoins. Good semi-circular doorway with original wheel fanlight and eight panelled door; blocked stone architrave with keystone. Good stone steps. Sash windows, all glazing bars missing.

Methodist Church: B. (1835/1862/1888) Architect for internal extensions 1862 - W.J. Barre; for extensions and new facade 1882-88 - J.J. Phillips.

Once more the street frontage is broken, this time to create an entrance court in front of the Methodist Church with low ashlar stone boundary wall and nineteenth-century railings.

The facade is of ashlar stone with banded rustication to the ground floor. There is a shallow pediment on scroll brackets above the panelled door surround; on each side are two small windows set within a frame of pilasters and segmental pediments. Above this a large elongated, vaguely Venetian, window with segmental heads and Ionic pilaster surrounds is set within a blank wall flanked at each corner by an Ionic pilaster and surmounted by the main frieze, cornice and pediment of the facade, with the words 'METHODIST CHURCH' in good incised lettering.

There is a quarter circle bay with balustraded cornice, all in painted plaster, behind each corner pilaster. The one on the left turns back gently to 'bump' into the narrow pedimented gable entrance of the church hall facing down the steep hill and detailed somewhat in the same manner as the main church facade. Blocking courses and quoins are in plaster.

Interior:

The entrance door leads into a snug vestibule just large enough to accommodate the coupled doors on either side, one of each pair opening on to an aisle, the others on to stairs to the balcony. There are good encaustic tiles on the floor and on the wall facing the entrance is an aedicule recess. This, with all the other chunky classical detail that binds together this well composed hallway, has been executed in warm-toned pitch-pine.

The intimate scale continues within the church. There is a balcony on three sides supported on seven slender cast-iron columns, with the balcony front of decorative cast-iron backed by maroon felt. The open pews are of pitch-pine, those nearest the wall on each side being slightly angled towards the pulpit so giving the illusion that each row is curved. The well-elevated mahogany pulpit is elliptically shaped on plan (wide enough to seat more than one minister) and reached by two flights of stairs. They are placed one at each side of the pulpit with Romanesque style miniature arcading forming the banisters and the pulpit front. The wall behind the pulpit is a wide arcaded recess and here a curtain backdrop is framed by mahogany pilasters crowned by small pediments set at each end of a mahogany frieze and cornice with central bracketed pediment. On the left of the pulpit in a large panelled box-like case is the organ (probably nineteenth century). Immediately below the pulpit are the communion table and communion rail.

The semi-circular headed windows have pale coloured stained glass. The set of lattice quarries is given variety by rectangular-paned margins and geometrical decoration in the heads. Probably the dominant feature in the church is the stained pine sheeted ceiling of large panels with pine fretwork ventilator grilles laid out in a geometrical pattern. So much of the detail of this interesting well-maintained interior must have changed little since 1862 when W.J. Barre remodelled the building.

The rear gable of the church and the three-sided end of the Church Hall (1859) are glimpsed, as one group, above the wall in Dawson Street, their coursed random rubble stonework and brick dressings unrendered.

(I.B. Vol.XXX 1 Dec.1888
Bassett p.95-96)

Church Hall: (1859) Architect W.J. Barre; builder Thos. Ross. Built as a Sabbath and day school, now used as a church hall. A four-bay, two-storey building, cement rendered and lined out, with quoins. Original paired windows with segmental heads to ground floor, unfortunate new steel frame windows to first floor. Railings missing to stone upstands which formed part of the entrance court are worth replacing.

(Lynn p.134.
Rogers (2) p.42.)

Former Protestant Hall: (mid-nineteenth century) An inn stood on this site in which James II lodged in 1689 and the Duke of Schomberg in 1690. Six-bay, two-storey cement rendered building, a flat but convincing essay in classicism. Stone plinth; pilasters between each window; recessed panel between ground and first floor windows; simple cornice and frieze. At top corner the pediment rises above top three bays. One doorway is in a similar opening to windows; ground floor windows now blocked up.

Round the corner, facing towards the Cathedral, the building becomes an important focal point; three-bay, two-storey, pedimented with six windows, all blind.

Rear elevation - see Dawson Street.

It is good to know that plans are being prepared for the restoration of the hall as a centre for the mentally handicapped.

(Rogers (2) p.21)

19-21 Abbey Street: Two-storey, two-bay roughcast dwelling with

asbestos slated roof and painted cement quoins. Sash windows, all glazing bars missing.
No.19 is being restored.

23-25 Abbey Street: Pair of three-storey, two-bay dwellings; elliptical carriage arch to no.25. No.23 has smooth plaster to ground floor and roughcast to first and second floors over originally exposed stone; cement quoins. No.25 random rubble limestone with ribbon pointing; large window on ground floor, all windows replaced and without glazing bars.
Ground floor of no.23 has later mullion and transom windows and moulded architraves; pretty,original doorway with fanlight of intersecting semicircles. Side approach to front door with three steps of precast concrete and modern railings.

27-31 Abbey Street: Prominently sited terrace of three two-storey, two-bay houses of random conglomerate with limestone; once whitewashed, then plastered and now stripped with stone re-pointed. Chimney missing to no.27.
All windows renewed; no.31 has top hung windows with glazing bars; unfortunately the tripartite window was not replaced.

Armagh City Hospital: B. (1774) Architect George Ensor.
Substantial nine-bay, two-storey building of coursed conglomerate. Basement and hipped roof with dressed stone eaves cornice. Centre three bays break forward with pediment.
Gibbsian doorway and window architraves and blocked quoins of ashlar stone. Later railings to basement.
Originally the entrance door was not in the centre of the front facade but sited at the third window from the right hand side; the third window from the left hand side was the door into the surgeon's house. The fanlight still exists as part of the window and inside the inner double doors still have their large and beautiful fanlight with Greek key-pattern frieze. There are good memorial plaques in the entrance hall and the fine original staircase is intact.
The plaques read:
'The Two Principal Wards of this Infirmary with the Entrance Hall, Board Room, Surgery and Staircase, have been reconstructed by Public Subscription in commemoration of the Great Services rendered by Surgeon Palmer and the staff of this Institution to the sufferers in the Railway Accident near Armagh 12th June 1889.'

'This tablet was erected by the Governors of Armagh County Infirmary to express their grateful thanks to the British Red Cross, who through the County Director, Mrs. Talbot O.B.E. of Castle Dillon, allotted part of the surplus funds collected in Co. Armagh to install electric plant and improve the X-Ray Apparatus for the benefit of ex-Servicemen and civilians. - 1921 - '

'This Hydraulic Lift was erected by Miss. Ellen Anne Eyre of Maydown Benburb, by substitution of a pulley lift given by Mrs. Cope, The Manor, Loughgall. The Governers place this tablet to express their thanks for the munificence of both these ladies. September 1906.'

On the right hand side of the building the roofless shell of the porter's lodge still exists serving as a screen for the oil tank and carrying a datestone 1826.

The lengthy extension to the north facing, pipe-infested elevation is in keeping except for the canopy and large window. Good chimney stacks; breakfront and pediment nicely repeated.

South side extensions are unobtrusive.

Dan Cruickshank points out that because infirmaries in the eighteenth and early nineteenth century had no distinctive architectural character some, like this building, resemble a 'country house stranded in town with only a central pediment for aggrandisement'.

(Cruickshank p.159-60 & 284.
Stuart p.532-35.)

Surgeon's House: A five-bay, three-storey L-shaped building. Traditionally proportioned sash windows. A flight of steps leads to front door between solid typically Thirties reconstituted stone walls. Fits in well.

Public Library, Abbey Street: A. (1771) One of the most perfect architectural set pieces in the City, built to designs by Thomas Cooley in 1771; it was extended by adding a bay to each end by John Monsarrat in 1845. Archbishop Robinson established the Library by an Act of Parliament in 1773, entitled 'An Act for settling and preserving a Publick Library in the City of Armagh for ever'. The Armagh Library Act was based on the one for the Free Library in Dublin founded by Primate Narcissus Marsh (1707). The preamble states:

'Whereas the Most Reverend Father in God, Richard Lord Rokeby Archbishop of Armagh, &c., out of his general inclinations to the public good of this Kingdom, for the propagation of the Christian religion as by Law established, and for the encouragement of Learning, hath at his own costs and charges erected and built a house upon a spot of ground, part of the estate of the see of Armagh, and hath fitted and prepared the principal part of the said house for a publick Library for ever, for the use of all persons who shall resort thereto at the hours to be appointed for the Library Keeper's attendance, and shall conform themselves to the rules, orders and directions of the Governors thereof for the time being; and hath also provided all things convenient for the better order, use, and standing of the books intended to be kept therein; and hath likewise fitted and prepared the remainder of the said house for the accommodation and habitation of a person to be appointed Library Keeper and his successors, Keepers of the said Library, for ever.' The keeper's quarters are on the ground floor and on three floors to the rear of the building.

The entire building is in ashlar limestone; the ground floor is rusticated and the remainder smooth. The elevation facing the Cathedral is three bays wide and unified by a subdued order carried up through both storeys. The parapet balustrade rises above a deep cornice overhang supported by modillion brackets. The rest of the entablature is only expressed in the central bay. This bay is slightly advanced and is topped by a pediment. The architrave is broken by a plaque bearing inscription.

Dean William Reeves in a pamphlet published in 1886 says that: 'A stone which was over the front door, till the alteration of 1848, bore the Greek numerals αψοα (1771). On a slab inserted in the wall was the Greek title ΤΟ ΤΗΣ ΨΥΧΗΣ ΙΑΤΡΕΙΟΝ, which also appears on a medal that was struck in commemoration, on silver and on copper, from a dye sunk by John Kirk of Piccadilly; having on the obverse his image beautifully cut, and the superscription 'RICH: HIBERN: PRIMAS BARO ROKEBY DE ARMAGH'. On the reverse is the front elevation of the building, then but three windows wide, and the inscription TO THS YUCHS IATREION.

The Primate was an Oxford man, of Christ Church, and was very generous to Alma Mater; but it was a mistake to depart from the form of inscription as given by Diodorus Siculus, who relates of Osmandyas, of Egypt, the originator of Libraries: 'ExhV d'υπαοχειν την ιεοαν βιβλιοθηκην, εφ' ης επιγεγοαφθαι ψυχης ιατοειον: 'Post haec sacrum esse Bibliothecam, cum inscriptione, Medicatorium animae'. But when our library was lengthened and refaced, in 1848, a new slab was inserted over the public entry, with the inscription limited to

Diodorus's two words, and these cut in archaic letter.'

The generally accepted interpretation of the inscription is 'the healing place of the soul'.

The two flanking bays have blind attic panels. All three bays contain recesses with semi-circular heads rising through two storeys and broken at mid height by a string course. The central bay has an arched niche at first floor level which is protected by a segmental pedimented hood on console brackets. Below this is the main entrance which has a straight hood mould also supported by consoles. In the flanking bays there are windows; at first floor these have triangular pedimented hoods and moulded stone architraves; at ground floor level there are only architraves.

The elevation facing Cathedral Close has five bays. The design is similar to the entrance elevation except that the first floor windows have semi-circular heads and there are no hoods of any kind. The central three bays are slightly advanced and express a complete entablature. The gable towards the hospital has two bays both of which are blind at first floor. The building is enclosed on the three public elevations by a low ashlar stone wall surmounted by railings.

Interior:

The library door opens into a hallway from which a cantilevered stairway ascends to the reading room that occupies the whole of the remainder of the first floor. Bookcases line the walls, rising in two stages. A narrow gallery with decorative iron balustrading reached by a spiral staircase gives access to the upper stage. The format is the standard collegiate pattern for the time. Thomas Burgh's masterpiece had been completed at Trinity College, Dublin, in 1732 and Archbishop Robinson's former college, Christ Church, Oxford, had a similar library designed by George Clarke and completed c.1739.

(Armagh Library drawings collection - folio of signed drawings, Thomas Cooley 1770. Irish Times, 3rd March 1981.Coote p.313.
'Irish Statutes' vol.X. pp.603-4.
Stuart p.449 and 535-539.
Rogers (2) p.24.
Bassett p.85-86.)

The Post Office yard, at the foot of Abbey Street, has created a very unsightly gap in the street frontage. An undistinguished wall, built of dreary pink concrete bricks, inadequately screens rows of bright red vans. The Post Office Coat of Arms mounted on the yard wall came

The City Hospital. Built as Armagh County Infirmary. The central entrance was moved from its original position where it balanced the closed up door on the left. (M. Campbell).

Armagh Public Library. The east end addition of 1848 to Cooley's building dating from 1771. The extension allowed direct access to the enlarged library room without going through the Keeper's residence. (M. Campbell).

Robinson's House, ABBEY STREET, demolished in 1911, the site is now occupied by the Alexander Memorial Hall. (Public Record Office (N.I.), Allison Collection).

BARRACK HILL and Armagh Savings Bank, 1975. Barrack Hill houses before reconstruction. In the circular enclosure grew the 'Orange Tree' removed because of its age, a new one has now been planted. (Historic Buildings Branch, Department of the Environment N.I.).

from the former building on the site, built c.1900, but would appear to be older. Over the top of the wall there are good views of the oldest Presbyterian Church in Armagh.

Presbyterian Church: B. Date stone 'Anno / Domini / 1722' beneath east window. Thomas Ashe writing in 1703 says, 'One croft and garden plot containing together about one acre. On this is built a large house with a retinue or angle which is called ye Presbyterian Meeting House.....this is one of the greatest meeting houses in ye North. There are in it three large galleries....This is at ye lowest end of Abbey Street.' (The street names have changed - see Rocque's map of 1760 - he is in fact referring to Sydney Place at the Shambles). The graveyard remains but this particular building was demolished in 1970.
The 'T' plan meeting house in Abbey Street, behind the Post Office, was known at this time as 'The New Meeting House'. Dean Swift remarks on the building of this 'New' meeting house with regard to the use that was made of stone robbed from the nearby ruins of the abbey of St. Peter and St Paul 'see how these fanatical Puritans are chiselling Popery out of the very stones.' However, not all the carved stones were defaced and some remain to be seen at the base of some of the windows. In the 1960s when plaster fell off the east end of the church the original window openings were revealed; two carved pilaster heads of fourteenth century date were retrieved and are now in the Armagh County Museum collection.
Stuart, writing in 1819, describes an 'excellent mansion' for the Minister then on the site now occupied by the Post Office Yard. The First Presbyterian congregation used the Meeting House for worship from 1725-1879, then they moved to the Mall. The Second Presbyterian congregation worshipped there until 1915; it was during this time that the gallery arrangements were altered and the gable windows enlarged. The congregation of Third Armagh took over responsibility for the building in 1915. The Armagh District Council plans to include the building in their tourist venture.

(I.B. Second Vol.XX 15 Jan 1878; Second Vol.XX1 15 Feb 1879; Vol. XX1 15 Jan. 1878.
Lundie.
Ashe.
Armagh County Museum Collection nos.127 & 128)

12-14 Abbey Street: Pair of three-bay two-storey houses; painted roughcast with cement architraves and vermiculated quoins. Ground floor architraves have cornices and on first and second floors there are shouldered architraves. Two sash windows survive in no.12 but without glazing bars; at ground level there is a distinctive modern bull's eye window. The top portion of the gable of no.12 has half-timbered decoration with fretted bargeboards.

The doorcases, with original eight panel doors, have cornices breaking forward over console brackets, set within rectangular openings.

The three-bay, three-storey return to no.12 (facing the lane way up to the old Presbyterian Church) has one original sash window with glazing bars, the remainder are modern. Adjoining it is a four-bay, two-storey block, no.12A, now divided into three houses with modern sash windows and dormers.

16-18 Abbey Street: Pair of three-bay, three-storey dwellings; roughcast ground floor, smooth rendering lined out to first and second floors. Moulded architraves to first floor windows; original windows with glazing bars have survived on first and second floor of no.18; top hung windows to no.16.

Attractive architrave and cornice to door of no.16 with trellis fanlight and five panel door; service entrance to no.16; new door to no.18.

20-22 Abbey Street: Pair of three-storey, two-bay houses, smooth rendered and lined out. Sash windows with glazing bars throughout; glazed doors with no embellishment. No.22 is unoccupied and dilapidated.

24 Abbey Street: Three-storey, seven-bay building, smooth rendered and lined out, with garage door crudely set into wall at lowest level. Sash windows but no glazing bars.

Flat-headed sandstone Gibbsian doorway with keystone; original door of eight fielded panels with similar panels to reveals and soffit of doorway with fanlight. House in a dilapidated condition.

26 Abbey Street: Three-storey, two-bay building, smooth rendered and lined out; original windows with glazing bars. Doorway has architraves with cornice and frieze with diamond-shaped panel; fielded seven panel door with similarly panelled reveals and soffit; good fanlight and stone step.

28 Abbey Street: Three-bay, three-storey building with carriage arch; newly painted roughcast; rather characterless modern windows and doors.

30-36 Abbey Street: (1904-25) Terrace of four two-bay, two-storey brick houses raised above the level of the street with a small flight of steps and little hanging gardens at eye level. Built by Samson Jervois on part of the garden of his house, no.40. It is possible that he was also the architect for the terrace. Two end and centre bays break forward as gables; carriage arch at one end of terrace in additional bay. Curious angled chimneys.

Well detailed brick arched porches; nos.32 and 34 have original door and side panel with stained glass.

Not at all typical of Abbey Street but a well composed group.

38 Abbey Street: Along the side of the street runs a roughcast wall screening the traditional two-storey outbuildings of no.40. In the wall are ashlar gate piers, which once sported fine stone balls with stems, and modern sheeted gates. Through them can be seen glimpses of a cobbled yard.

40 Abbey Street: Three-bay, two-storey roughcast dwelling set back from street; centre bay projects to pavement providing little cobbled stone entranceway to front door at 90 degree angle to street. Simple stone pediment to top of centre bay with eaves course and cement quoins; small lunette in pediment, windows below not original but in scale.

Very fine doorway with robust cornice breaking forward above panelled architrave; original six panel door.

42 Abbey Street: Imposing three-storey, three-bay red brick building with two canted bay windows rising through all floors; stone cills and eaves cornice and purple brick string courses to windows. Ornamental drip courses and bosses to doorway with bracketed cast-iron and stone balconette. Fine stone steps and upstands to the missing railings.

Architecturally more at home in the south end of Mall East or Victoria Street.

44 Abbey Street: Two-storey, six-bay building with carriage arch; cement rendered and lined out. Two-storey canted bay window containing entrance doorway. Cement moulded architraves to windows and doorway; cement blocking to doorway; stone cills.

Recent re-painting is good except for the black chimney stacks.

Church House (Church of Ireland Diocesan Hall): B. (1913) Architect
W. Samson Jervois MRIAI. (Armagh) Consultant R.Caulfeild Orpen
FRIAI (Dublin). Builder McLaughlin and Harvey, Belfast.
Erected in memory of Archbishop Alexander and built of coursed,
square-cut, rough-faced limestone with flush ashlar quoins. The
Collegiate-Tudor style Diocesan Hall is two-storey, the hall is on the
first floor above the offices and meeting rooms. The building is
cruciform shaped on plan, the four tall roofs of Westmorland slates are
surmounted by a stubby, louvred cupola. The gable walls of three of
the arms of the cross carry handsome, four-centred arch windows,
subdivided by stone mullions and transoms. Below the window in the
gable facing the road (built tight against the footpath) is a stone
memorial tablet, surmounted by the arms of Archbishop Alexander.
Attached to the south-east gable, with no window, is the lower
entrance wing, set back from the road with a double gable roof, small
gabled entrance porch and pointed-arched entrance doorway. The
steps are approached, castle-style, by a stone parapeted walkway
across the garden below.

Interior:
Through the entrance door a short flight of steps, dignified by a stone
capped solid balustrade, leads up to the hall. One of the most unique
public rooms in Armagh and, interestingly, showing the influence of
Lutyens and also the Arts and Crafts movement at the beginning of this
century on a local architect and his metropolitan consultant. The
cruciform plan is celebrated by the great plaster barrel vaults that
spring from the low cornices of the four arms and meet in the groined
vaulting over the crossing. There is also a subtly inferred ecclesiastical
layout in the plan. The arm nearest the road and the central square is
the nave, the arm with the platform is the choir and the other two
arms, one containing the balcony, are the transepts.

BALLYNAHONE HOUSE

A two-storey country house of modest scale set over a basement. The
front elevation is of three structural bays, the roof is pitched and
gabled, the gables each crowned by chimneys. The head of the walls is
capped by a dressed limestone corbelled eaves course, the central bay
is advanced and pedimented; in the tympanum are armorial bearings,
now very badly eroded but almost certainly of the Cust family. The

main entrance is set in this bay and is decorated only by a semi-circular fanlight, but the bay is further emphasised by rusticated ashlar limestone casing the complete ground floor through the full bay width. Above, at first floor and in the flanking bays, the dressed limestone is limited to quoins only, the rest of the wall surface is roughcast plaster. The approach to the entrance is up a grand flight of nine cut limestone steps, stretching the full bay width. The entrance door is flanked by single windows and at the same level in each of the two side bays there are two windows. At first floor and basement level there is only one window and above the door at first floor is a single window.

The building has undergone a number of refurbishments throughout its history; in the absence of reliable documentation it is difficult to date exactly. There is a sundial on the gable with the date 1685 on it. It is quite possible that the house has its origins in the late seventeenth century but what we see today is either a rebuild or a very drastic remodelling carried out for Henry Cust sometime between 1770 and 1776. Ballynahone is stylistically similar to George Ensor's other recorded work.

Henry Cust had been appointed revenue collector for the Armagh excise district in 1738 but he soon began to neglect his duties and was forced to resign in 1760. Henry was also a member of the Barrack Board having the responsibility for building and maintaining buildings under the direct control of Dublin Castle. He amassed a small fortune so that by the time of his death in 1781 he leased in excess of 4,000 acres including the 600 comprising Ballynahone town land which he held from the Primate. In 1769 he was appointed High Sheriff of the County and served on both the County and City Grand Juries. He also held the appointment of Sovereign nine times. During his public office he oversaw the first provision of street lighting in the city, a scheme which cost the Corporation £40. Before his death he left Ballynahone and returned to live in the city.

(Clarkson & Crawford p.64-66
Taylor & Skinner p.26)

BANBROOK HILL

This was the old way into the city from Loughgall, Moy and Blackwatertown. The name is a corruption of Bondbrook (as it appears on a lease in 1740) originating from the Bond family, who owned

BANBROOK HILL

Drumsill and lands in the area.

Banbrook Hill runs up from the lower English Street/Railway Street junction along the lower slope of Knockadrain Hill then down to 'the Railway Street roundabout'.

On the Cathedral side of Banbrook Hill, below St. Patrick's Grammar School, the two-storey terrace houses are approached by steps or ramps. The most recent Housing Executive brick terraces are decorated with bands of yellow brick and curious little triangular shaped porches.

On the east side of the road there are single-storey old people's dwellings with stepped roofs. They form part of the large Housing Executive development that occupies nearly all the land between Banbrook Hill and Railway Street. The Northern Bar, a traditional two-storey public house overlooking the roundabout, has survived in the angle between the two roads.

(Paterson (B) p.71)

BARRACK HILL

Formerly known as Wellington Place, it acquired its present name because it was the approach road to the barracks which was moved here in 1773. The part restoration and part recreation of the long terrace of houses is of special interest. As in the case of Castle Street this work became necessary because of prolonged neglect of historic fabric.

6 George's Street: No.6 George's Street and nos.1-33 Barrack Hill were refurbished for Gosford Housing Association in 1990. Architect Ian Donaldson.

The first house in the terrace has its entrance porch and two bays to George's Street and three bays to Barrack Hill.

Its gable wall, like that of the Savings Bank, is a focal point coming from the Mall and Barrack Street. Concern about the prominence of the gable caused the architect to decorate it with an inset arch, keystone and pediment in concrete 'heritage' brick.

Maisonettes are reached from the back of the terrace.

Original street nameplates have been re-used.

1-5 Barrack Hill: A group of three-bay, three-storey terrace houses of random rubble limestone with brick trim to openings, stone cills. Hanging basket brackets are also flag pole holders.

7-13 Barrack Hill: A two-bay, three-storey terrace of coursed rubble limestone with brick trim to openings and stone cills. Nos.7,9 and 13 have sixteen light sash windows; no.11 has twelve light sash windows.

15-33 Barrack Hill: A two-bay, two-storey terrace of random rubble limestone with stone soldier arches to openings. Original doors and windows faithfully reproduced with frames set close to front face of stone.

35-47 Barrack Hill: (c.1965) Seven three-bay, single-storey old people's dwellings in concrete brick with pantiled roofs and modern windows.

49-51 Barrack Hill: (c.1965) Pair of houses, one three-bay and one four-bay, similar in design to nos.53-71.

Marantha Church: (1972) A six-bay church in red brick and smooth render. Tall pointed windows with shallow pitched, hipped roof and obelisk shaped finial.

53-71 Barrack Hill: (c.1965) Terrace of two-bay, two-storey grey concrete brick buildings. Flat roofed canopy over entrance door and side lights. The terrace is raised above road level and approached by a high level walkway.

109 Barrack Hill: (Victoria House 1841) Three-bay, two-storey smooth rendered Regency style villa with hipped roof and overhanging eaves. There is a suggestion of pilasters and frieze in the raised plaster banding. Small flat roofed later addition to side with decorative ironwork balcony rail like Charlemont Place. Simple fanlight and portico with Tuscan columns. Original sash windows with square panes, interesting keystone heads to ground floor windows.
Lions couchant on gate piers, the replacement gates are inappropriate. Although much repaired the original charm of the building has not been lost.

The old stone wall which continues along Barrack Hill is breached by new entrances to deluxe bungalows.

On the north side of Barrack Hill the great stone wall of the barracks is of coursed and squared limestone with semi-circular coping stones. Khaki-coloured high level metal sheeting has been installed covering much of the wall and giving it a bleak appearance. It is relieved by a small brick and concrete observation tower peeping out at the main entrance gate; altogether an example of Eighties siege architecture. There are several fine cut stone entrance piers and at one corner an observation post corbelled out from the wall. On it an inset label stone is inscribed 'O B No 1'.

Gough Barracks: This complex replaced a short lived barracks on the site of the Gaol at the head of the Mall. The first group of buildings (demolished about twenty years ago) stood in the south-west corner of the present site and appear to have been erected in 1773. This makes them the earliest purpose built barrack buildings in Ulster. All these early buildings were constructed of pink rubble conglomerate with cut limestone dressings. The section of the perimeter wall, facing Barrack Hill, dating from this period is easily identified because the later work is exclusively limestone. The main accommodation block was an impressive fifteen-bay, three-storey block facing west over the city. The central bay was advanced and pedimented. It may well have been the work of the architect George Ensor. The two-storey block behind remains but its pitched roof was replaced by a concrete flat roof during conversion for Civil Defence use about 1960. The officers' stables adjacent to the old gate is more or less intact.

In 1874 a lease was taken out between John McWatters, bookseller, and Her Majesty's Secretary of State for War. This enlarged the site but it is clear, from O.S. map 1863 and certain other documents, that the military were making use of the land prior to the date of this lease. A new perimeter wall of squared rubble limestone was built and decorated with flankers that allow, from the inside, a view of the outside face of the wall. They perform the same function as modern television surveillance.

The next building erected was a magazine site opposite the gatelodge of St. Mark's. The north-east corner of the site was cordoned off and a hospital was built. It consisted of a main hospital block, a separate ward for infectious diseases, a mortuary and a gymnasium. The complement of the hospital, at the time of handover in 1921, was six officers and one hundred and ninety three men. The main hospital block has been replaced by a two-storey brick building for the Territorial Army. Also built at this time were two eight-bay, two-storey barrack blocks, probably married quarters. These buildings remain but like the earlier buildings now have flat concrete roofs. The most impressive building of this period is the Armoury which has a central gabled tower with an attic and two flanking staircase towers with pyramid roofs. All these buildings are of squared rubble limestone construction with brick dressings. A particularly fine feature is the robust shouldered stone chimneys with canted caps. The ventilators in the side of the flues are a reminder that these blocks were originally lit by gas.

In 1908 several other buildings were added including a separate house for the Regimental Sergeant Major, a miniature range on the site of the older magazine building and two more two-storey blocks. In c.1930 a canteen and recreation building was erected between these two blocks. All the buildings of this period are smooth red brick with yellow brick string courses. A little later a new sergeants' mess was built behind the guard room. This is in the Arts and Crafts style with a bell caste roof interspersed with dormers that light the bedrooms. The original windows have leaded panes. Inside is an inglenook fireplace, built-in bench seating and an oak panelled staircase.

Gough Barracks was so named to honour Field Marshal Hugh, 1st Viscount Gough, who commanded the 2nd battalion of the 87th Regiment of Foot at the Battle of Barossa during the Peninsular War. In 1881 the 87th and 89th Regiments of Foot were amalgamated to create the Royal Irish Fusiliers - the Armagh Militia were also combined into the same new regiment.

(Coote p.322
Irish Military Archives
R.U.C. Museum
Police Authority Archives
Stuart p.532
Armagh Guardian 6th Jan. 1950)

10-38 Barrack Hill: A group of fifteen single bay two-storey terrace houses of random rubble stone with brick trim. A few original windows and doors remain. Nos.10-16 are on level ground, the remainder step down following the slope of the hill.

40-48 Barrack Hill: Five two-bay, two-storey terrace houses with painted roughcast in various tones of chocolate and cream.

At the bottom of the road are the Kingston Memorial playing fields with a scattering of playground equipment surrounded by a low wall and an ugly corrugated iron fence with chain link fencing.

BARRACK STREET

This street was so called because it led to the military barracks built at the south end of the Common in 1736. In 1780 this building was demolished and the Gaol was erected on the site. The barracks were moved to their present site on Barrack Hill in 1773.

Bridge House: (1970) Architects G.P.& R.H.Bell for N.I.Housing Trust. Two five-storey blocks in grey concrete brick with single pitch roofs linked by a central open stairway. Their tower like appearance with forlorn metal balconies dominate the view from Scotch Street. A dire example of Sixties housing.

1-15 Barrack Street: (1970) Architects G.P.& R.H.Bell for N.I.Housing Trust. Eight single bay, two-storey terrace houses in grey concrete brick. Single pitch roofs hidden from view; each house has a lower lean-to roofed staircase projection.

17-19 Barrack Street: A two-bay, two-storey house in grey concrete brick with shop extension attached.

21 Barrack Street: A two-bay, three-storey end of terrace house of squared and coursed limestone. Sash windows with glazing bars; oculus window to ground floor; side facing entrance door. (See Gaol Square)

2-4 Barrack Street: A five-bay, three-storey building of random rubble limestone with ashlar soldier arches; rendered finish to ground floor. Splendid segmental carriage arch. Sash windows remain except to first floor of no.2; glazing bars to second floor of no.4 only. Basic modern shop fronts with plastic signs.

6-20 Barrack Street: Eight single bay, two-storey houses similar in scale to many of the Dobbin Street houses; nos.6-18 of random rubble stone; nos 16-20 smooth render finish. Originally all first floor windows were tripartite, those to nos.18-20 survive but without glazing bars. Original opening to ground floor no.6 remains with modern frame and door. The rest have large shop fronts with a medley of signs of varying quality.

22-24 Barrack Street: A five-bay, one and a half storey building with smooth render finish; chimneys missing. Coupled sash windows to no.22. Basic shop fronts.

BARRACK STREET in 1946. The site of the Armagh horse fair. All the houses are now shops but many were then private dwellings and it is noticeable that there is not a motor vehicle in sight. The buildings to the left, at the bottom of Scotch Street, were demolished to make way for a car park in 1963. (M. Craig).

BARRACK STREET. A view taken in 1991 showing the houses now in use for commerce and facing a widened roadway. The other side had been completely rebuilt by 1970. (M. Campbell).

St. Patrick's Church of Ireland Cathedral. A view from the chancel with the stone screen erected by L.N. Cottingham during his restoration and removed in 1888. National Library of Ireland, Lawrence Collection).

26-28 Barrack Street: A pair of two-bay, two-storey buildings; roughcast finish with smooth render to ground floor. Parapet wall with segmental curved feature above windows, probably originally tripartite. No.26 has a modern aluminium shop front.

30-34 Barrack Street: Three single bay, one and a half storey buildings with modern windows and blank first floor wall to no.30. Basic shop fronts.

36-38 Barrack Street: Two-bay, three-storey tower-like block; smooth rendered with blocked quoins. Modern windows in original openings. Ground floor pub front extends to corner as flat roofed block with modern plastic fascia.

CALLAN STREET

This is a very ancient way which led from the the hilltop westwards across the River Callan via the fourteenth century stone bridge built on the site of an earlier ford. It was the main road from the west, past Navan Fort, until the construction of the new route to Killylea and Caledon in the nineteenth century.
It is now a Y-shaped street connecting Irish Street, Abbey Street and Windmill Hill.

Culdee Crescent: Ten-bay, three-storey block of flats in roughcast set back from the original street line. External access walkways protected by a curved plastic canopy run the full length of the building. Two access bridges link with the footpath and grass area in front of building.
The crescent expresses clearly the functional design philosophy of the Sixties.
Across the street are the remains of small houses and blocked up garage entrances associated with Vicar's Hill.

47-75 Callan Street: A terrace of two-bay, two-storey dwellings in roughcast render with pantiled roofs and metal windows; some have been individualised by new doors and windows. The roofs step down to follow the slope and in some cases flights of steps lead up to entrance doors.
On the opposite side of the street is a dilapidated two-storey roughcast

block with a shop and shelter.

70-74 Callan Street: A terrace of two-bay, two-storey dwellings in concrete brick with timber windows and pantiled roofs.

CASTLE STREET

This picturesque street takes its name from a castle erected on ground granted to King Henry III by the Archbishop in 1227. Its circular contour preserves the outline of the inner ring of the ancient hilltop fortress.

The houses on the east side of the street are either being restored or have been replaced by new houses in the local traditional style. It is unfortunate that replacement became necessary, such neglect of historic fabric was a scandal that should not be allowed to happen again in Armagh. The datestones, now lost but previously recorded, establish that the earlier buildings were erected in 1828.

Only two houses remain under the cathedral 'ramparts' on the west side of the street. Many old stone walls remain, mostly party or boundary walls, which have been sensitively repaired and three gardens have been created. These were designed in the 1960s as a morning, afternoon and evening garden for the use of local people. There are parking bays this side.

53 Castle Street: All that remains of a terrace backing on to the cathedral walls. Three-bay, two-storey building of coursed rubble conglomerate and limestone; originally two houses. Good ashlar stone to window surrounds, heads and flush quoins. Datestone '1830' over doorway; datestone '1730' on corner. Rendered gable wall.

The Armagh conglomerate kerb to pavement each side of no.53 is worth a glance.

The remainder of the street on this side consists of car parking space and mown grass slopes bounded by stone walls.

Where no.2 Castle Street once stood is an open, grass covered site with new trees.

4-38 Castle Street: (1986) Designed 'in-house' by N.I.H.E. architects. A long curving terrace of generally two-storey, two-bay houses (nos.12 & 32 are three-storey) of coursed rubble limestone. Carriage arch between nos.22 & 24. Traditional style sash windows with glazing bars; tripartite windows to the ground floors of nos.4,6,22 and 24. A number of houses have 'mouth-organ' fanlights, all have six panel doors; pleasant colour scheme. An excellent example of total re-build.

At the rear of the terrace much of the yard space is taken up by steps to ground floor level. The car parking space is well sited.

The rear aspect of the terrace is very important and well handled particularly when seen from Friary Road.

40 Castle Street: Three-bay end of terrace house with quoins. Around the corner, in Chapel Lane, a hipped roof and four-bay elevation with steps and railings.

48-50 Castle Street: B. (c.1750) A most handsome pair of robust and stylish three-bay, three-storey houses of coursed random conglomerate. Ashlar stone blocked architraves to windows and semi-circular Gibbsian doorways; four steps enclosed by solid ashlar stone parapets; cut stone eaves parapet. Basements blocked up and railings missing.

The restoration of 48-58 Castle Street as part of a larger scheme by Hearth Revolving Fund has commenced.

52-54 Castle Street: B. (c.1760) Pair of two-storey houses of random rubble conglomerate; no.52 is three bay, including carriage arch, no.54 two-bay. Ashlar stone surrounds with keystones to doorway and segmental arched carriage entrance. Segmental soldier arches to first floor windows. Carved stone eaves cornice.

56-58 Castle Street: B. (1773) Five-bay, two-storey corner building; two houses of random rubble conglomerate, partly roughcast; chamfer-edged quoins at corner. Ashlar stone surround with keystone to doors. Cut stone projecting eaves cornice with urn pedestal block at the corner inscribed 'Whaley's Buildings Castle Street 1773'. The pedestal block awaits replacement of the urn.

CATHEDRAL CLOSE

Shown on earlier maps as Church Lane, it got its present name when the large stone houses were built in 1854 in the Cathedral grounds for the use of the clergy.

The Cathedral Church of Saint Patrick. (C.of I.)
This ancient building has been the focus of the city for over 700 years. The castellated parapet of its central tower crowns the summit of the hill. It is claimed to be the church in Ireland that has remained in use for divine service the longest of any in the land. The foundation of a Christian church on this site was the work of St. Patrick (445 AD). This preceded St. Augustine's foundation of Canterbury by more than a century.

The present building has at its core the work of Archbishop O Scannail, who rebuilt the church between the years 1268-1270. He chose the Continental model as established first in Ireland by St. Malachy (born in Armagh in 1094, died in Clairvaux 1148), at Mellifont in 1142. At Mellifont, masons and craftsmen were sent to Ireland to help St. Malachy by his friend St. Bernard of Clairvaux. At Armagh there is no reason to doubt that the work was by other than local craftsmen. The new church incorporated St. Patrick's, Damh-liag Mor (Great Stone Church), and also covered the ground previously occupied by two other smaller church buildings.

This construction has been subject to many ravages and changes since. The outward appearance to-day is very much the legacy of Archbishop John George Beresford who employed the architect, Lewis Nockalls Cottingham, to refurbish the building in 1834. At a meeting of the Lay Subscribers on 14th March 1835 under the chairmanship of the High Sheriff, Edmund Bacon, it was resolved:

'lst - THAT we cannot view with indifference the munificent Grant of Eight Thousand Pounds, made by His Grace the Lord Primate, and the liberal Contributions of the Dean and Chapter, and of the Diocesan Clergy, towards Restoring The Ancient Cathedral Of Armagh to its original beauty and splendour.

2d - THAT the Restoration of this Cathedral should be considered a National object, and, as such, should be supported by National Subscription; it being impossible to expect that any Local Subscription by the Clergy and Laity, however liberal, could be adequate to the completion of so important and costly and undertaking.

3d - THAT ARTHUR I. KELLY Esq., Sovereign of Armagh, WILLIAM BLACKER, and WILLIAM PATON, Esqrs., be appointed a Committee for soliciting Subscriptions, and carrying into effect the Resolutions of this Meeting; and that they be requested to apply to the most distinguished Noblemen and Gentlemen connected with Ireland, for permission to enrol their names as Honorary Members, in order that a General

Committee may be formed, suited to the National character of the undertaking - no Honorary Member, so enrolled, to be liable to risk or responsibility, of any kind whatever.

4th - THAT our said Committee be requested to solicit the patronage of THEIR MAJESTIES to the undertaking, as being an object of Public Interest, and also of the LORD Lieutenant of Ireland; and to forward Subscription Lists to our most Influential Countrymen at Home and Abroad - to all those distinguished persons who have held office in Ireland, or their immediate Representatives - to the Irish Societies in London, and to all other non-resident Proprietors of Irish Estates; and, generally, not to neglect any means which may appear conducive to the successful accomplishment of the undertaking, in a manner creditable to the Country and all those concerned.

5th - THAT we highly approve the Plan of Restoration furnished by L.N.COTTINGHAM, Esq., of London, and adopted by His Grace the Lord Primate; and that the funds collected in pursuance of these Resolutions, shall be laid out in the excution thereof, in such manner as may meet His Grace's approbation.

6th - THAT the Public Press be requested to give free insertion to these Resolutions, and of such Lists of Subscribers, as may, from time to time, be forwarded for publication by the Committee.

MR. KELLY having stated that the EARL of CALEDON, SIR THOMAS MOLYNEUX, Bart., and COLONEL WILLIAM VERNOR, M.P., had consented to become Honorary Members of the Committee, and having handed in a List of Subscriptions to the amount of £12,812 5s. - Resolved,

7th - THAT the meeting is highly satisfied with successful commencement, and feel entire confidence in obtaining the liberal support of the country at large, towards the completion of this National Undertaking.'

(SIGNED)   EDMOND BACON.

John Davidson Junior records that Thomas Hopper (architect of Gosford Castle c.1818) drew up plans in 1823 for a new church. However, due to the cost involved, this idea was abandoned and the restoration was entrusted to Cottingham.

Cottingham had set up his own practice in 1814 under the guidance of the medievalist scholar, John Carter. He quickly became accepted as a leading medievalist himself and in 1842 was elected to the Oxford Society for Promoting the Study of Gothic Architecture. Cottingham's work was meticulous and scholarly. His major restoration works in the Gothic style can be seen at Rochester Cathedral, St. Alban's Cathedral, Hereford Cathedral and Magdalene College Chapel, Oxford as well as at Armagh.

Except for the tower, the entire building was encased in ashlar sandstone. The West end was re-modelled removing the medieval carved doorcase; the spire was taken down and the pre Christian stone circle sited on the south-west slope of the graveyard was dismantled. Fortunately some of the carved stones taken from the building were not destroyed and are now preserved in the chapterhouse. Some other earlier features were not altered at this time, for example the traceried windows of the aisles as installed by Archbishop Hampton 1612-1613, also the sundial set on the south transept dated 1706. Some of the remaining smaller windows in the flanking walls of the transepts may be even earlier in date.

Even if we did not have the testimony of the seventh century book of Armagh (now in TCD) backed up by much other documentary evidence, the roughly circular form of the graveyard would itself confirm the early foundation of this site. The ground adjacent to the south transept is said to be the royal plot used in the tenth and eleventh centuries for burials of the Kings of Ulidia and close to the corner of the north transept a slab commemorates the interment of the High King Brian Boroimhe (Boru) in 1015 following his victory and death at Clontarf in 1014. The graveyard was fortified by a battlemented wall under the direction of Archbishop Hampton in 1613. This enclosure was replaced by the present walls and railings in 1834.

Interior:

The interior has also undergone an evolution through the years. Most recently the arches at the crossing were raised in height and the ceiling in the chancel replaced and redesigned (1903). The body of the nave and aisles remain very much as constructed by Archbishop Sweteman about 1365. The slight change in angle from choir to nave is a representation of the inclination of Christ's head as he hung upon the cross. Another feature of interest in the nave is the setting of the clerestory windows to the centre over the columns below. The ceiling in this section of the building is eighteenth-century plaster work and probably forms part of the works executed by Thomas Cooley in 1765. In the transepts and choir much of the thirteenth century construction remains. The gable windows have been enlarged and other alterations made but there is every reason to believe that the general format is still the work of O Scannail incorporating the earlier work of St. Patrick.

The Royal Irish Fusiliers chapel (1950) is the work of Major George Pace of York (1915-75), architect for the George Vl Mortuary Chapel, Windsor, and restorer of Llandaff Cathedral.

Monuments:

There are some notable monuments, in particular to Sir Thomas Molyneux by Francois Roubiliac, to Doctor Peter Drelincourt by Michael Rysbrack, to Archbishop Marcus Gervais Beresford, by John Taylor, to Archbishop Lord John George Beresford by Marochetti, (both Beresford monuments are full length recumbent figures) to Archbishop William Stuart by Sir Francis Chantrey, to Archbishop Richard Robinson by Joseph Nollekens and to Lt. Thomas Kidd by Thomas Farrell. On the wall on the north side of the Cathedral is a bust of Primate Knox and near the west door one of Archbishop Alexander. There is also an interesting group of monuments to the Caulfeild family set in the north transept, the earliest of which is dated 1698.

The organ is dated 1840 and is the work of Walker of London. (The first organ was installed in 1721). Another important relic preserved within the church is the remains of the eleventh century High Cross from Market Street, brought here for safe keeping in 1813 after it had been broken during rioting in the town. The remaining sculptured panels depict on the one side - Christ in Glory - a group possibly David with a Choir - three figures thought to be Hananiah, Mishael and Azaraih - the sacrifice of Isaac - the Ark - the Fall. On the reverse side the Crucifixion - below three unidentified figures - below that another unidentifiable group - the Baptism - the Presentation - the Nativity.

Stained Glass:

Several well-known English firms were involved in the installation of stained glass in the Cathedral.

Heaton, Butler & Bayne, of London, provided a number of well-researched and carefully painted incidents and figures. The series starts with Ascension in the east window, a Beresford memorial of 1903, and continues along the north side with the Archbishop Gregg window, obit 1896, which illustrates Jehoida the priest paired, unusually, with St. Paul. On the other side of the crossing the openings contain Three Marys at the Tomb, installed in 1914 in memory of a son of Archbishop Crozier; Christ carrying the Cross, a Royal School World War I memorial; Transfiguration, an Archbishop Crozier memorial post 1920 and the Adoration of the Wise Men and

Shepherds, in memory of Archdeacon Irwin obit 1920.

Much of the glass has been damaged by explosions. Repairs were carried out by Caldermac Ltd., Lisburn; they have inserted new windows also. In the chancel Archbishop Ussher appears with Archbishop Bramhall and Archbishop Robinson is shown with his Armagh buildings. Beyond the transept a Clutterbuck design of 1858 has been replaced by illustrations of the armorial bearings of the Irish Sees. The Evangelists in the chancel, painted by Miss Dunbar niece of Primate J.G.Beresford, survived the blasts; perhaps the superfluous Dorcas inscription from St. Mark in the Mall could be accommodated here. One of the angel windows has been retained in the chancel, it was erected in memory of Dean Jackson of Armagh, obit 1841. Along side Caldermac have provided a modern depiction of Ferdomnach, compiler of the Book of Armagh, and Primate Torbach, under whom he completed his first gospel in A.D.807.

The work of Lavers & Barraud, of the mid 1860s, occupies the south transept. There are two richly patterned lights and then an extraordinary memorial to Primate J.G. Beresford in which he appears twice. The narration moves from Solomon's Temple, via its restoration by Ezra and Nehemiah, to St. Patrick laying the foundation stone at Armagh in A.D.445 and culminates with Primate Beresford examining a plan of the cathedral. The armorial bearings of benefactors in the 1834 restoration, including Lord J.G. Beresford, are exhibited in the north transept and a further set of bearings are displayed in the west window.

Clayton & Bell's two windows in the south aisle were judged, in 1876, to be 'poor specimens of artistic skill and taste', but they are now of historic and iconographic interest. Raising Jairus' Daughter, incorrectly assembled, Wise and Foolish Virgins and Christ with Disciples all appear in the memorial to Rev. Cosby Stopford Mangam of Derrynoose, obit 1862. A musical theme was chosen for the memorial to Rev. Richard Allott, precentor, obit 1858; Jonathan and his sisters look on and scenes from the life of David appear at the base. A contrast is provided by the next window which depicts St. George, St. John and St. Patrick, in memory of Lord Armaghdale, obit 1924, by James Powell & Sons (Whitefriars) Ltd. The firm moved to Wealdstone, Middlesex, in 1923 but retained the little white friar mark which appears in this window at the bottom right. The windows flanking the entrance were the work of William Warrington, London, in 1852 and 1854. To the south are Good Samaritan and Acts of Mercy of the sick and the prisoner, an appropriate memorial to

William Lodge Kidd, Medical Inspector of Prisons. On the opposite side an opportunity was missed to devote a whole window to Moses; the right leg of the boy in the central light terminates in a left foot, an unusual deformity.
(Cathedral Guide.
Myles p.23-38
Weatherup (2).
Davidson.
Dixon - (3).
U.J.A. Vol.XXXXVII 1984. pp.109-161.
City of Armagh by James Black. 1810.
Drawing of West end of Cathedral by Francis Johnston 1785.
Drawings in the Armagh Public Library.
de Paor.
Documents in the Irish Architectural Archive:
-water colour sketch view of the city. Wm. Greenlees 1838.
-interior photograph. E. Chandler circa 1885.
-drawing for the new tower proposed by Robinson (undated)
-drawing for work on the spire 15/7/1784 signed F. Johnston.
I. B. Vol. XXX 1st October 1888
Rogers (1)
Rogers (2) p.33-36
Stalley pp.25 & 172-3.
Stuart p.518-523.
Gazeteer of Irish Stained Glass, 1988.
Ryan D'Arcy.
Coote p.307-312
Potterton.
Paterson (A) Vol. XXI. p.261.)

Vicar's Hill.

Takes its name from the houses which were principally occupied by cathedral choirmen and clergy widows. It appears on Rocque's map of 1760 as Pound Hill, being the site of the cattle pound. On Livingston's map of 1766 it appears as Church Street.

1-4 Vicar's Hill: B. (1724) A terrace of four houses built for Archbishop Boulter to accommodate the widows of Church of Ireland clergy. Evocative and picturesque three-bay, two-storey roughcast houses with pitched roofs and square chimney stacks. All windows have glazing bars except one window in no.2; the tiny first floor windows are a distinctively early feature. The Gibbsian doorways have flat heads, fan-shaped keystones and panelled doors.
'Side-on' steps with railings to front doors of nos.1-2 turn to face each other in a friendly fashion.
(S.A. Vol.6 No.l. 1971. pp.94-130)

5-6 Vicar's Hill: B. (1776) Both houses were built for Archbishop Richard Robinson, no.5 as a Metropolitan Registry Office. The Registry was a repository for ecclesiastical documents and registers until they were removed in 1935 to Armagh Public Library. They were returned to the Registry in 1958 but were subsequently withdrawn and are being replaced in the Public Library.

Two and three-bay two-storey houses with larger windows. Doorways have Tuscan pilasters on pedestal and no cornice; semi-circular fanlight with blocked architraves and keystones; six panelled door; two steps.

7 Vicar's Hill: B. (1776) As for 5-6 but with wheel fanlight.

Nos. 8-11 including the spacious music hall in no.9, were built for Archbishop Robinson.
(Paterson (A) Vol.IV. p.15 & 46)

8 Vicar's Hill: B. (1780) Three-storey, three-bay house with additional bay on third floor. Simple Gibbsian doorway of ashlar limestone

9 Vicar's Hill: B. (1780) Entrance to music hall within an elliptical archway consisting of a large single doorway flanked by half Tuscan columns and full cornice above, surmounted by three light fanlight. Small high level segmental-headed window above entrance. The presence of the hall in the terrace is expressed by three tall vertical nine pane windows, two-storeys high.

10 Vicar's Hill: B. (1780) Four-bay three-storey house. Eight panelled door with Tuscan pilasters on pedestals (as in no.6). Glazing bars missing to windows. Original built-in foot scraper.

11 Vicar's Hill: B. (1794) Three-bay three-storey house. Doorway similar to nos.6 and 10. All windows are, at present, blocked up.

The street is terminated by a good wall, steps and railings; re-opening would be an improvement. The undulation of the original Armagh limestone paving is attractive.

The See House. (1975) Architect Edwin Leighton, Diocesan Architect. Tucked into the northside of the Cathedral Hill, behind a high stone wall, and on the site of a former rectory garden is the official residence of the Primate of All Ireland. Built in 1975 after the Palace was sold to Armagh District Council, the house is no more than a two-storey

VICAR'S HILL from the Cathedral churchyard showing the 18th century houses and Music Room with beyond those built for the clergy widows in 1726. (M. Campbell).

CATHEDRAL CLOSE and St. Mark's Rectory. The former rectory, photographed in 1969, was demolished to provide a site for the new See House built in 1975. (Armagh County Museum).

Elevation of a proposed tower by Francis Johnston for ST.PATRICK'S CHURCH OF IRELAND CATHEDRAL. This was commissioned in 1782 by Archbishop Robinson as a copy of the Magdalen College tower in Oxford. (Irish Architectural Archive).

modern villa. The panes from the inside porch door of the Palace were removed and re-erected at the See House. These depict the arms of twenty-four Primates.

The Gates to See House: A. (1780) Architect Thomas Cooley.
It is only the handsome entrance gates that evoke any kind of primatial grandeur. They consist of two tall piers of blocked ashlar limestone embellished with Greek key pattern banding above which is a frieze with carved stone swags, heavy cornices and ball finials on stem pedestals. Two side gates and side piers join the high curved stone walls of the sweep in. The fine iron gates are probably nineteenth century or later.
Originally sited on the Newry Road at the principal entrance to the Primate's Palace, the gates framed the building which had a most impressive approach with a curving drive. The present gateway to the Palace was then a service entrance to Dobbin Street Lane. The gates were removed when the R.U.C. Barracks were built in 1963 and re-erected in Cathedral Close.
(Paterson (A) Vol. II. p.121.
Drawings in Irish Architectural Archive)

Lady Anne's Gate: B. (c.1840)
A fine early wrought iron gate giving access from See House to Church House. It was moved from the Palace demesne where it was the gate to Lady Anne's garden. Lady Anne Beresford was a sister of Lord John George Beresford, Primate from 1822-62. A photograph of the gate appears as the frontispiece to Alexander E. 'Lady Anne's Walk' (London 1903), the author was a daughter of Primate Alexander.

15-16 Cathedral Close: B. (1854) Architect John Boyd. Architects for 1991 renovations - Leighton Johnston Associates.
An important pair of semi-detached three-bay, two-storey houses, with basements, of coursed and squared limestone. Built in the Collegiate-Jacobean style and positioned on a steep and prominent site overlooking the north-east side of the Cathedral precinct. The confident massing of the houses and the splendid flourish of their tall Tudor-style brick chimneys, punctuated by curious vertical see-through slits, all create a perfect visual 'lead-in' from Market Square to the East end of the Cathedral.
The houses are entered from the narrow Cathedral Close roadway and here the double-pile central block has three stepped gables with

coupled entrance doors approached by two full flights of stairs symmetrically arranged on each side. At ground level are the service entrances and yards cleverly screened from the main entrance and the public roadways. On the south side facing the cathedral lawn the south half of the double pile block extends east and west to make a facade six-bays long. The two central bays are marked by a pair of stepped gables and two storey canted bay windows with the transom and mullions common to all the larger windows in the group.

Built to a scale and style suitable for clergy of the Victorian age the two houses have recently been skilfully converted into spacious flats. This has been achieved without in any way altering the exterior appearance of the houses.

(I.B. XIII, 5th May 1871 p.209)

CATHEDRAL ROAD

Mill Street, which ran from the Shambles to the Manor Mill, was renamed Cathedral Road when the Roman Catholic Cathedral was built in the nineteenth century.

1-4 Cathedral Road: Two three-bay and two single bay two-storey buildings of roughcast and smooth render with basic shop fronts.

5-11 Cathedral Road: Six-bay, three-storey stone buildings, now roughcast. Variegated brick chimneys and eaves course. Sash windows to first and second floors of nos.6,7 and 8; top hung windows to nos.5, 9, and 10. Fine hanging sign bracket.

15-17 Cathedral Road: Terrace of three two-bay, three-storey red brick houses. Ornamental moulded brick eaves cornice. Bay windows rise through two floors. Original sash windows to nos. 16 and 17.

19-27 Cathedral Road: Squat little terrace of seven two-bay, two-storey smooth rendered houses, all converted to shops except nos.23 and 25. Very small window openings suggest considerable age. Ugly proliferation of signs.

St. Patrick's Hall: (1954-5) Builder, P.McKenna & Sons, Armagh.
A cement rendered building set at an angle to the street line. The recessed entrance doors, with flat canopy, are centrally placed in the

gable front. Above is a group of small windows linked together by vertical concrete fins in a typical Fifties manner. Flanking the entrance feature are triple slit windows surmounted by shields worked in concrete - one an 'M' (1954 was a Marion Year), and the other 'St P' on a shield. There are regular quoins to the corners and around the entrance. High up near the apex of the gable is a simple cross.

The Lodge at St.Patrick's Cathedral: B. (1884) Architects, Ashlin & Coleman.

A single storey building with Gothic detail harmonising with the cathedral. It is built of squared rubble limestone brought to courses and left quarry faced. Dressed limestone is used for the coping of the plinth, the quoins, the dressings to windows and door, the eaves course, the coping of the gables and for the chimneys. There are two chimneys with chamfered caps and below them, on the shaft, a moulded string course. The roofs are steeply pitched and slated.

The principal elevation containing the entrance door faces the driveway to the cathedral. The entrance and lobby is advanced from the main body of the building and has its own narrow pitched roof and coped gable, crowned by a foliated finial, and carried on carved kneelers. Above the door is a panel depicting Christ as the Good Shepherd with a border of shamrock all contained within a trefoil. The bay to the right of the entrance is also advanced and gabled. The decorative iron finial is broken, otherwise the coping detailing is similar to the entrance bay. In the gable is a single Gothic arch in the form of a label mould; the stops are the carved heads of bishops (possibly St. Malachy and St. Colman). A quatrefoil in the tympanum contains the date 'AD 1884' and is flanked by trefoils filled with floral decoration; below is a pair of sash windows.

On the north face of this bay, facing the cathedral, is a carved panel containing the Papal Tiara and the keys of St. Peter. In the return wall, on the south side of the entrance lobby, is a single window and on the face of the main wall beyond is a carved panel containing an Irish harp. The other main elevation faces south towards Cathedral Road. The main feature of this face is a similar large gable, the finial in this case is complete. The stops to the label mould are, to the left the head of an abbess (probably St Brigid) and to the right a bishop (probably St. Patrick). Within this tympanum is a trefoil containing the arms of Primate McGettigan surmounted by the mitre and cardinal's hat bordered by floral designs with his motto 'PRO DEO ET ECCLESIA'.

CATHEDRAL ROAD

The gate screen is in a similar style and detailing. The four main piers carry the symbols of the evangelists.

St Patrick's Cathedral: A. (1838-1904) Architects Thomas Duff and J.J. McCarthy.

The Roman Catholic congregation in Armagh worshipped at Tullysaren when the Penal laws were in operation. This chapel was a long way from the city and was set alight on at least two occasions by rioting Orangemen. However in December 1750 a lease was negotiated with the Annesley estate for a site within the city in what is now Chapel Lane. The first chapel on this site was consecrated in 1752 and remained the centre for Catholic worship in the city until after Emancipation.

Plans to build a new Cathedral followed in the wake of the 1829 Act. Dr. Crolly registered a lease from the Earl of Dartrey for seven acres on the northern boundaries of the city including the hill top described in the seventh century Book of Armagh in relation to St. Patrick who, when he and his followers went to mark out the site for his church on the hill, where now stands the Church of Ireland Cathedral, disturbed a deer and its fawn. His followers wanted to kill the animals but St. Patrick took up the fawn and, followed by the mother, gave them sanctuary on this northern hill.

The committee set up to oversee the building work for the new Cathedral first met in Setember 1839 and construction began on St. Patrick's Day 1840. A target figure of £20,000 was agreed for the Cathedral. Great pains were taken by the building committee to select a source of building stone; they investigated seven quarries before selecting Ballybrannan, adjacent to Navan Fort.

The approved designs were the work of the Newry architect Thomas J. Duff, who had recently completed the fine new cathedral building of St. Patrick and St. Colman in his home town. As for the former building, Duff chose English Perpendicular Gothic as his style. The contractor for the foundations was Mr John Gribben and the architect apointed Mr Marron as Clerk of Works on 10th May 1841. By 1844 work had reached the top of the arcade but famine and cholera brought a temporary stop to the work; soon Duff himself was dead (1848).

An entry in the Dublin Builder of June 1851 indicated that Joseph James McCarthy had been chosen to carry on the work. In fact his appointment was not confirmed until 1853. The contractor appointed on 16th March 1854 was Thomas Byrne of Belfast. McCarthy had been

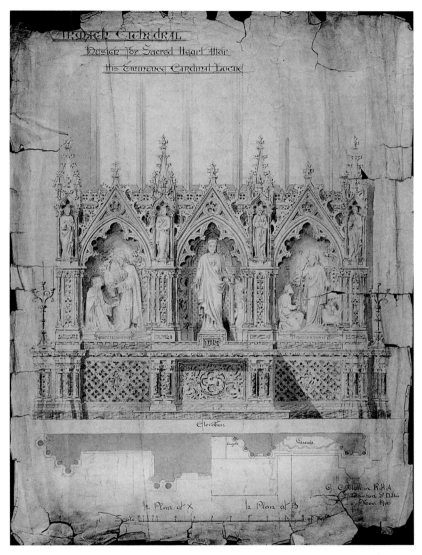

Drawing of the Sacred Heart Altar in St. Patrick's Catholic Cathedral by G.C. Ashlin, 1900. (Irish Architectural Archive).

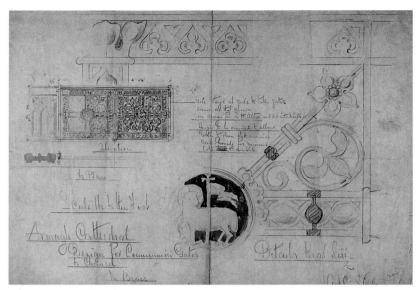

Detail drawing of the communion gates in St. Patrick's Catholic Cathedral by Ashlin and Coleman, circa 1900. (Irish Architectural Archive).

Macan Asylum for the Blind, CATHEDRAL ROAD. Opened in 1854, now demolished and the site developed for housing. (Armagh County Museum).

a pupil of the architect William Farrell and dubbed the Irish Pugin. He was himself a Catholic, a member of the Young Ireland Movement and a founder member of the Irish Ecclesiological Society. In 1847 he had published an article in the 'Irish Catholic Magazine' criticizing Duff's work in Armagh and so it can be no surprise that he set about a reappraisal of Duff's designs.

McCarthy chose an earlier form of Gothic as his model and based his new conception on Continental rather than English models. The proposal for a crossing tower was abandoned and a much greater emphasis was given to the towers flanking the great west door by the addition of spires. Generally the building was given a more vertical emphasis both inside and out by adding a triforium and increasing the pitch of the roof. One of the most interesting architectural features of McCarthy's building is the timber framed ceiling, based on the hammer beam principle but with the first stage rising from the walls as though to form a conventional groined vault. It is only at the step of the hammer beam that the true nature of the construction is revealed leaving the span of the central section to be completed in a coffered form. The building was finally dedicated for use on 24th August 1873 by Archbishop Dr. McGettigan.

J. Sheehy exlains the work of the two architects as seen on the exterior 'on the west front, the lowest stage with pointed openings set in rectangular frames is unmistakeably Duff, as are the windows above the aisle doors, with their ogee hood-moulds. The arcade with twelve apostles above the main doorway has very much the stamp of McCarthy, and so has the great seven-light west window. The window tracery, which is mostly what is called 'flowing', is McCarthy's. He completely changed the appearance of Duff's design by getting rid of the pinnacles on the buttresses, the battlemented parapets on nave and aisles, and by making the pitch of the roofs steeper.'

Interior:
Dr McGettigan's successor, Archbishop Logue, set about the suitable adornment of the interior. He appealed for funds across the world in the form of the 'National Cathedral Bazaar' of 1900. His efforts were suitably rewarded. The artists he employed included Cesare Aureli for the high altar, Oveste Amici for the ceilings, John Earley for the mosaics and Meyer for the windows and their work was directed by the Dublin architects Ashlin and Coleman. When he considered his work complete he celebrated the achievement by a 'Solemn Consecration' on 24th July 1904. It is a matter of great regret that so much of this

priceless work has so recently been removed in the name of the Second Vatican Council. Neither the quality of the replacements nor the skill of the craftsmanship can disguise the total alienation of the new work from the spirit and meaning that was McCarthy's ecclesiological architectural inspiration. In this setting, these modern intrusions appear dispassionate and irrelevant. The architects who won the competition set up by Cardinal Conway in 1971 to undertake this work were McCormick Tracey Mullarkey. The work was completed in 1982 in Cardinal o Fiaich's primacy.

The grand approach from Cathedral Road was the creation of Cardinal D'Alton.

Stained Glass:

Almost all of the window openings are filled with stained glass provided mostly by the firm of Mayer of Munich which became involved after the appointment of Dr Logue as Primate. Prior to this a few lights had been installed in the chancel by a Dublin company. Of these the east window, erected in 1879 at Dr McGettian's expense, illustrates a Crucifixion above incidents from the life of St. Patrick. It commemorates Primate William Crolly, obit 1849, and Primate Joseph Dixon, obit 1866. In the north aisle, after the crossing, the remainder of the glass is by Mayer, with the exception of the first two windows which are by an English firm.

Mayer was founded in Munich in 1827 as the Royal Bavarian Glass Painting Studio and by the early 1870s was doing enough business in England to justify opening an office in Holles Street, London. 'Munich glass' became despised through time but the firm has produced distinguished work depending on the artists involved. William F. Dixon, from Clayton & Bell of London, joined the studio in 1894, and his influence is apparent in the windows installed after that time, for example the St. Dympna or St. Patrick panels at the west end of the north aisle. Taken as a whole the stained glass complements the architecture and makes a positive contribution to the splendour of the interior.

The following list sets out the windows in the format used by the international Corpus Vitrearum, wherein the sequence starts at the east end and proceeds along the south side before returning to the east to repeat the process on the north walls. (If some of the detail appears remarkably fresh this is because it has been renewed recently by Caldermac Studios using a special enamel.)

South Side

St. Clare and St. Veronica with Sacred Heart.
Incidents from the life of the Blessed Virgin Mary.
St. James the Great, St. John and St. Peter.
Sorrows of the Blessed Virgin.
Incidents from the life of the Blessed Virgin.
Apparition of the Sacred Heart, Last Supper and Sacrifice of Melchisedech.
Come unto Me...and St Aloysius receiving Communion from St. Charles Borromeo.
Distribution of rosaries and a scapular with St.Oliver Plunkett saying the rosary.
St. Patrick and Kin Laoghaire at Tara.
St. Malachy receiving the last sacrament and curing a boy's arm.
Apparition at Lourdes and a procession of the Blessed Sacrament.
Martyrdom of St. Catherine and St. Philip Nervi attending the sick.

North Side

St. Michael, St. Malachy, St. Elizabeth of Hungary.
St. James the Less, Madonna and Child, St. Elizabeth with John the Baptist.
St. Benignus, St. Joseph, St. Malachy with Good Samaritan. St. Theresa, St. Brigid, St. Dympna.
St. Mel gives the veil to St. Brigid and offers her a crozier at her convent.
Assumption and Council of Ephesus A.D.431.
St. Malachy received by St Bernard with St. Malachy curing Prince Henry of Scotland.
St. Patrick with the Princesses Fedlimin and Eithne.
Espousal of Mary and Joseph and budding of Joseph's staff.
Dream of St. Patrick and St. Benignus placing flowers on St. Patrick.
Flight and martyrdom of St. Dympna.
St. Patrick receives his mission from Pope Celestine and death of St. Patrick.
Suffer little children with Moses striking the rock.
St. Patrick baptises King Laoghaire.

Ara Coeli: (1877 and 1928) The first section was built in 1877 for Archbishop McGettigan, four years after the completion of the Cathedral. It was altered and extended for Cardinal McRory in 1928 and it is his arms that appear carved above the entrance with his motto

'FORTIS IN FIDE'.

Generally the composition is two storeys; it is rendered with a dressed stone eaves course supported by modillions. The sills and quoins are also dressed limestone. The projecting single storey porch is constructed of dressed limestone and has granite pilasters flanking the doorway. The porch is the most architectural element of the building. The roof is hipped and the chimneys are placed at random.

The Synod Hall and Sacristy: B. (1896)
The two-storey building provides for a sacristy on the ground floor and a synod hall (or chapter house) and a library on first floor.
The building is cruciform in plan and the main axis is five bays in length. The main door is in the transept facing Ara Coeli. It is recorded that this doorway was built from stones dressed for the proposed entrance door into Thomas Duff's cathedral but put aside when McCarthy was appointed architect. It seems likely that some of the other cut stone in this building has a similar origin as the whole feel of the place is of the English Perpendicular style that was the basis of Duff's design.
The body of the masonry is punched ashlar fielded. On the north face the corners are decorated with the symbols of the evangelists. On the other three faces foliated bosses are carved in similar positions. The windows are tripartite with cusped heads to each light and the entrance is marked out by the addition of a label moulding with foliated stops.
A closed curving corridor, in similar architectural style, links the sacristy to the cathedral. Approximately half way along the corridor is an exterior door cased by a three centred Tudor arch. Above this is a crow-stepped gable in which are displayed the arms of Cardinal Logue with his motto 'IN PATIENTIA SALUS' and the date '1896'.

St Patrick's College: (now St Patrick's Grammar School) (1838, 1870, 1907, 1955 and 1975)
This austere building also forms part of the complex on the Cathedral Hill. The college was founded by Archbishop Crolly in 1838 to train students for the priesthood. In 1988 amalgamation took place with the Christian Brothers School (founded in 1851) and it became known as St Patrick's Grammar School.
The original building was extended in 1870 and again in 1907. The main front is symmetrical and of two storeys with an attic. The central entrance bay and the gabled wings are advanced. The architectural

detailing is sparse but the little there is originates in the Tudor Revival style. This is most clearly expressed in the individually shafted chimney stacks, the turrets that flank the entrance and the heavy kneelers at the base of each gable.

Subsequent additions have generally echoed the original forms.

(O'Fiaich.
Sheehy p.39-42.
Stuart.
Dixon (2) p.17.
Set of drawings in Architectural Archive Dublin from the office of Ashlin and Coleman, interior photographs c.1904.
I.B. - Vol. XV. 1st Sept. 1873.
    - Vol. XLV. and XLl 1904.
Builder - 7th Jan. 1854. 18th Nov. 1854. 21st June 1851.
Dublin Builder - 1st Aug. 1859. 1st Sept. 1859. 1st Oct. 1859. 1st and 15th April 1863.
The Two Cathedrals and their Founders - a public lecture given by the Rev. Father R. Murray on 22nd November 1990.
Cathedral Archives including Minutes.
Rogers (2) p.38-39.
Gazeteer of Irish Stained Glass
Ryan D'Arcy.)

1-4 Cathedral Terrace: An elegant and well proportioned terrace of four cement rendered houses. Nos.1 and 2 are three-bay, two-storey, nos.3 and 4 are two-bay, two-storey; no.2 has a carriage arch. The bay windows to no.1 rise through two floors; two single storey bays with little pitched roofs survive to nos.2 and 3. Original sash windows remain, except to no.4; nos.1 and 2 have original horizontal glazing bars. No.2 has original entrance door with delicate little sidelights. There are canopies over the doors of nos.2,3 and 4 with fretted fascia surviving to nos.2 and 3. Segmental arched doorway to no.1 with sidelights is probably not original. Original door and ventilators to carriage arch.

Unfortunately no.4 has been substantially altered.

Cathedral Villas (Nos.5-10): Six two-bay, two-storey red brick villas, four with attic storeys. Nos.9 and 10 have bay windows rising through two floors and no attic; nos.5-8 have single storey bay windows with a delicate curved roof and single windows in gabled dormers. Segmental headed windows and semi-circular doorways with brick keystones. Small gardens enclosed by ecclesiastical looking railings.

Padua House and Eskragh Eouse: Two semi-detached two-bay two-storey red brick houses with dormers. Single storey bay windows and entrance porches combined; moulded eaves course and door surround. Eskragh has original sash windows and railings.

68 and 69 Cathedral Road: Two detached three-bay, two-storey villas. Windows and entrance doors have been replaced but original interior stained glass door remains to no.69.

Corn Market: A. (1827) (see Dawson Street) Three-bay single storey elevation in coursed squared limestone with ashlar dressings. The pedimented centre piece breaks forward with central rectangular opening (with original gates) set in segmental headed recess. Vertical blind round headed recesses on either side.
(Brett p.36)

Public lavatories in dark artificial stone with hipped roof. A small building which blends in with its important stone built neighbour.

The open market area is separated from the road by a length of railings with upstands in coursed squared limestone. There are four entrances with octagonal gate piers with domed caps; the first entrance with modern mesh gates has been reconstructed and widened. It is good to see the market in use once again with a row of banners announcing this fact.

8 Cathedral Road: B. Architect possibly J.H. Fullerton.
A very attractive two-bay, two-storey red brick building with attic; yellow brick surrounds to openings and ornamental moulded brick string courses. Original sash windows with vertical glazing bars. The bay window rises through two floors and terminates in a balustrade of delicate recast stone semicircular arches on columns. This forms a balcony reached by coupled elliptical headed windows in the gable dormer.
Original entrance door with semi-circular blank fanlight. Fine chimney stack with corbelled brickwork at ridge level and steeply pitched roof with embellished cresting. Original railings to small garden.
The whole ensemble is unchanged since it was built and is full of charm.

10 Cathedral Road: Three-bay, two-storey building in smooth render with window surrounds and quoins. Sash windows with glazing bars.

A modern service station and railings to a public park and playing fields mark the end of the built up section of Cathedral Road.

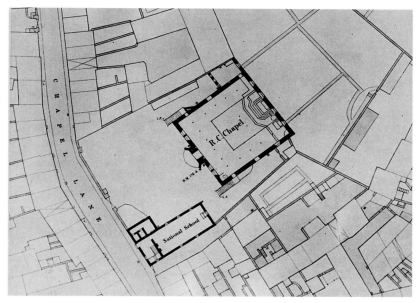

Ground plan of St. Malachy's Church and National School from the ordnance survey map of 1863.

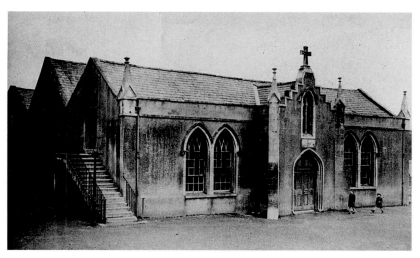

St. Malachy's Catholic Church in CHAPEL LANE; demolished in the early 1950s after standing derelict; shown as it was before 1935 with the front built in 1819. (P.J. Hamill).

Children playing in CASTLE STREET, 1963. The houses on the north side below the Cathedral churchyard had already been demolished at that date. (M. Craig).

Stable block at the back of CHARLEMONT PLACE on the Mall in 1987 with the Royal School in the background. (Armagh County Museum).

CHAPEL LANE

This steep narrow laneway connects Castle Street and Ogle Street. It was called after the Church of St. Malachy which was erected in 1752 and demolished in 1955, twenty years after it ceased to function as a chapel.

1-5 Chapel Lane: Three single bay two-storey small scale dwellings with slated roofs. Uninhabited and blocked up.

St. Malachy's Primary School: (1956) This building was erected on the site of the original St. Malachy's Church (see Irish Street). The main block is six bays with a two bay low wing in painted render with brick gable and base and metal windows. The building is set back from the lane with a brick retaining wall and railings. At the south end the blank brick wall is higher than the eaves of the adjoining houses and this gives it a somewhat forbidding appearance.

A vacant site with an untidy boundary wall leads to a terrace of five two bay, two-storey Housing Executive dwellings. The buildings in painted roughcast with cement quoins have traditionally proportioned doors and windows, small gardens with railings and pitched roofs which step up the slope.

This side of the lane is terminated by the end of terrace stone house, 40 Castle Street, and by a view of the Cathedral beyond.

From the gable of 27 Ogle Street a painted render wall with segmental carriage arch leads up the steep slope to a yard wall with garage entrance.

16 Chapel Lane: Two-bay, two-storey modern dwelling in dry dash render with projecting canopy.

18 Chapel Lane: Three-bay, two-storey modern dwelling in painted render, similar in design to the Housing Executive houses in the courtyard to the rear.

A recently constructed stone wall, well built and pointed with two openings and good capping, screens the development behind.

32-34 Chapel Lane: A pair of three-bay, two-storey early houses of random rubble conglomerate with soldier arches to openings. Currently undergoing restoration.

CHAPEL LANE

36-40 Chapel Lane: Three dwellings of three-bays and two-storeys in course of construction in traditional style; they replace an earlier hall on this site. Roofs step up following the line of the lane.

A curved coursed rubble stone entrance, under construction, leads to a central courtyard at the rear of houses in Castle Street and Irish Street. This side of the lane is terminated by the rear view of 48 Castle Street with its semi-circular bow window rising dramatically through three floors.

(S.A. Vol.1 No.2 1955 pp. 169-75)

CHARLEMONT GARDENS

This mid-Fifties development was built on the gardens of Charlemont Place in an attractive setting with St Mark's Church in the background. The main part of Charlemont Gardens was developed in a fairly straight sweep up to the top of the hill where it terminates in a wide circular turning space. Around it a pair of semi-detached houses and four detached houses are arranged to form the centrepiece of the development.

Halfway down the hill a shorter side road runs south in a curve close to the driveway of St. Mark's Church. This whole cul-de-sac development (architect George Taylor) is interesting because the houses are of a similar design with common features like the corner windows which create a pleasant harmony. The low garden walls give the development a commendable unity.

Further down the hill the road which runs north was once a laneway serving the splendid rubblestone coach houses to the rear of Charlemont Place, now demolished, and the rear entrance to the Royal School. Portions of walling remain and will provide screening for the proposed car park behind. The large modern extension to the Southern Education and Library Board's offices is a dominant feature of the lane. On the other side is a disappointing new Masonic Hall (1991 - architect Clive Henning) with a three-bay facade set at right angles to the lane. It is cement rendered with a shallow pediment and projecting porch. An old high stone wall screens much of the lower part of the building.

The long side elevation of the County Museum dominates one side of the road which leads to the Mall. Built in the Fifties, this extension of brick with precast concrete dressings is two-storey, twelve-bay; the centre three bays and last bay break forward with pediments.

Opposite the Museum extension are two interwar, semi-detached, two-storey, rendered houses with inset arched porches and all their original doors and windows intact. The site where these houses stand is shown on early maps as a formal pleasure garden associated with Charlemont Place. Further along two large bungalows, with half timbered gables, stand one on each side of the lane.

(O.S. map 1835 and town maps 1846 & 1863)

COLLEGE HILL

A section of the road referred to on Rocque's map (1760) as the 'Road to Castle Dillon' was later renamed College Hill. It runs from the north end of the Mall past the College, or Royal School, to Dean's Bridge. The bridge was named after the Deanery, built by The Very Reverend Hugh Hamilton, Dean of Armagh from 1768-96.

1 College Hill: A five-bay, two-storey roughcast building attached to the porch and slate-clad gable of the Sovereign's House. Modern plastic windows with implied glazing bars. Original blocked stone door surround now painted. Traditional style panel door.

3 College Hill: A three-bay, three-storey roughcast dwelling set back from the road line; modern metal windows. It is seen through three large arched openings cleverly integrated in a very high wall of random rubble conglomerate spoiled by cement capping.

5-7 College Hill: (c.1920) A pair of substantial semi-detached three-bay, two-storey roughcast dwellings set back from the road with gardens and a low wall in front. Metal windows to no.5, plastic windows with implied glazing bars to no.7. Canted bay windows with pitched roofs on either side of entrance doors. Glazed panels beside each entrance door give the impression of double entrances.

The Royal School: A. (1774) Architect Thomas Cooley.
The removal of the Royal School from the site in Abbey Street, where it is delineated as 'The Free School' on Livingston's map of 1776, to its present site was made possible through a gift of £4,000 from Primate Robinson. The Royal was one of five schools founded by King James I in 1608 as part of his scheme for the Plantation of Ulster. There was a

re-assignment of the lands with which it was endowed by a charter of Charles I dated 1627. The move to College Hill was, along with the foundation of the Public Library and the Observatory, part of Archbishop Robinson's unsuccessful plan to establish a university in Armagh. James Black's painting of the City in 1810, shows the school buildings on the edge of a built-up area in a rural landscaped setting. The armorial bearings of George III adorn the south wall of the quadrangle between the escutcheons of Primates Robinson and Beresford.

The principal buildings are grouped in a traditionally collegiate form to create the four sides of a quadrangle. The original entrance was from College Hill through the blank screen wall that backs a cloister range spanning the whole northside. The arcade of this cloister was originally open to the quadrangle but was blocked up during the nineteenth century, at which time a square office building was added in the north-east corner. All these later inappropriate features were removed during recent renovations and the cloister arcade re-opened, although the openings are now glazed. The east and west sides of the quadrangle are formed by three storey ranges which contain school rooms and dormitories and the headmaster's former lodgings. The south side is now closed by a two-storey building containing the library. In the original design it was a single storey with the Royal Arms on a crenellated gable facing north. When Archbishop Lord John George Beresford enlarged the building in 1849 it was raised to its present height. The transition of floor levels between the two-storey and three-storey buildings is handled by recessed linking wings each with a door from the quadrangle. The western doorway was closed up after the Second World War and skilfully re-opened during recent alterations. Against the south side of the library there was, in 1872, a further enlargement by the addition of a big schoolroom and the lower classrooms. To the west is a further two-storey range, erected in two different periods which, with a wing of domestic offices, encloses a service courtyard entered separately from College Hill. The whole group is built with rubble conglomerate while the dressings of the later buildings are ashlar limestone. The shape of each building is simple, roof lines are relieved only by a series of chimneys set at regular intervals along the ridges of the wings and rising from the southern face of the south block. The proportions of the buildings are classical while Gothick dressings give an added air of scholastic respectability. All the parapets that face College Hill are crenellated, the entrance doorways from the street and the cloister arcade have Tudor Gothick dressings and the windows of the south block have label mouldings in the same style.

To the south and east were large walled gardens and orchards which gave the school a degree of self-sufficiency. The enclosing walls of conglomerate stone are still evident, although no longer intact. Much of the space has been used to provide sites for additional school buildings, added at a variety of dates. The most sympathetic is the range recently constructed to the designs of Belfast architects Samuel Stevenson and Sons and the Head Master's house designed by Major W.A.Johnston in 1967. Behind this building is the Preparatory Department converted in 1940 from the Sanitorium (1872) and extended in 1957 to designs by Major W.A.Johnston.

The long wall to College Hill is interspersed with entrances and decoratively designed wrought iron gates.

(Coote p.317.
Rogers (2) p.25.
Stuart pp.449 and 541-545 and Plate p.366.
Northern Life Vol.6 No.3.
Irish Architectural Archive - drawings from the McCurdy + Mitchell collection.
Armagh Public Library (three drawings) one signed Thomas Cooley Sept. 28th 1775.
Ulster Gazette Supplement 15th Nov.1990.
James Black - oil painting of the city of Armagh 1810, Armagh County Museum).

After the entrance to Tower Hill the road continues over the rise with a high bank and trees screening the almshouses and the new development in the foreground. College Hill is terminated on this side by a garage forecourt with a long canopy and a standard modern shed-like showroom.

Observatory entrance and gatelodge: The gate piers are of punched ashlar stone with a frieze of studded banding and cornice. Side walls of coursed roughcut conglomerate terminate in outer piers. Simple wrought iron gates. In front of the gate piers are two good original octagonal and domed buffers.

The gatelodge, of random rubble stone, is built against a gate pier; seen from the Mall the pointed window with shutters catches the eye. The extension is in scale though the glazed section inside the gate is ugly.

Observatory: A. (1789-91) Architect Francis Johnston.

From the gate lodge at the bottom of College Hill the drive winds up Knockboy to the Observatory buildings sited at the top. The buildings form an important element in Primate Robinson's overall plan, both as an element of his university project and as a practical ornament in the landscape he was creating, to give the whole city an environment of cultured serenity and good taste. Work began on the construction in 1789; as Cooley had died in 1784 the design was entrusted to the archbishop's new protege, Francis Johnston. This was to be Primate Robinson's last completed scheme for a public building in Armagh. He secured its perpetuity, as he thought, by the endowment of the lands of Derrywaught and the tithes from the parish of Carlingford and he placed its management with a Board of Governors and Guardians. These arrangements were given the formal approval of the Irish Parliament. To mark the achievement Mossop was commissioned to strike a medal, the inscription on this commemorative piece reads 'The Heavens Declare The Glory of God'.

The orientation of the Observatory buildings is the same as that of the Palace and the Royal School, with the entrance on the north face. The buildings are stone with conglomerate rubble for the main walling and ashlar limestone for the dressings. The proportions are classical, the decoration is minimal; the architectural effect is achieved by the subtle relationships of solid to void.

The dominant element of the group is the astronomer's lodging. This building is roughly square on plan, has a double pile structure and is formed of two storeys over a basement. The main elevation is three-bay, the entrance is central and approached by a fanned flight of seven stone steps. The doorway is cased by a Tuscan prostyle porch in ashlar limestone with block parapet and projecting cornice mould set over modillion brackets. The frieze is decorated by triglyths separated by unadorned metopes. The only decoration of the architrave is the guttae that give emphasis to the triglyphs above. A pair of doors with small pane glazing above the lock rail and timber panels below close the entrance. The windows are all small pane sliding sashes each with a dressed limestone cill, lintel and stepped dressings to the jambs. Chimneys crown all four gables. Between the pitches of the roofs is a wide platform that has been used to mount various instruments. There is a block parapet delineated by a projecting string course; a second string course defines the basement. All four corners have stepped fielded quoins.

The main feature of the south face is the circular telescope tower which bears the same inscription as the medal. Approximately two-thirds of the bulk of the tower projects beyond the body of the building and the observation room at the top creates an attic storey.

The whole feature is capped by a hemispherical, copper-clad dome. The telescope is supported on a central limestone pillar rising through the full height of the tower and braced against the outer wall by the stone treads of the spiral stairway. The final ascent into the observation room is via a straight flight below a copper roof with a semi-circular section that rises out of the main roof and is lit by a single curious roof light.

In the interior the detail is restrained and minimal, the joinery is the main architectural element. The tower naturally introduces curves, however other curves have been purposely created for purely aesthetic reasons. In particular the astronomer's study is beautifully lined with curved bookcases and cabinets. The same form is echoed in the shape of the chimney breast. An amazing proportion of the original doors, windows, encasements and fittings have survived decades of every day use. The recent work to convert the lodging to office use and the need to accommodate computers has been skilfully handled with minimum loss of historic fabric.

Adjoining the east gable there is a single storey wing now connected to the lodging but probably originally designed to be separate. It features the square two-storey sector tower built in 1841; the south face is adorned by the arms of Primate Beresford. The slot, in the adjacent pitched roof (now covered) was to allow readings from the Mural Circle. The range is terminated at its eastern end by a second circular tower built in 1827 to house an Herschel telescope. This second tower is very similar to the main one in both size and shape.

Most of the other buildings on the site are relatively modern and not of any particular architectural merit. However there is one exception, the free standing structure, built in 1885 to protect the new Grubb built Robinson Memorial Telescope. It is formed by cast iron columns of minimal section held erect by iron diagonal tension braces. These elements support an iron ring beam that in turn provides a rail for the wheels that allow the dome to be rotated. The compression members of the dome are a series of cast iron quadrant ribs. The tension element is provided by the weather skin of the dome. The whole assembly is an exceptionally elegant engineering design based on the structural principle of a tent and is very economical in its use of materials.

The original tree planting, mostly of beech and chestnut, is now beyond maturity. Other specimen trees were added to this group towards the end of the nineteenth century. Lower down the slope, as a screen to the boundary with the Armstrong County Primary School, further trees were planted. These are reaching a height where the two way view between the Observatory and the Palace is becoming obscured. The most recent addition to the landscaping is a garden of radiating paths and beds on the south side of the lodging. There is no doubt that the original conception was for the buildings to rise directly out of the green sward. From this vantage point the Palace is poised with the obelisk rising from the trees behind it.

(Moore.
Coote p.314.
Stuart p.45 and 523-527.
Rogers (2) p.26.
Bassett p.89.
Photographs dated 1869 and 1963 in the Irish Architectural Archive.)

Armstrong Primary School: (1929) Architect J.St.John Phillips.
The school is built around a courtyard as a series of single storey brick pavilions with hipped roofs in a well composed but rather mechanical Thirties style. The main elevation facing due west is nine bays long with the five central bays having a higher roof line and also breaking forward with pilasters, cornice and a blocking parapet and other dressings in fawn faience (a hard wearing substitute for stone popular at the time). The centre panel of the parapet is raised to carry the inscription 'THE ARMSTRONG SCHOOL'. The south elevation to College Hill is twenty bays long including the hipped gable ends of the west and east pavilions.
Modern flat roofed brick extensions on the north and east sides are carefully linked to the main building so as to form separate units set clear of the original block. Unfortunately modern extensions into the courtyard have altogether compromised the original architectural conception.
In the tarmac surfaced grounds are two attractive loggias with fat Tuscan columns in faience.
The low galvanised security fencing on the College Hill retaining wall is worth a mention for being unobtrusive.

Planetarium: (1965-7) Architects G.P.& R.H. Bell. Contractors A.C. Simpson & Partners.
In 1950 the Planetarium Board was formed after many years of endeavour by Dr.E.M. Lindsay. Originally it was intended that the erection of the building and provision of finance for the Planetarium

should be an internationally funded project. However the necessary support was not forthcoming and financial assistance was obtained from H.M. Government, the Armagh County and City Councils with a grant from the Carnegie Trust for exhibits. A site near the Observatory stables was chosen for the Planetarium.

The two-storey entrance feature takes the form of a doorway recessed below a large and curious chequer-board panel of black and white squares. This is attached to the ribbed auditorium drum crowned by a tall sheet-metal dome. At the side is a later wing, the Hall of Science, with roughcast render walls and tall slit windows.

While many of the finishes are appropriately modern for this space age building, local stone has also been used and here the workmanship is particularly good. However it is a pity that the unique shape of the Planetarium building, a distinctive landmark in Armagh, was not allowed to speak for itself with more clarity.

(Lindsay.)

Within the grounds are two pleasant staff houses, one single storey and the other two-storey, of painted roughcast rendering with red tiled roofs and painted metal windows.

A good stone wall runs along College Hill. Below and behind the wall are the playing fields of the Royal School.

Dean's Hill gate lodge: (c.1860) A three-bay cottage ornee of informal design set on sloping ground with the entrance at the higher level. Roughcut stone with punched ashlar flush quoins; hood moulds to windows. Now a shell but undergoing restoration. Note the re-built triple chimney stacks in the traditional manner.

This building replaces an earlier lodge located on the opposite side of the road.

Tall punched ashlar stone entrance gate piers with stems of missing balls, the gates have been removed. Two curved wing walls of roughcut stone terminate in smaller piers.

Dean's Hill: B. (1772)

A symmetrical double pile house of three storeys over a basement with classical proportions and the barest of decoration. The centrally placed entrance door is approached by seven cut stone steps bridging the basement area and fanning out towards the foot. The flight is guarded by iron railings, elegant but without decoration of any kind. The door has eight panels, the top and bottom panels are full width, the rest are arranged in two rows of three. Above is a semi-circular fanlight consisting of a semi-circular eye and four radiating geometrical panes. The doorway is encased in limestone; Doric pilasters support an unembellished entablature and triangular pediment.

The body of the building is roughcast rendered. There are quoins at basement level, a string course above the basement and a corbelled eaves course, all of dressed limestone. The chimneys are set on the gables and are in two stages, apparently raised with the introduction of coal as a fuel. All the windows are small pane sashes, in the piano nobile they are five panes in height, at first floor level they are four and in the attic and basement two. In the entrance front there are four sets while facing the garden there are five. Extending to the left of the main front there is a two-storey wing, in similar style, that links to the contemporary service yard. With some very minor exceptions all the interiors are also contemporary.

(Stuart pp.528-529)

COLLEGE STREET

On Rocque's map of 1760 it is known as the Road to Castle Dillon. The name College Street derives from the Royal School, locally called the College or Classical College, which was moved to its present site from Abbey Street in 1774. College Street is short and straight and links the Mall to English Street; at the junction there are good views down College Street and up College Hill. On the south side of the street is an outstanding group of houses like those in Beresford Row, Mall East.

1 College Street: Two-bay, two-storey building of incised painted render; cut-stone doorway with pointed arch; windows with pointed heads to first floor.

3 College Street: (c.1804) Originally a gospel hall built for the Secession congregation and now stripped of all its character. Rogers refers to it as 'the Tabernacle in College-street used by the Independent denomination'. Four-bay, two-storey building, incised smooth render; semi-circular headed first floor windows. New traditional style shop front being inserted at upper end.

(Rogers (2) p.44.
Paterson (A) Vol.III, p.17.
O.S. map 1839.
Lundie.)

5-7 College Street: Pair of three-storey smooth rendered houses; carriage arch to no.7. Sash windows with glazing bars except to ground floor of no.7.

9 College Street: B. (1820) Three-bay, three-storey coursed rubble building with segmental headed carriage arch; keystone of arch inscribed 'W.B.1820'. Semi-circular Gibbsian doorway; stone step. Stone cills to windows; all glazing bars intact.

11-21 College Street: B. (c.1820) Splendidly intact terrace of two-bay, three-storey houses of random rubble limestone; no.21 is painted render. All have ashlar limestone semi-circular headed Gibbsian doorcases; nos.13-19 have 'spider's web' fanlights; nos.11 and 21 have plain quartered fanlights; good replacement doors; most have foot scraper recesses. The ground and first floor windows are tripartite with soldier arches; most windows have glazing bars.

23 College Street: B. (c.1820) Three-bay, four-storey rendered building; unusual rectangular fanlight to door. The two windows on the second and third floors are not centred on the windows below. All windows have glazing bars except on ground floor. Recessed foot-scraper.

25 College Street: B. (c.1820) Two-bay, three-storey building of coursed random rubble limestone with windows and doorcase of ashlar limestone. The segmental headed arched doorway with fanlight, simple cornice and frieze is supported by half columns all set within the arched opening. Recessed foot scraper.

The one-bay, three-storey side elevation of 3 Rokeby Green faces College Street; smooth render finish with window arrangement paying regard to its next door neighbour and the street.

Nos. 1-25 College Street form a cohesive group of good quality buildings. It is important that, if alterations are planned to any individual unit, the group quality should be a paramount consideration in the judgement of the proposal.

A vacant site where the first of the Seven Houses, English Street, once stood.
A seven-bay, three-storey block finished in smooth render; partly blocked up awaiting re-development.

COLLEGE STREET

An undistinguished run of single storey sheds and a sleek modern spare parts garage shop; all ripe for re-development.

First Presbyterian Church Lecture Hall: B. (1857) Architect W.J. Barre. Contractor Mr John Farr.

A handsome six-bay, two-storey rendered building erected as a Sabbath and day School; smooth plaster with blocking courses to ground floor. Hipped roof with projecting eaves on paired scroll brackets.

At each end there is a segmental headed arched recess containing a doorway with a wide fanlight above a scroll bracketed cornice. The first floor has semi-circular headed windows over a continuous stone cill course. The eaves are raised in the centre two bays in a segment to contain the text 'TRAIN UP A CHILD IN THE WAY HE SHOULD GO' around an open book carved in stone.

(Rogers (2) p.40.
Paterson (A) Vol.IV. p.22)

CONVENT ROAD

Mount Saint Catherine was the name chosen by Archbishop Dixon for the new Sacred Heart Convent at Tullynasney, in the townland of Lurgyvallen, to the west of the city. The section of Desart Lane, connecting Cathedral Road with Callan Street and Windmill Hill, which forms the eastern boundary of the property then became known as Convent Road.

1-21 Convent Road: A modern development of single and two-storey detached and semi-detached dwellings.

The remainder of the road on this side is an open area of grass. The siting of the ancient city is dramatically seen from this viewpoint.

The fine coursed rubble perimeter stone wall to the Convent runs almost the full length of the road on the opposite side. It is breached only once to allow entrance to the Convent rounds. Some sections of the wall form part of the buildings located in the grounds.

Gatelodge: A two-bay, two-storey red brick building with yellow brick dressings and string course; modern timber windows. Brick ridge tiles to roof with cresting. Modern extension. The brickwork to the gabled side elevation is worth a second glance.

Convent of the Sacred Heart: (1859) Contractor Mr McCaughey.
The foundation stone was laid on 30th April 1857.
The nuns of the Sacred Heart opened a school in Abbey Street in 1851. Before the Convent was completed they moved first to the Pavilion, then to Charlemont Place. .
The Convent is set back some distance from the road on an elevated site. The original building of three bays and three storeys was a symmetrical classical composition, it was later extended to eleven bays. It is built of coursed and squared stone; the three centre bays are advanced with an open pediment above. In 1874, the clock, by G. Borell of Paris, was added. At the top of an elegant flight of steps is a porch with cornice and blocking course. The doorcase has an elliptical fanlight and sidelights between pilasters, over which is a statue of Our Lady in a niche. The ground floor window heads are square, first floor serm-circular and the second floor segmental.
In 1885 a new wing in the Tudor Revival style was added. This building was badly damaged by fire in 1964, its replacement in brick looks incongruous. Behind the main building there are several Sixties blocks, all of expressed frame construction. At the bottom of the hill close to the entrance gates is a more recent brick dwelling.
(Coleman p.436-9
Paterson (A) Vol.4. p.116
S.A.Vol.9. No.2. pp. 350-61)

The convent wall continues to the end of the road and extends around the corner up Windmill Hill. It is good to see such a fine feature of this part of Armagh so well maintained.

CULDEE STREET

This street connects Irish Street and Navan Street and now consists entirely of modern housing of a typical Sixties design. Once a street of small terraced houses called 'Primrose Hill' to commemorate Lady Primrose who left money in her will to give Armagh its first piped water supply.

1 Culdee Street: A modern five-bay, two-storey block of maisonettes in roughcast render with pantiled roof.

3-11 Culdee Street: A terrace of modern two-bay, two-storey dwellings in roughcast render with timber windows.

13 Culdee Street: An end of terrace house with a panel of windows on the front and the entrance door around the corner on the gable.

15-17 Culdee Street: Three blocks of brown brick maisonettes with flat roofs and painted render panels below windows.

2-16 Culdee Street: Similar to their counterparts on the opposite side of the street, the exception being no.8 which has been individualised by the addition of a projecting porch and new windows.

18 Culdee Street: A three-bay, two-storey detached dwelling on an open site at the corner of Culdee Street and Navan Street. Red brick to first floor and dry dash render to ground floor. Gable entrance at first floor with outside steps and porch; modern plastic windows.

CULDEE DRIVE

On Livingston's map (1766) it is called New Lane, later it became known as Gas Lane. It took its recent name after redeveloment was undertaken by the N.I. Housing Trust in the Fifties. Culdee Drive now consists entirely of modern housing with the exception of the gasworks.

Gasworks: T.G.F. Paterson states that the gas producing plant was installed in 1834 and that by 1840 most of the shops and houses were lighted by gas. He says that 'a prehistoric monument was demolished on the ground now held by the company, a structure that would have made Armagh unique among Irish towns had it been preserved'.
The gasworks closed in 1986 but the former Manager's House (1893), offices, weighbridge house and part of the fine perimeter stone wall remain.
(Paterson (A) Vol.4, p.95.
Paterson (H.H) p.54.
Map of gasworks (1877) in Armagh County Museum)

DAWSON STREET

The street was named after Thomas Dawson an ancestor of the Earls of Dartrey and a burgess of the city in the reign of James I. On Livingston's map of 1766 it is shown as Abbey Lane.

Armagh Gas Works in 1967. Gas was piped around the town from here from 1833 until 1966. (Armagh County Museum).

The Shambles Grain Market, erected in 1827 as seen from Dawson Street in 1946. (M. Craig).

No.17 DAWSON STREET. A mid-eighteenth century house, not visible from the street, which looks across playing fields to the Convent grounds. (M. Campbell).

The Corn Market: A. (1827) Architect Francis Johnston.
Nine-bay, single-storey block in coursed, squared limestone with ashlar dressings. An impressive facade with a squat tower as centrepiece rising above the roof ridges and terminating in a robust cornice and blocking course. The segmental arched recess in the front face of the tower is pierced by a semi-circular arch with gateway and original gate. Above is an inset plaque inscribed 'Erected 1827 Lord John George Beresford Archbishop Arthur I. Kelly Sovereign'. Above the cornice a curious timber sheeted and panelled cupola on two steps rises above the blocking course. There is a clock face on all four sides and above each an oval louvred opening set in a round-headed dormer forming part of the domed roof with arrow weather vane. The blank walls each side of the tower are relieved by three thin semi-circular headed recesses carrying arrow slit openings. The bay at each end breaks forward with a segmental recess below a simple pediment. The doorway at the Cathedral Road end is blind, at the other end it is a gateway.
It is interesting to note the treatment of the fall in ground level; the projecting base of the centrepiece has become a string course by the Cathedral Road corner.

(Brett p.36)

The remains of very fine boundary walls of random squared limestone with ashlar quoins and some new openings with crude brick infilling. Behind are sheds with the corrugated iron and asbestos roofs of many insensitive extensions.

Nondescript group of single-storey roughcast warehouse buildings with corrugated iron roofs lead into the brick gable wall of no.1 Edward Street. Note the angled corner.

9-15 Dawson Street (no.13 does not exist): All that remains of a terrace of two-storey houses. Nos.9 and 15 are three-bay; no.11 is two-bay. Window openings survive apart from ground floor of no.9. Existing sash windows in first floor in nos.9 and 11; windows with glazing bars to ground floor of no.11. No.15 is unoccupied and boarded up.

17 Dawson Street: (c.1760) Down a little laneway between stone walls is a delightful two-storey, five-bay vernacular farmhouse of the Georgian period with a single storey wing. The building has a painted roughcast finish, simple three pane fanlight and moulded cement architrave to doorway, thin cement surrounds to windows, hipped, slated roof and stone eaves course. Aproaching the front of the building the view of the Roman Catholic Cathedral on the hill beyond is spectacular.

(Livingston map 1766 (Noble copy))

Side elevation of fire station: Tall four-bay, two-storey building, totally blank on ground floor except for a small door at one end. Good random rubble stonework with ashlar quoins; painted roughcast to first floor level. Three large windows are detailed in a typical Sixties manner.

An untidy assortment of garage stores. One garage has utilised an older building with ashlar stone to the front; behind a little hipped roof building remains. A lively and very explicit hanging sign of an exhaust piercing a tyre hangs outside.

Further up there are a number of screen walls, some roughcast, some of stone with raised pointing and topped with spiked security fencing.

10-14 Dawson Street: (1870) A terrace of three two-bay, two-storey red brick houses; no.14 has a vehicular entrance. Moulded brick eaves cornice; string course at first floor sill level. Sash windows.

High roughcast screen boundary wall with gate piers.

16-20 Dawson Street: Blocked up remains of three two-bay, two-storey stone houses, some roughcast rendering still remains.

22 Dawson Street: Three-bay, two-storey cement rendered building. Semi-circular heads with moulded surrounds to window and door openings; sash windows.

Fine stone boundary wall, part to Methodist Church and part to Protestant Hall. Intriguing traces of very old windows and doors suggest an original terrace like nos.16-20.

DOBBIN STREET

The street was named after Leonard Dobbin who laid it out in 1811 as part of a commercial development. The street curves around to link Scotch Street and Thomas Street.

1 Dobbin Street (also part of 24 Scotch Street): Prominent four-bay, three-storey building of random rubble limestone with ashlar stone quoins and soldier arches. Stone work continues as a screen wall to an overgrown yard. Original sash windows with glazing bars. Modern over large shopfront fascia turns the corner into Scotch Streeet.

3 Dobbin Street: Thirteen-bay, two-storey building with parapet wall and capped pedestal blocks at intervals. The two bays nearest Scotch Street are lower and the parapet wall has an elegant 'hump-back' profile that catches the eye. Modern windows with glazing bars. Considerable care has been taken with the design of the new shop fronts in the refurbishment of this building.

3a Dobbin Street: Single-storey flat roofed shop with a door and window.

5-11 Dobbin Street: Three single bay and one two-bay, two-storey buildings with two flat headed carriage entries of coursed and squared rubble limestone. Original segmental headed tripartite windows to first floors.
No.5 has a shop front with two windows, small scale and well proportioned, ruined by an unrelated fascia board. No.7 has fine first floor tripartite window and original crown glass; replacement door with reveals and fanlight. No.9 has modern windows in old openings; door not original.
No.11 has roughcast rendering; all windows have been widened and modernised so affecting the character of the whole group.Now undergoing careful restoration.

Community Centre: Small modern, flat-roofed, single storey infill building; roughcast with curved corner and large wall of glass. Inoffensive apart from the tank block on roof but incongruous beside the free-standing gatehouse/clock tower.

The Old Buttermarket: (1820) Built by Archbishop Stuart. Architect possibly Francis Johnston.
The site is almost completely cleared except for the clock tower and one gateway arch, which was moved from its original site. This totally destroys the ambience of the street on this side. Originally there was a linen hall on this site which subsequently became a butter and egg market.
The clock tower has a substantial semi-circular archway of ashlar

limestone with chamfered blocking courses and rusticated voussoirs and quoins. Above the arch is a string course followed by a deep band of ashlar and over this the clock. There is a simple cornice and blocking course to the flat roof from which rises a cupola crowned by a metal sheeted domed weather vane. The gateway contains the original gates, part wrought iron with cast iron fittings and decoration. The segmental arch is of punched ashlar limestone with rusticated quoins and a broad impost course; simple frieze and cornice surmounted by robust ball finials.

The present low boundary wall, curving round into Linen Hall Street, does not compensate for the loss of the original high stone wall. The Dobbin Street clinic to the rear of the site is a long low single storey modern brick building.

(Paterson (A) Vol.I, p.79 and 96)

13-21 Dobbin Street: Three single-bay and two two-bay buildings of coursed and squared rubble limestone with ashlar stonework to ground floor soldier arches carried the full length of the buildings. Ugly raised pointing to nos.13,17 and 19. Brick soldier arches and quoins to first floor windows.
No.19 has sash windows without glazing bars and other windows of various types. The carriage arch is ruined by an ugly galvanised metal door.
No.21 retains its original sash windows with glazing bars.

23 Dobbin Street: Handsome three-bay, three-storey building of coursed and squared rubble limestone with ashlar stone to soldier arches and string course and simple stone eaves cornice. Original sash windows with glazing bars. Nice ornamental cast iron protection grille to ground floor. Unfortunately there is a modern flush front door and the segmental carriage arch now contains a roller shutter and a petrol pump.

25 Dobbin Street: Two-bay, single storey shop of coursed and squared rubble limestone. Most of the front of the original building has been removed and large horizontal shop windows inserted. It is particularly unfortunate that this building is the view of Dobbin Street as seen from the Palace gates.

27-29 Dobbin Street: Five-bay, three-storey building with smooth render above first floor string course and painted ashlar limestone

The Butter and Egg Market from DOBBIN STREET in 1951. The wrought iron railings, gates and lamp standards were removed when the clinic was erected. The Market Hall built as a flax market for Leonard Dobbin in 1820 was also demolished and replaced by a low wall. The entrance arch with its cupola still stands. (M. Craig).

The Royal Hotel, DOBBIN STREET, in 1963. A former coaching inn on the corner of Scotch Street., it was demolished to provide a site for a car park and public lavatories. (Armagh County Museum).

The Manager's House, behind the Belfast Bank, ENGLISH STREET in 1959. Note the skylights of the tunnel from the house to the offices and the railings and lamp standards destroyed when the property was converted to a Tourist Information Centre. (Armagh County Museum).

below. A medley of painted lettering and zizag painted half timbering. The building is in a dilapidated condition.

Two-bay, two-storey extension of 38/40 Thomas Street at corner of Dobbin Street.
2-6 Dobbin Street have been demolished and replaced by a car park with screen wall and a flat roofed public convenience.

8-44 Dobbin Street: B. (1812-14) Architect believed to be Francis Johnston.
A very attractive curving terrace of coursed rubble limestone dwellings. There are three clear construction breaks in the stone work of the front wall. The sequence of building appears to be :
Phase I - Nos.8-10.
Phase II - Nos.12-26 and 34-44.
Phase III - Nos. 28-32. In this group is a carriage arch bearing the date '1814', it would appear that it took two years to build the terrace and it was the insertion of the central group which completed it.
(Paterson (A) Vol. IV, p.79)

8-10 Dobbin Street: Pair of two-bay, two-storey buildings with carriage arch to no.8 and blocked doorway to no.10; original sheeted doorway to no.8. The ground floor of no.8 has a sixteen pane sash window; the first floor tripartite window consists of a twelve pane central unit flanked by two four pane units.

12-26 Dobbin Street: Nos.12-14 are two-bay, two-storey, nos.16-24 are single bay.
No.12 has a new flat headed carriage entry. No.16 has modern sash windows with glazing bars and an ugly cement surround to openings. No.18 has modern windows. No.20 has modern sash windows with glazing bars to ground floor. No.22 has original sash window with glazing bars to first floor. No.24 has original window to first floor; original six panel door with fanlight and panelled reveal. No.26 has original first floor window and doorway with panelled reveal and 'mouth organ' fanlight. Ground floor opening greatly enlarged to become a garage doorway. Ugly raised pointing to stonework and cement surround to openings.

28-30 Dobbin Street: Pair of three-bay, two-storey buildings. Modern paired sash windows without glazing bars replace the original tripartite format. Ugly cement surrounds to openings and poor pointing. No.28 has a Gibbsian doorway with new semi-circular headed fanlight. No.30 has replacement door and panelled reveal. Carriage arch has datestone '1814'.

32 Dobbin Street: Two-bay, two-storey building. Modern paired sash windows with cement surrounds replace the original tripartite format. Semi-circular headed Gibbsian doorway with fanlight. The ground floor of this building has been reorganized but it is still in keeping.

34-42 Dobbin Street: Five single bay, two-storey buildings.
No.34 has a tripartite window to first floor without glazing bars and doorway with rectangular fanlight and sheeted door.
No.36 has modern sash windows. Arched opening to doorway with an aedicule consisting of fluted Tuscan columns with frieze and cornice above; modern door with crude cement arch.
No.38 has a sheeted door and plain blank fanlight. No.40 has new hardwood sash windows which would be improved by painting. Cement surrounds to openings.
No.42 has modern sash windows and cement surrounds to openings. Altered entrance with modern panelled door, reveals and fanlight.

44 Dobbin Street: Single bay, two-storey building. Replacement casement windows to first floor and modern sash windows to ground floor. At the side of the building is the original entrance with a simple slated triangular gable head above. In the service yard behind is a former office consisting of an interesting church-like gable end with good stone work and a steep pitched roof.

46 Dobbin Street: Once a very fine seven-bay, three-storey building now spoilt by modern openings and a plethora of signs. Built of coursed and squared random limestone with brick surrounds to windows and archways and ashlar quoins. Two segmental headed archways to ground floor, one is bricked up. Original windows, many retaining their original twenty-four panes. Large brick chimney stack at each gable end.

48 Dobbin Street: Dull seven-bay, two-storey building in brick and roughcast. Gable facing Wellworths has modern windows with grilles and protective fencing to yard walls. Zig-zag pattern to doorway at side.

The remainder of the street consists of a recently completed five-bay dark brick supermarket wall, blank except for a few narrow lancet windows at first floor level. A bleak and forbidding end to the street relieved only by the entrance tower at the corner.

EDWARD STREET

An attractive right-angled street which borders the Shambles Market on two sides. In 1887-88 Mr.George A. Edwards J.P. built twenty houses in Edward Street.
(Bassett p.109)

1-2 Edward Street: (1873) Pair of two-bay, two-storey houses. Modern windows and modern traditional type doors; painted brickwork.

3 Edward Street: (1873) Three-bay, two-storey smooth rendered building with carriage arch. Moulded plaster surrounds to ground floor windows; original sash windows with horizontal glazing bars; original door.

5-17 Edward Street: Terrace of two-bay, two-storey red brick houses; some now smooth rendered and some roughcast. No.14 has original windows, original door and carriage door with shamrock shaped ventilating holes.

18-31 Edward Street: Terrace of two-bay, two-storey red brick houses, happily with facades unchanged. The unaltered elevation provides a valuable architectural unity, the balance of which even the smallest alteration could destroy. Nos.21, 23, 24 and 26 have yellow brick dentils and eaves cornice.
The street concludes with the return block of no.8 Cathedral Road which is linked by the roof of an outbuilding.

The market wall is of squared and coursed limestone. The section facing nos.1-17 has original wrought iron railings with square deep upstands and chamfered coping. It has five pairs of octagonal gate piers with shallow domed capping but only one pair of the original gates remain. The wall facing nos.18-31 is partly grey rendered.

ENGLISH STREET

This street name is recorded as early as 1671 and presumably commemorates the Trian Saxon, one of the earliest divisions of the city. It may also have been an English settled area in the seventeenth century. Many of the eighteenth century two and three storey buildings still survive, following the gentle curve of the street line around the Cathedral Hill. In some cases the rear outbuildings and former gardens running down to the flat lands of the Mall can still be traced.

At the beginning of the nineteenth century some of the houses would have served as shops also, with only a nameboard to distinguish them. Later buildings, like nos.7,9 or 34, were designed with a shop on the ground floor and a separate entrance for the living quarters above. Banks were planned in a similar manner.

3-5 English Street: Two-storey five-bay building; smooth render with incised blockwork and parapet wall. First floor windows do not line up though shop front conforms to company house style.

7 English Street: Architect John Quinn. Erected by William and Thomas McWilliams.
Three-storey, four-bay painted stone building. An example of how a splendid stone facade, with cornice, blocking course and quoins, can be almost lost by painting, removal of glazing bars and the insertion of a thin, over-deep fascia and splayed vaguely "moderne" frame. Original interior shutters have been retained.
(Paterson (A) Vol.IV p.77 & Vol.XXI p.257)

9 English Street: B. Architect John Quinn. Erected by William and Thomas McWilliams.
Excellently restored, well proportioned, three-storey, three-bay building. Ashlar stonework with cornice and blocking course; projecting quoins chamfered on one side; first floor cills continue across front as a string course. New sash windows with glazing bars. Well designed shop front incorporating entrances to shop below and offices above. Ugly and inappropriate temporary boutique sign.
(Refs. as above)

11 English Street: B. (1717) This building was occupied by the Reverend Nathaniel Whaley in the early eighteenth century and later by the Reverend Henry Jenny. It became an hotel, called "The King's Head", in c.1769 under the ownership of Mr George Parks. In 1792 its name was changed to "The Molyneux Arms" and a year later stage coaches began to depart from the building. There was another name change in c.1808 to "The King's Arms" and in 1824 it became "The Royal Hibernian". In 1843 Thackeray stayed there. It became known as "The Beresford Arms Hotel" in 1844. It was badly damaged by an IRA bomb in 1972.

Immediately prior to its demolition in 1990, though blocked up, it was a three-storey, four-bay building of considerable importance in the street. Built of fine coursed random rubble limestone and conglomerate with ashlar soldier arches to wide segmental headed windows on the ground floor.

It had an ashlar limestone Gibbsian doorway with built-in foot scrapers on either side.

The restoration of the facade of this building, re-using much of the original ashlar stonework, is eagerly awaited.

(Ulster Gazette 7th Feb.91)

13-17 English Street: Three-storey, six-bay smooth rendered building with incised blockwork; quoins to corners; carriage arch to west end of building. Corner bay eaves line slightly raised; wall slightly canted out. Well proportioned windows; a few glazing bars remain on the top floor. First floor window nearest the corner set in a segmental arched recess, an important eyecatcher in the street.

Nos. 15-17 are due to be demolished and will be re-built, hopefully, in a manner in keeping with the streetscape.

19-23 English Street: Three-storey, six-bay smooth rendered building with incised blockwork and good quoins. Modern aluminium windows in traditional openings.

This building demonstrates how lack of chimneys and traditional windows can give a hard, empty appearance even though the main form and scale of the old building is repeated.

25 English Street: Three-storey, three-bay building; render finished in an all over pattern of wide vertical fluting. Tired looking ground floor of aluminium and black tiles.

27 English Street: Three-storey, two-bay smooth rendered public house with shallow smooth quoins and metal sash windows. The pub front and doorway are unremarkable.

29 English Street: Three-storey, three-bay building; painted roughcast finish and plaster quoins. Glazing bars retained in first and second floor windows.
New shop front with traditional air and pleasant, sparkling, shiny paint.

31-33 English Street: Very fine three-storey, six-bay block of coursed rubble limestone; blocked ashlar window surrounds to first and second floor. Sash windows; glazing bars remain on second floor of no.33.
Smooth render to ground floor of no.33; ugly ribbon pointing to the stonework above. Elaborate door surround in vaguely Venetian manner with cornice and balustraded frontispiece supported on bracketed dwarf columns. Nice ornamental cast iron protection screens to ground floor window cills.
The shop front of no.31 is in need of replacement.

35 English Street: Three-storey, three-bay smooth rendered building. Attractive architraves to first and second floors; one segmental and two pedimented architraves 'float' between first and second floors. Part of the original robust polished granite shop front remains and some ornamental tiles survive on the left hand side of the doorway.

37 English Street: Three-storey, three-bay smooth rendered building. Sash windows; glazing bars remain on the second floor. The shop front is disappointing.

39-41 English Street: Three-storey, seven-bay smooth rendered building; original windows replaced throughout.
The two shop fronts are of little interest.

45-55 English Street: B+. (1768-1770) A terrace of six, originally seven, houses erected by Dean Averell, then Rector of Tynan later Bishop of Limerick, for occupation by his seven sisters. No.43 was burnt in 1955 and subsequently demolished.
Handsome three-storey buildings, with basements, of coursed random conglomerate with parapet walls to roof. Sash windows retained in all houses, glazing bars notably in nos.49 & 51.
Noble doors with architraves and bracketed over doors all in ashlar stone.
Handsome railings with corner columnette balusters on pedestals surmounted by urns, unfortunately removed from no.53. The intrusion

of a three sided 'Quality Street' shop front extension to no.53 somewhat debases the currency.

Interesting 'front door' in the basement of no.45 with a segmental arched fanlight and fluted columns.

Behind the service entry from College Street the stone built coachhouses can be seen.

57-59 English Street: B. (c.1870) A most distinctive and well composed seven-bay facade with curious flattened bracket pilasters at each end. Probably remodelled from three older buildings as two original doorways and a carriage arch remain. Huge yellow brick chimney stack with recessed panels to the side and a strong cornice.

Splendid architectural window surrounds with free style brackets and cornices above a long fascia, stretching the full length of the facade and terminating in bracket supports. Brackets below cill string course on second floor. Painted stone Gibbsian doorway; heavy blockwork to the smooth rendering on the ground floor.

The building is empty and boarded up; if renovated and re-painted this unique Italianate facade could contribute much to the visual quality of the street.

61 English Street: Three-storey, two-bay smooth rendered building; quoins and moulded architraves to windows and door. Well painted. The proliferation of lettering spoils an otherwise pleasant facade.

63-65 English Street: Charlemont Arms Hotel. Before becoming an hotel it was the residence of a Dr Atkinson. Originally called 'The Caulfeild Arms', it was re-named in 1763 when the Fourth Viscount Caulfeild was created Earl of Charlemont.

Pleasantly traditional three-storey, seven-bay smooth rendered building with banded rustication to ground floor. Architraves and cornices to first and second floor sash windows; five small dormers to roof and large chimney stacks. Small Ionic porch of glass reinforced plastic is a recent addition (old photographs show an elaborate cast iron canopy over the pavement).

(Paterson (A) Vol.4, p.3.
Weatherup (1) p.62)

67-69 English Street: Two-storey four-bay building of smooth render and dry dash. Flat elliptical archway with chamfered reveals. Modern aluminium shopfronts.

71 English Street: (1939) Architect W.A. Johnston. An interesting and lively three-bay, two-storey traditional style brick building with vertical timber sheeting to the ground floor. The shop front is concealed behind a long concertina shutter, in a deep opening, flanked by a decorative pilaster at each end. The cornice and fascia above carry three segmental panels for lettering. The shop is now closed.

73 English Street: Three-storey four-bay smooth rendered building, tiled ground floor; sash windows.

75 English Street: Two-storey, three-bay modern brick building with ornamental copper fascia and a beaten copper mural/panel below each ground floor window.

77-79 English Street: Four-bay, part two-storey with flat roof, part three-storey with pitched roof.
Shop front in need of renewal.

81 English Street: Three-storey, four-bay building of coursed random limestone; smooth render to ground floor. Three original sash windows survive but not the glazing bars. Shop front is currently boarded up.

2 English Street: Well painted smooth rendered shop on corner site; three-storey three-bay to English Street and three-storey four-bay to Market Street. Well proportioned windows with glazing bars, moulded architraves, blocked quoins to the corner and bracketed eaves. Top floor windows altered to front opening.
Relics of the original plaster decoration survive in places; probably also behind the horizontally boarded fascia below the original shop front cornice. The building deserves a decent shop front.

4-6 English Street: Three-storey, four-bay smooth rendered building; modern window insertions and two indifferent shop fronts.

8-10 English Street: Three-storey, four-bay building with eaves level much lower than nos.4 and 6. One simple shop front and one smart shopfront of polished granite with incised lettering.

12 English Street: Three-storey, four-bay red brick building with two shop fronts. The eaves line steps up to match nos.4 to 6.
14-20 English Street: Three-storey, fifteen-bay smooth rendered block containing four shops and one house. Three of the original substantial

chimney stacks remain. A few of the original sash windows survive as do the moulded architraves on no.16. Gibbsian doorway with simple fanlight to no.20.

22 English Street: Three-storey three-bay smooth rendered building, with quoins, continuing the eaves height of no.20. Original doorway with panelled door and reveals, minus architrave; glazing bars to windows missing.
In view of its strategically important position, terminating the view up Russell Street from the Mall, this building urgently needs to be restored.

24 English Street: Three-storey, three-bay smooth rendered building. Sash windows remain though glazing bars missing. Original doorway with panelled door, reveals, architrave and steps.

26 English Street: Three-storey, two-bay building of smooth render with elliptical arched carriage entrance. The tripartite sash windows on the first and second floor have moulded architraves.
This building has been heavily restored. If the cement-rendered walls were painted and a new, well-proportioned shopfront installed it would improve the facade enormously.

28-30 English Street: Three-storey, four-bay roughcast building; simple smooth plaster architraves and quoins. Tripartite windows on first and second floor appear to be original. The cornice to the new flat roof is too heavy and is uncomfortably set above the eaves. Chimney stacks missing; basic shop front.

32 English Street: B. (c.1780) A very attractive two-storey, three-bay house and shop. First floor portion of the bow and moulded eaves cornice remain intact; but on the ground floor the bow has been chopped off to provide a crude shop front. A high proportion of the window glazing bars remain.
Original doorway with stone surround and three steps of Armagh conglomerate; panelled door with reveals and pretty fanlight; interesting interior. A building that cries out for a sensitive restoration scheme.

34 English Street: B. An attractive three-storey four-bay building; segmental carriage arch with a portion of the original sheeted gate. First and second floor red brick, ground floor ashlar limestone. Sash windows remain, most glazing bars missing.

It would be relatively easy to restore this important building to its original form.

36 English Street: Two-storey smooth rendered building; half timbered shop front with original clustered columns and fascia. Originally a motor garage and showroom.
This building is due for demolition to make way for the entrance to the St.Patrick's Trian car park. It is hoped that the original shop front will be salvaged and re-used somewhere nearby.

40 English Street: A. (1851) Built for the Belfast Banking Company to designs by Charles Lanyon.
In Baroque Revival Mannerist style of ashlar stone work and conceived on a monumental scale. The three-bay elevation is based on the triumphal arch theme, the main deviation being that all three arches rise to the same height. The parapet is a pierced balustrade with blocked ends set above an overhanging cornice supported by modillions. The frieze is unadorned except in the centre where a cartouche, designed into the architrave, breaks upwards into the frieze and below rests on the head of the central arch. Between the architrave and the moulded impost course the ashlar work is lightly rusticated. The arches all have radiating voussoirs. Margined glazed windows are set into the two flanking arches encased by moulded stone reveals and capped by carved keystone heads. The central arch encases the arms and bearers of the Belfast Banking Company carved in bass relief and set above a pedimented doorway. The stonework to the dividing piers is fielded and rock faced. The cills to the windows are developed to create a continuous moulded string course broken only by the doorway.
The building is linked to its neighbours by cut stone arches of similar styling but of a smaller scale, the cornice line relating to the impost of the main building. The arch to the left is the smaller and is blind; to the right the arch gives access to buildings at the rear, including the former manager's residence.

Interior:
Inside, the banking hall is full height. It has recently been tastefully converted for use as a Tourist Office. The counters have been removed and a new central doorway constructed following the style of the original work. This is to give access to other facilities at the rear.
The space in front of the building is enclosed by railings. A new ramp, to provide access for the disabled, has been constructed in matching

stone as part of the conversion works.
(Dixon (1) p.61)

Bank House: (c.1800) A three-bay dwelling, two floors above a basement. The walls are harled and detailed with stepped quoins. The Gibbsian doorcase has a moulded hood over a rectangular fanlight and a panelled door. The entrance was originally approached by a flight of eleven stone steps flared towards the bottom. They bridged the basement area and were flanked by decorative railings that terminated in lamp standards. The re-modelling of 1990 has removed all these attractive features.

42 English Street: Three-storey, three-bay building of smooth render, painted bright yellow to ground floor, dry dash to first and second floors.
Unusual flat-headed Gibbsian doorway with panelled reveal and original door.

44 English Street: Three-storey, three-bay smooth rendered building. Dumpy carved stone columns bracketed out to support end of original fascia board. Ornamental plaster pilasters and segmental arched mouldings form surrounds to the composition of two small windows between a large one on first floor only.
A facade of considerable potential spoiled by crude lettering and signs.

46 English Street: Two-storey, five-bay standard Sixties Ministry of Finance Works Division public building with flat roof which, unfortunately, occupies a most prominent site at the top of College Street.
This building replaces an earlier Post Office and a pair of dwelling houses.
(Lundie)

48 English Street: B. (1896) Architects Watt & Tulloch.
This building originally belonged to the Provincial Bank. Built of brick with ashlar sandstone to the ground floor and sandstone dressings throughout. In the three-bay, three-storey elevation facing English Street is an entrance doorway with a robust semi-circular hood on brackets. All windows on the ground floor have carved stone architraves and keystones, those on the first floor have flat pediments while the second floor windows have shouldered architraves and keystones. At both levels the horizontal centre line of the windows are

marked by flush ashlar stone string courses. Above the corner entrance is the beautifully integrated sign 'board' consisting of a cornice and convex curved stone fascia with intermediate blocking pieces now sadly devoid of lettering.

At roof level a bold bracketed cornice with heavy corner blocks support the great decorative brick gable facing English Street and the balustraded parapets. There is also a fine architectural chimney stack.

It is fortunate that such a splendidly confident building occupies this very dominant site where English Street, Abbey Street and College Street meet.

(see also Abbey Street)

52 English Street: An unsightly gap screened from the road by a cement-rendered wall fronting the bank car park.

54-56 English Street: A pair of two-storey houses of random conglomerate, once a terrace of three; sash windows have blocked cement surrounds.

Doorways have canopies with original decorative cast-iron brackets.

58 English Street: A gap site formerly occupied by the City Hall, now a car park. What of its future?

60 English Street: Three-storey, three-bay smooth rendered building; pitched roof and modern windows; chimneys missing.

62 English Street: Two-storey, three-bay building; rough rendered above modern shopfront; chimneys missing.

64 English Street: Two-storey, three-bay building; smooth rendered; sash windows.

66 English Street: Two-storey single bay building.

68 English Street: Evocative remains of a monumental entrance way with segmental arch, cornice, and blocking piece of ashlar stone. Coursed rubble limestone screen walls contain a semi-circular niche and keystone.

A most attractive incident in the street but the proliferation of signs is unfortunate.

70 Upper English Street: (Fire Station) A well intentioned but unimaginative three-storey flat-roofed building on a dominant three sided site at the junction of four streets.

ENGLISH STREET, circa 1895 showing the original Provincial Bank of Ireland before being rebuilt in 1901 with the Tontine Rooms beyond before conversion to the City Hall in 1908. To the right is the slated gable of No.1 The Seven Houses built circa 1770 and burned in 1956. (National Library of Ireland, Lawrence Collection).

Beresford Arms Hotel, ENGLISH STREET. A view about the turn of the century showing the original fenestration and rendered and lined walls.
(National Library of Ireland, Lawrence Collection).

UPPER IRISH STREET in 1946, with the police barracks to the right. Already the proliferation of poles and overhead wires is evident. (M. Craig).

The Pavilion. Built by Captain W.W. Alegeo, circa 1820 and demolished to provide a site for Armagh County Secondary School about 1960. (National Library of Ireland, Lawrence Collection).

The opportunity to make something of the monumental fire-engine doorways has, alas, been missed.

FOLLY LANE, FOLLY ESTATE AND ROSEMOUNT

This triangular area bounded by the Newry Road, Ballynahone River and Barrack Hill is a post-war development which started with the N.I. Housing Trust Folly estate. This was followed by private development in the Sixties and Seventies.

Folly Lane is lined with two-storey and single-storey semi-detached brick houses, some of them pebble-dashed, built in the Twenties and Thirties. A number have attractive stained glass in the bay windows and porches. There are two pairs of good Thirties ex-servicemen's semi-detached houses to a standard pattern with oriel windows.

As a contrast to this at the end of the Lane and at the top of the hill is the uncompromising bulk of the Orchard Leisure Centre. The building is comprised of two large flat roofed boxes, one for the swimming pool (1964 - Architects Manning and Clamp) and one for the sports hall with a separate glass-clad block for the entrance/cafe (1985 - Architect Ian Donaldson). It comes as a surprise to find a large public building like this set down in the middle of housing, but architecturally it enlivens the scene and car parking has been unobtrusively tucked away.

The Folly estate, north east of the Orchard Centre, built in the Fifties by the N.I. Housing Trust was probably designed in-house. It is typical of the sober, well-proportioned, decent-looking, colour-washed, two-storey, semi-detached houses and short terraces which the Trust produced at this time. Worthy of note is their policy of retaining existing trees and here the beech-lined Folly Glen on the east side makes a small linear park.

South of the leisure centre, with fine views over the city, Folly Estate leads to Rosemount Avenue which in turn becomes Ashley Estate. Here a lively variety of house types, including chalet bungalows and two-storey detached houses with finishes including white horizontal boarding, dry dash and pre-cast stone are set amidst profusely planted gardens.

IRISH STREET

The area of the city in which the Irish mainly lived and so named on Rocque's map of 1760. As it was the road south it was evidently earlier called Dundalk Street. Much of the original character of the street has been lost because of road widening, a new road junction, a high level road bridge and extensive new housing which created a new street line.

Nos.1-33 are set considerably back from the original line of the street and were built by the N.I.Housing Trust in the Sixties in their recognizable style with pantile roofs, roughcast rendering and casement windows.

1-3 Irish Street: A pair of two-bay, two-storey dwellings which step forward from Callan Street to join the line of Irish Street at no.5.

5-13 Irish Street: Five two-bay, two-storey dwellings. No.7 is individualised by a clipped cupressus arch and good nineteenth century railings.

On either side of Culdee Street is a five-bay return; on both sides the first two bays break forward with a feature panel.

15 Irish Street: Two-bay, two-storey dwelling.

17-19 Irish Street: Pair of two-storey dwellings set back from streetline.

21-33 Irish Street: Seven two-bay, two-storey houses; each one stepping up the street. Small front gardens.

65-69 Irish Street: A very handsome and important group of three-bay, two-storey buildings. No.65 is a public house with lined out rendering and cement quoins. The three first floor cills are joined to form a cornice for the hand painted fascia sign. The lively painted gable is a feature. All have Gibbsian door surrounds; no.67 with original fanlight and fine carriage arch with cut stone surround. Original sash windows throughout; no.69 has original glazing bars.
(Note: first floor window on right hand side is same height as ground floor windows.)

71 Irish Street: Three-bay, two-storey brick building with two dormer windows and moulded brick eaves courses. Original door with semi-circular fanlight and ornamental semi-circular brick hood mould and keystone. Segmental headed brick soldier arches to windows; original sash windows with vertical glazing bars and stone cills. Good dormers with round headed pediments on brackets.

An attractive unaltered building.

A group of single-storey shop units with a brick gable and utility shop fronts to Irish Street is set back from the street.

The new access lane to Friary Road forms part of the Sixties Road Improvement Scheme that broke the old streetline and swept away a group of fine stone terrace houses opposite the entrance to St. Malachy's.

1-4 Greenpark Terrace: (c.1900) Four three-bay, two-storey dwellings; roughcast finish with smooth cement corner edging and string course uniting first floor cills. Three houses retain original 'Arts and Crafts' detail - projecting front door porches with cornices; sash windows with small panes to the top sash, single vertical glazing bar to the lower sash; narrow window over door. A basic design enhanced by good detailing.

Unfortunately the windows in no.1 have been modernised.

Two-bay, two-storey and basement return block of no.58 Castle Street currently undergoing restoration. (See Castle Street.)

2 Irish Street: (mid eighteenth century) Three-bay, two-storey building with smooth rendering lined out and ashlar stone eaves cornice. Cast cement fascia cornice; semi-circular blocking pieces above cornice with traces of original lettering in label panel over door. Two enlarged ground floor windows with moulded architraves. New sash windows with vertical glazing bars to first floor.

4 Irish Street: (mid eighteenth century) Four-bay, two-storey building, smooth rendered and lined out. New replica sash windows with glazing bars.

6-8 Irish Street: (mid eighteenth century) A pair of two-storey dwelling of five bays in coursed Armagh conglomerate with soldier arches to windows and ashlar stone surrounds to door; stone cills and eaves course.

10-12 Irish Street: A pair of two-bay, two-storey houses being rebuilt in original style.

Nos.2-12 Irish Street are presently being restored by Hearth Revolving Fund, the descriptions refer to work in progress.

14-22 Irish Street: Three three-bay and a pair of two-bay, two-storey houses, smooth rendered and lined out. Modern front opening windows; hard wood panelled doors; plaster quoins. Small front gardens with light railings. Pleasant, well-painted new development in traditional style, except for overhanging eaves.

A gap leads into a neat courtyard of one and two-storey modern dwellings.

24-28a Irish Street: Four two-bay, two-storey dwellings similar to nos.14-22.

32a,32b and 34 Irish Street: Pair of two-bay and one three-bay, two-storey houses. Smooth cement rendering; flat headed entry; modern windows and small front gardens.

Return to 57 Ogle Street: Five-bay, two-storey building with stepped roof. New brick extension forms first two bays; original brickwork to remaining three bays with moulded brick eaves cornice. Modern replacement windows. A welcome refurbishment marred by ugly pipework.

36 Irish Street: Single bay, two-storey brick building incororating the third gable on the corner site. Segmental headed coupled sash windows on first floor. Basic shop front within plastered brick piers.

38 Irish Street: Four-bay, three-storey building, smooth rendered and · lined out. Two windows sheeted over; two sash windows; chimneys removed. Two traditional style panelled shop fronts.

42-44 Irish Street: A pair of two-bay, two-storey buildings, smooth rendered and lined out. Three doors with blocked out surrounds and small cornice. Tripartite sash windows to ground floor; sash windows without glazing bars throughout. These houses could be made very attractive with little effort.

48-50 Irish Street: Four-bay, three-storey building in coursed limestone with fine segmental headed carriage arch in punched ashlar stone; soldier arches and cement edging to windows; ugly ribbon pointing. The carriage arch is partly obscured by an inappropriate mosaic facing. Good hand painted sign.

52-54 Irish Street: Five-bay, two-storey building with central flat headed entry and dry dash finish. Sash windows to no.52; plastic windows to no.54.

St. Malachy's Church: B. (1935-38) Architects Ashlin & Coleman, Dublin.

In the early Thirties old St. Malachy's Church in Chapel Lane which had served the Roman Catholics of Armagh since 1750, and had been much altered and extended in 1820, was deemed to be no longer practical. The decision to build a church on a new site in Irish Street was taken. Although vacated in 1938 this distinctive Gothic style chapel with its triple gable roof and outside balcony staircases was left standing until 1955 when it was demolished to make way for St Malachy's Boys Primary School (see Chapel Lane).

The new St Malachy's Church, built of Navan limestone in coursed rubble with ashlar dressings, is in the Romanesque style on a simple basilica plan - nine bays long with nave, side aisles and apsidal sanctuary. The tall nave gable wall forms the west front facing Irish Street and here the main entrance doorway in ashlar stone is inspired by Irish twelfth century Romanesque. It is arched with three orders, columnettes with blank capitals and an undecorated tympanum over the heavily framed doors. High in the gable is a group of tall triple semi-circular headed windows the cills of which form part of a long frieze of small blind arches mounted above the inscription: SANCTE MALACHIA ORA PRO NOBIS 1935'. The doorway, windows and arcaded panel are all set within a tall arched recess of snecked rubble limestone framed by flat ashlar buttresses and stepped corbelled ashlar arcading to the gable slopes.

The aisles have steeply pitched lean-to roofs, built against the west gable of the nave. They are similarly detailed with a group of triple semi-circular headed windows in each. Along the north and south sides of the building double gables project forward from the aisle roofs; there are also shallow flat-roofed projections and side doors as well as a small building with a separate hipped roof housing the church offices. The great blank semi-circular snecked rubble stone wall of the apse is the distinctive feature of the east end with the apex of the gable surmounted by an empty bellcote. Curiously the bell is mounted at low level on a stand on top of the flat roof of the north side entrance.

Interior:

Inside the rugged splendour of the basilica plan is impressive. On each side of the nave is an arcade of six polished silver granite columns with undecorated capitals carrying arches with chevron decoration. Above this the semi-circular headed coupled clerestory windows light the great coffered barrel vault over the nave, the ends of its arched trusses are carried down the walls between the windows as wallposts. There is a balcony for choir and organ over the narthex. The aisles have plaster groin vaulting and, carefully placed, along the side walls are oak confessionals in a Greco-Roman Revival style of interior architecture which adds much distinction. Equally distinguished are the mosaic and marble panels in the sanctuary behind the high altar and the geometric marble paving in front. It is questionable whether the walls and vaulting of the aisles should have been painted a dark, turf-brown colour. The Stations of the Cross are by Franz Mayer of Munich.

Stained Glass:

The firm of John Hardman, of London and Birmingham, was responsible for the scheme of stained glass in 1938. The stained glass department of this company opened in 1845 and became one of the largest provincial studios in England. To the north of the apse Apparition of the Sacred Heart and Suffer Little Children are illustrated. Annunciation and Nativity appear on the south side with Immaculate Conception on the adjoining wall.

The west window, larger in scale and partly obscured by the organ, contains representations of St .Malachy, St. Patrick and St. Brigid and contains a panel showing St. Patrick's vision of tne Children of Ireland appealing to him to return.

Quarries with bright coloured margins are used to glaze the remainder of the openings. Any attempt to alter this ideal arrangement by the insertion of modern glass should be resisted.

The only item of interest in the rather bleak grounds is the enclosure of four memorial slabs to four former parish priests who died in the early part of the last century. These memorials from old St Malachy's church are mounted together in an enclosure.

(O'Muiri)

74-94 Irish Street: Ten two-bay, two-storey houses, except no.78 which is three-bay; there is a gap between no.76 and no.78. Nos.74 and 76 are roughcast, the remainder are smooth rendered and lined out.

Windows mainly modern; nos.90 and 94 have sash windows with single vertical glazing bars.

A modern high level road bridge concludes this section of the street.

JENNY'S ROW

This narrow lane which connects English Street and the Mall was called after the Reverend Henry Jenny, Rector of Armagh from 1738-59, and Archdeacon of Armagh from 1733-38. The oldest houses were situated on the south side of the lane; the ones on the north side were built 1831-35.

The entrance from English Street is through a segmental headed archway, the buildings on the right hand side are undergoing restoration, the ones on the left are due to be rebuilt.

There is a second segmental headed archway half way down the lane making a frame for a narrow view of the Mall. Further down on the right, on the site where a picturesque row of little white washed houses once stood, is an attractive terrace of single-bay, two-storey, replacement dwellings of painted roughcast with stone soldier arched heads to openings and random rubble conglomerate gables and chimney stacks. (Architect - Ian Donaldson 1989) On the opposite side the open site is scheduled for housing.

At the end of the lane there is a good view of the crow-stepped gable at the back of the gospel hall which will be partly hidden when the houses are built. It is worthwhile pausing to look at the side elevation of the building.

On the right hand side the new terrace is terminated by a modern random rubble stone wall partly screening the next door garage.

(Map by J.T. Noble. Armagh County Museum 93/84.
O.S. 1835)

LINENHALL STREET

The street takes its name from the flax market erected as part of the commercial development of that area of the city by Leonard Dobbin. Linenhall Street, which connects Dobbin Street to Scotch Street, has lost much of its character through demolition and the introduction of a long low modern building.

Corner of Dobbin Street: Three-bay, two-storey elevation to no.13 Dobbin Street, the first two bays are of squared and coursed limestone with ugly raised pointing; the third bay is a roughcast modern extension. Crude modern windows and an ugly illuminated box sign.

Roughcast wall with yard gates to a cleared site.

17-19 Linenhall Street: Three-bay two-storey building of squared and coursed limestone with soldier arches to openings; all that remains of a small terrace of houses.

Roughcast yard wall with entrance gate. Then the two-bay gable to no.27 Abbey Lane; smooth rendered with cement quoins to one side. No windows to ground floor; two windows with glazing bars to first floor. Pretty original fretwork bargeboard; building '1857'. Marked on 1864 O.S. Town Plan as Fire Engine Station.

Vacant site used for car parking with low random rubble conglomerate stone wall and some trees. This open space destroys the sense of enclosure in the street and opens up an unattractive view of the rear of some adjacent buildings.

The two-storey gable of 46 Scotch Street, close to the front of the pavement line, of random rubble stonework with cement quoins. The wall is blank except for one shop window and a small sash window on the first floor. Two bay extension, cement rendered with incised joints, two doors and two modern sash windows. Nondescript yard and outhouses behind in need of screening or refurbishment.

Clinic: Eight-bay, single storey modern red brick building with metal windows. The two end bays break forward creating an uncertain symmetry which is not resolved.

20 Linenhall Street: Two-bay, three-storey building of random rubble limestone with roughcast to ground floor. Tripartite sash windows to first and second floors.

22 Linenhall Street: Two-bay, two-storey roughcast building with tiled surround to shop window. Modern tripartite windows to first floor.

24 Linenhall Street: Two-bay, two-storey building of painted roughcast and smooth render. Ground floor shop front and window in need of attention.

26 Linenhall Street: The roofless shell of a new incomplete six-bay, two-storey building.

28 Linenhall Street: Three-bay, three-storey building of random rubble with raised pointing. Traditional sash windows with glazing bars. Good modern shop front in traditional style with painted name board.

Two-bay, three-storey return to 42 Scotch Street of random rubble limestone with raised pointing; segmental soldier arches to openings. Traditional sash windows with glazing bars; one attic sash window in gable. Panelled side door and foot scraper recess. A good colour scheme completes a pleasant and well restored building.

LISANALLY LANE AND ALEXANDER ESTATE

Lisanally Lane was formerly a rural roadway running from the junction of English Street and Banbrook Hill through fields to the north-east of the city. Albert Place, a terrace of houses on the right hand corner, was built by 1864. Later a row of nine terrace houses called Winder Place was added across the lane. These are two-bay, two-storey slated dwellings, recently rendered with, in most cases, replacement doors and windows. In 1907 the terrace was extended to the junction with the newly opened Lonsdale Street by two rows of two-bay, two-storey brick slated houses. The creation of Lonsdale Road in 1984 cut off the earlier portion, containing Winder and Albert Places, from the remainder of Lisanally Lane.
Lonsdale Villas, a row of seven square red brick detached houses which stand out on account of their simple, pleasant proportions and good detailing, were erected in 1907 also. It is good to see that nos.2,5,6 and 7 have retained the original fenestration. The lane was little developed otherwise until after the Second World War when the construction of the Alexander Estate and the Armagh Girls' High School commenced. The school was designed by W.R.Thornton, County Armagh Education Architect, and built by Hyde of Portadown. It opened in 1954 and closed in 1990, following amalgamation with the Royal School. A number of detached houses and the private estate of Knockamell Park represent more recent development.
The section of the College of Further Education facing Lisanally Lane was built in 1964 and designed by County Armagh Education

Committee Architects' Department. Further along this side of the lane, at the second sharp bend, are two interesting, semi-detached, two-storey Modern Movement houses with white walls and flat roofs. They were designed by G.P.& R.H. Bell who built a number of houses in this style just before and after the Second World War. At the next bend is the College's most recent building. It is a four-storey, L-shaped block clad in dark brown brick, incorporating classrooms and workshops, and was designed by Ferguson & McIlveen, Belfast (1983).

Further along on the same side is a Fifties, architect-designed, deluxe bungalow, wing-shaped on plan (for the view and the sun) once occupied by the manager of the Bairnswear factory. Next door is a handsome lodge in coursed and squared rubble stone, T-shaped on plan, with a steep pitched roof and fretted barge boards, tall chimneys and hood moulds to the window and door. There is an arrowslit recess in each main gable and a small quatrefoil window to the gable facing the road which also carries a date stone '1846'. The stone gate piers close to the lodge have flat pedimented caps. The lodge has been extended at the back and the gates no longer lead anywhere - it is said they never did.

On the crest of the hill is Alexander Crescent, part of a post-war housing estate built by Armagh Urban District Council in 1953 to the designs of architects G.P. & R.H. Bell. All the original houses in the estate are semi-detached or in short terraces with flat roofs, part rendered and part brick walls, steel windows and glass bricks forming side lights to the front doors. In Alexander Crescent six little flat-roofed blocks of rendered semi-detached houses are set around a semi-circular green. Each block is T-shaped with the party wall running down the centre and there is a small flat-roofed porch in each internal corner. This very attractive and well-maintained group was clearly influenced by the International Style of the early Thirties and has considerable rarity value and interest today.

(History of Armagh Girls' High School
Dixon (1) p.85)

LONSDALE ROAD

This road replaces Lonsdale Street named after J.B. Lonsdale, M.P. for Mid-Armagh from 1899-1918, who became Lord Armaghdale in 1918. During the construction of Lonsdale Street (1907), in order to obtain access, the west screen wall and gates of the Court House were removed thus destroying the symmetry of the building. Most of Lonsdale Street disappeared when the new road was constructed though a section remains as car parking for the College of Further Education. When opened, in 1984, Lonsdale Road replaced Railway Street as the main route to Moy and Dungannon.

The road is dominated on one side by the buildings of Armagh College of Further Education. This is a large school complex of system built teaching blocks, mostly with a dry dash finish and low pitch felt roofs, assembled in tiers. The setting is enhanced by the grassy slope and trees behind; the car parking is generously landscaped.

There is a good modern development of two-storey brick dwellings, also a few post-war prefabricated bungalows, located below the level of the road and beyond Lisanally Lane. They are entered from the lane though visually they belong to Lonsdale Road.

On the opposite side of the road views of the rear elevations of buildings in English Street predominate. Little of the old gardens remain and while there is some utilitarian development on a small scale there is little sign of any planning control.

THE MALL

On Rocque's map of 1760 it is named 'The Common' and 'The Horse Course' skirts it round. The starting point was near Barrack Street and the finishing post at the bottom of Jenny's Row. The race course was removed by Primate Robinson and in 1773 he leased the commons to the Sovereign and Burgesses for the purpose of utilizing them as a public walk for the inhabitants of the city. In 1803 Coote writes that 'a very fine wall, or terrace, has been lately enclosed with a dwarf wall, dyke and iron gates, within which is a neat gravel walk, encompassing a lawn, for the enclosing of which Lord Rokeby procured an act of parliament, and is but lately finished.' G.H.Bassett writing in 1888 says that the transformation into a public walk 'was accomplished by subscription, in a creditable manner. The trees then planted, and some added by a citizen, are now of majestic proportions. Football and cricket matches are played on the green, and the country in the town feature is furnished by the presence of grazing cattle.'

The Mall, which is one of Ireland's most attractive urban parks, is appropriately encircled by a number of Armagh's best classical buildings that include the Court House and the Gaol ('speaking' to each other across its full length), Charlemont Place, the Savings Bank and the Scotch Church. The Mall is also embraced by a pleasant variety of nineteenth century terraces and Gothic-style churches and gospel halls, all unified by the generous parkland landscape of trees, grass and the low boundary wall around the Mall promenade some three feet below road level.

(Paterson (A) Vol.V p.38-49.
Bassett p.91.
Maps - Bartlett's 1601, Rocque, Livingston, OS 1835 & 1864)

Notable features in the Mall Park:
The low perimeter retaining wall of rough-faced coursed rubble stone with robust cut-stone coping. Also the pairs of original wrought-iron lamp standards carried on wrought-iron pedestals decorated with scroll work; one pair to each of the three entrances into the park opposite the Court House and the Gaol. Simple iron railings link these standards at the Gaol end and the missing railings have recently been restored at the Court House end by the Armagh District Council. On the inner face of the gateway wall, opposite the Courthouse, there is a date stone inscribed 1798 and a distance stone giving the length of the perimeter walk as four furlongs.

The 1914-18 War Memorial, facing the Court House, has a bronze figure of Mourning Victory (sculptor C.L. Hartwell R.A.) on a buttressed plinth of granite on top of a square of three granite steps. As part of the upgrading scheme for this area, carried out in 1990-91, the wide podium on which the statue sat has been replaced by granite paving with generous granite steps.

Some distance east of the 1914-18 War Memorial is a memorial 'Erected in memory of the Officers, NCOs and men of the Princess Victoria's Royal Irish Fusiliers who fell in the service of their country during the South African Campaign 1899-1902'. Two steps and a plinth of Newry granodiorite and, on top of this, a huge boulder of Shap granite supports a young capless bugler, like a figure out of 'Boys Own Paper', sounding the Last Post. The sculptor for this statue, which was unveiled on 6th October 1906, was Kathleen Shaw. There is a similar statue in Brighton by the same sculptor, but the bugler is wearing a cape. The model for the statue was a local youth Edward (Ned) Stevenson.

(Armagh Guardian 12th Oct.1906)

The White Walk across the Mall with its pleasant lamp standards was constructed in 1836 on 'receipt of a memorial from certain inhabitants of the City requesting that a communication may be made across the Mall commencing at the bottom of Russell Street. It was agreed that a walk should be constructed and that it should be properly lighted'.

(Paterson (A) Vol.IV. p.96. and p.99)

The circular bandstand seen in old photographs near the South African War Memorial and the elegant little cricket pavilion, with its veranda, have long gone. To-day the cricketers occupy a clubhouse, erected in 1964, on the west side of the Park that looks like a Sixties semi-permanent primary school. The Mall deserves better.

The gun, with carriage, placed near the South African War Memorial, was captured from the Russians in 1854 during the Crimean War.

THE MALL EAST
From the Court House and past the Sovereign's House the line of stone-built three-storey terrace houses in Beresford Row, dating from the 1820s, is magnificently halted by Charlemont Place, heroic in scale and superb in detail. After this the two pairs of semi-detached inter-war villas follow as something of an anti-climax. Then comes the smaller scale temple front of the Museum followed by more three-storey stone-built terrace houses; then the line of building is punctured by the tree lined vista to St Mark's Church. Next comes a large hall, a cottage ornee in polychrome brick, then more three-storey houses dating from the 1880s, this time built of brick or faced in stucco. Finally there is another single-storey house, a long stretch of garden and, as a visual full stop, the Savings Bank on its dominant island site between Victoria Street and Barrack Hill.

Special note should be made of the mews originally provided behind the Mall East houses. These substantial coach-houses and outbuildings are reached through carriage arches and are a feature of Armagh.

Sovereign's House: A. (1809-10) Designed by John Quinn and possibly Francis Johnston.

The name 'Sovereign's House' dates only from the establishment of the Royal Irish Fusiliers Museum. Prior to this it was known as No.1 Beresford Row, before that as No.10 Beresford Row and earlier still was part of Rokeby Green.

It was the first house built on the Mall and local tradition states that materials used were surplus to the Court House contract. The house was built for Arthur Irwin Kelly, the contractor for the Court House.

John Claudius Beresford, uncle of the Primate Lord John George Beresford, made a public comment on the coincidence of Mr Kelly's good fortune after which the Court House and Mr Kelly's house were known as 'The Cat and Kitten'. Kelly was created a Burgess in 1805 and at the end of the same year was appointed Sovereign, a position he held almost continuously until 1837. Kelly was the ground landlord of Beresford Row, which was named in honour of Lord John George Beresford, Archbishop of Armagh (1822-62).

A fine two-storey three-bay building of squared coursed rubble limestone with ashlar dressings and slate hanging to gables. Originally the front door and entrance steps were in the centre bay but, about 1820, the entrance was moved to the College Hill side of the building. The porch has a very fine ashlar doorcase with half columns supporting the cornice and fluted frieze with paterae breaking forward over the columns, all set within a segmental-headed archway. The door is six-panel and the segmental spider's web fanlight is a modern reproduction.

The two-storey, five-bay outbuilding at the rear is of coursed rubble limestone with flush ashlar quoins. The centre bay breaks forward with a segmental-headed archway and simple pediment with bull's eye window.

Outside the house is a curious pillar-box without a cipher.

(Wm. Blacker's Diary 1786-1817 in Armagh Guardian 24 and 31 Jan.1936)

Beresford Row.

By 1819 nos.2 and 3 were the homes of Michael Magee and Joseph Marshall, while the occupant of no.4 (now no.5) was John McKinstry; it remained in that family until acquired by Dr H.H.G. Dorman. The building by Robert Baxter of two houses sometime before 1836 (to fill the gap after no. 6) completed the terrace. Remodelling of the houses before 1840 introduced a third house, which was then no.4 and had Miss Heaney as tenant. Nos.5 and 6, now nos.6 and 7, were in the names of Mrs Colthurst and Mrs Carpendale, they belong to the Southern Education and Library Board. The last two houses, then nos.9 and 10, now nos.10 and 11, remain private dwellings. Prior to occupation by the S.E.L.B. these buildings were used by the Armagh Girls' High School and the Ministry of Labour. In 1915 Miss E.J. Hogan moved her school from Victoria Street to 9, Beresford Row under the title of Richmond High School. In 1925 amalgamation took place with Miss Best's Russell Street School to form the Armagh Girls' High School, at the same time no.8 was acquired. It remained there until the former Girls' High School was built at Alexander Road in 1854.

1 Beresford Row: (c.1920) Two-storey two-bay building of coursed rubble limestone with hipped roof and cast stone mullions and transomes. Sympathetic infill except for the ugly ribbon pointing.

2-4 Beresford Row: B. (1826) Three-storey Georgian terrace of coursed, squared, rough-faced limestone. Nos.2 & 4 have original Gibbsian semi-circular headed doorcases. The large scale OS maps of 1839 and 1864 indicate that the extra house, no.3, was carved out from nos.2 and 4 between these dates. The entrance to no.3, originally a common entry to the rear, is now filled by a decorative elliptical fanlight, door and side lights. All three houses have sash windows with exposed sash boxes and glazing bars.

(Paterson (A) Vol.V. p.40).

5 Beresford Row: B. (1827) The gateway to this house has two date stones 'RB 1827' and on the rear arch 'MDCCCXXVII John Quinn Fecit'. The 'RB' is identified as Robert Baxter who also built nos.7 and 8. A three-storey, three-bay terrace house of coursed squared rubble limestone with ashlar dressing, Gibbsian doorcase and exposed sash boxes. First floor windows were remodelled in late nineteenth century, and a decorative Victorian cast-iron balcony running the full length of the building was added.

6-9 Beresford Row: B. (1840) A group of three-storey dwellings in squared rubble limestone of a slightly inferior quality compared to nos.1-5. Gibbsian doorways have eight panelled doors that are original but only one original fanlight survives. All windows refitted as undivided sashes, all openings have ashlar dressings. The arch bears 'R.B. 1836' on the keystone.

10-11 Beresford Row: B+. (c.1830) A pair of three-storey five-bay terrace houses in ashlar stone, the ground floor is embellished with quoins and a string course. The encasements of the entrance doors and common entry have been advanced to form a central feature - this is an early alteration. At ground floor level there are tripartite windows. Three of the first floor windows of no.11 have ornamental cast-iron balconies.

(Paterson (A) Vol.V.)

1-5 Charlemont Place: A. (1827-30) Architect William Murray.

The name of the terrace commemorates Francis William, 2nd Earl of Charlemont. Part of an incomplete terrace, designed to house officers of the provincial headquarters, built as a speculation by the Earl of Charlemont. The builder was John Barnes, a relation of Sir William Barnes, Wellington's Quarter Master General.

In the valuation of 1834 the four houses in Charlemont Place were occupied by Sir Thomas Molyneux, Dr W.L. Kidd, Col. Bainbridge and Col. Napier, with no.5 apparently empty. By the next year Dr Kidd had moved to no.1 and by 1864 the row was inhabited by Margaret Kidd, Thomas Dobbin, Hugh Boyd, Rev. Benjamin Wade and William Patton. In 1839 Miss Heaney had moved from Beresford Row to Charlemont Place where she ran a select boarding and day school in no.2, then known as no.12 Charlemont Place. At this time Charlemont Place started at the Diocesan School House, now the Orange Hall, and included St. Mark's Church and St. Mark's Place. Dr Kidd was still resident in no.1, no.3 was occupied by Col. Roberts and no.5 by William Blacker, while Col. Napier remained in no.4.

The nuns of the Sacred Heart Convent, who had opened a school in Abbey Street in 1851, moved temporarily to the Pavilion and then to Charlemont Place before the convent was opened in 1859. No.2 was the manse of the First Armagh Presbyterian congregation from 1891 to 1960, while in the early 1930s Armagh County Council moved into no.1. When the Council was abolished because of local government re-organisation in 1973 they occupied nos.1-3 with the Masonic Hall in no.4, from 1947, and the Armagh City Club in no.5. By 1990 the complete terrace was in the possession of the Southern Education and Library Board.

Superbly regal in scale, a three-storey terrace of five dwellings with basement and attic storeys. Ashlar stonework, blocked parapet, overhanging cornice with dentils and modillions, stepped quoins. First floor balconies are contemporary.

Cut stone Doric doorcases, cornices decorated with paterae. The doors of nos.4 and 5 are original, the interiors of these two units also remain practically intact.

The terrace is terminated at both ends by a single storey pavilion; these were later additions, the 1864 map shows only the north pavilion. The whole group is fronted by fine railings casing swept stone stairways leading to each entrance. There is very little in all of Ireland that could match the style and quality of this exceptional terrace.

Date stone in back entrance gate pillar of Armagh Royal School 'LK

1835' (Leonard Kidd) was the arch keystone of no.1 yard entrance, closing off the back lane.

In April 1989 a 500lb bomb exploded beside Charlemont Place. It caused extensive damage to the terrace and surrounding buildings. Restoration work on Charlemont Place involved rebuilding of the north pavilion, replacement of windows, fanlights, roof re-instatement and cleaning of stonework. Indiana limestone was used for stone replacement. Southern Education and Library Board architects for the project R. McMullan and N. Robinson.

(Paterson (A) Vol.V. p.36-46.
Lundie.
History of Armagh Girls High School.
Government Valuations 1834, 1839 & 1864 and sundry directories.
Ulster Architect Oct 1990.
Ulster Gazette 13 April 1989.
Belfast Telegraph 5 March 1959)

1-4 Charlemont Gardens: Four semi-detached pebble-dashed 1930s infill buildings erected on the large garden of no.5 Charlemont Place.

Armagh County Museum: B. (1834) Design attributed to William Murray.

Built as a single-storey school-house, the Charlemont Place School. In 1856 became Armagh Natural History and Philosophical Society's Headquarters, name changed to 'The Society's House'. Interior converted from a schoolroom to two rooms at ground floor level and balcony above in 1856-7, architect Edward Gardner. Taken over as Library Headquarters and County Museum by Armagh County Council in 1931. Extended 1956-7 by architects John McGeagh and Alan Dorman when the long brick return was built over the former school play-yard and garden.

A two-storey building with three tall arched windows behind the ashlar limestone tetrastyle Ionic portico and matching doorways in screen walls at each side of the portico. Side extension of coursed random limestone with pedimented gable linked to 1950s brick extension is in a subdued classical style.

1-5 St Mark's Place: B. (1834) Built by the Reverend William Carroll. A three-storey terrace of coursed rubble conglomerate with brick dressings to windows and doorcases; cut stone quoins. Nos.4 and 5 have a parapet and a later tripartite bay window was added to no.2. All windows except two have glazing bars.

Doorcases of nos.1-3 have semi-circular fanlights and scrolled console brackets. No.4 has a wide segmental fanlight with bracketed cornice and sidelights. No.5 has a side entrance between two rectangular bay windows, added later, all under a single slated lean-to roof. The stone cills are stooled.

At the back a fine range of outbuildings in coursed rubble conglomerate with an open pediment and bull's eye window to central bay. Well converted to living accommodation.

St Mark's Church: B+. (1811) Architect Francis Johnston, rebuilt (1830) architect William Farrell.

Built as a Chapel of Ease by Primate Stuart, consecrated in 1814 and described in Stuart's 'City of Armagh' 1819 as follows:

'A new Church or Chapel of Ease has been lately erected by his Grace the Most Rev. Dr. William Stuart near the public walks to the Eastward of the Cathedral. It stands on an eminence fronting the city and forms a conspicuously beautiful object. There is a chasteness and correctness in the design and a harmony in the parts of this edifice, highly equable to the spectator and the effect is heightened by the very vivid colour of the hewn calcareous stone with which it is constructed. Perhaps the addition of a spire to the tower, which ornaments the church might have rendered it a more complete and finished piece of architecture.'

St. Mark's was also known as the Garrison Church and the army actively assisted in its building.

In 1821 trees were planted in the Church Walk and replaced early this century; in the late 1820s the church, except for the tower, was rebuilt with side aisles, balconies and probably a new roof. In 1866 a chancel and two side aisle extensions were added to the east end, architects Slator and Carpenter. Finally in 1896 much refurbishment, including a new pulpit and and new pews, was carried out.

The square tower, built of Navan limestone, with the main door facing West down Church Walk is a most accomplished architectural work in late 18th century Gothic Revival style and both stonework and carving are of a high standard. It rises in three levels terminating in a bold cornice and solid panelled parapet with corner pedestals and finials to the clasped buttresses, (note the stepped junction with tower and diagonal stepped buttresses). Over the pointed arched entrance doorway is set the Primate's arms framed by an extended hood moulding with the date 1811 carved in the frieze of the intermediate cornice. Elongated arrow-slits punctuate the flat buttresses, there is a square louvred window opening with hood mould on the three sides of the tower at the second level and tall pointed windows with louvres behind a mullion and transom screen with lozenge tracery at the third level. The nave of the church is five bays long articulated on the outside by ashlar stone stepped buttresses with diagonal buttresses at each corner and all terminating in finials on pedestals which form part of the castellated parapet wall. (It is interesting to note that the detail of the finial with its Chinese-like swag ornament is similar to those on the tower so, either Farrell copied Johnston or else replaced Johnston's finials by his own). Each bay has, at high level, a tall pointed window with hood mould, the window subdivided by a timber mullion and transom with glazing bars. Below is a small square window with mullion and glazing bars. There are ashlar stone window surrounds and the walls of pink conglomerate rubble limestone show signs of being originally rendered in roughcast. At the junction of the tower and nave it would appear that the present gable is part of the original 1811 church and in 1830 was given a castellated parapet and diagonal buttress to match in with the new side aisles, the front gables of which are well set back from the front gables of the older nave.

At the East end is the cluster of 1866 extensions, all two bays in length with a three-sided chancel apse. The style is Early English Gothic Revival with steep pitched roofs, plain buttresses and plain pointed windows with plate and geometric tracery and a little projecting gabled porch on the south. All in total contrast to the delicate Gentleman's Gothick style of Johnston and Farrell.

Interior:

Two tiers of cast-iron clustered columns support the balcony and roof. The ceiling overall is of shallow plaster ribbed sexpartite vaulting carried on flat arches spanning between the columns and back to the outside walls. The balcony extends over the side aisles and the west end of the nave where the balcony front, panelled in pine and kingwood to a Gothic pattern, breaks forward in the centre in a shallow bow.

In the chancel the Early English Gothic Revival style is evident in the open collar braced roof sheeted in pine and the squat stone columns that divide off the chancel from the side aisle extensions (one side the organ loft, the other the choir robing room).

The 1896 refurbishment is to a high standard and the oak panelling, its buttresses and finials repeating in miniature the buttresses outside, and the encaustic tiles are of particular note. But the most splendid item of this period is surely the pulpit and steps designed by the architect J.J. Phillips and made up of a white and pink marble arcaded front carried on a broad marble stem surrounded by a cluster of little marble buttresses.

Stained Glass:

The early glass, three neo-medieval patterned windows in the apse, is in memory of John Young Rutledge, rector, obit 1872.

Ideally the remainder of the openings should have remained clear but it is difficult to fault the inclusion of two windows by Ethel Rhind of the Tower of Glass Studio, Dublin. On the south wall the subjects are St.Cecilia about to receive her crown of thorns and the Good Samaritan below which is the inscription normally reserved for Dorcas. The window was installed in 1920 as a memorial to Muriel Tichborne who died on active service at Aldershot in 1918. Opposite, in 1926, Miss Rhind painted St. Luke and Virtuous Woman in memory of Robert Gray FRCPI and his wife Harriett.

There were no further insertions until the 1980s when Caldermac Studios, Lisburn, provided a St. Patrick, holding a model of the church, and St. Mark as a memorial to Major Frederick Charles Armstrong, Chairman of the Armagh District Council, obit 1983. In 1985, on the opposite wall, the firm was responsible for Suffer Little Children in memory of Mrs Jean Mercer and Good Shepherd, a memorial to Alfred K. Stinson, obit 1988.

The windows are small, well-spaced and of good quality but the atmosphere of the interior will be affected seriously if the installation of more than one other coloured composition is permitted, that is in the north-west corner.

The use of simulated early glass, both in the church and in the Crozier Hall, is welcome.

In the church grounds the entrance to the Mall East has been widened so that a decorative wrought iron gate with side screens gives a full view of the beautiful vista along the avenue of limes to the church tower. The gates were replaced in 1961-3 following a report to the Vestry that they were beyond repair 'to any state of perfection'. The medallion at the top centre bears the arms of the See of Armagh. The architect was George Taylor of Armagh, the work was executed by Messrs McKee of Dungannon and the gates were erected by A. Quinn of Tandragee. At the Victoria Street entrance south east of the church there are cut stone gate piers and an L-shaped gabled lodge of stone.

(I.B. Vol.X 15 Sept 1868.
Bassett p.93.Rogers (2) p.33.
St. Mark's Vestry Minutes June 1961-3.
Armagh Guardian 20th June 1963.
Gazateer of Irish Stained Glass.
Ryan D'Arcy.
Stuart p.547-9)

Crozier Hall, Church Avenue: B. (1850) Built as The Church Walk Infant School but now used as a church hall. It has three inscriptions - on the left hand gable '1850 erected by John George Beresford, Lord Primate', on the right hand gable '1850' and in the centre, under the mitre, 'The Crozier Hall/ 1932' . The single storey building has gabled projections and mullioned cast-iron windows with unusual geometric glazing subdivisions. Drip mouldings over the doors and windows in the gables. Recent additions are in reasonable harmony with the original. Ornamental bargeboards have been replaced by plain timber.
(Ulster Architect Feb/Mar 1990)

The Mall School (Previously the National Model School now an Orange Hall): (1818) Architect, possibly Francis Johnston.
Erected by Primate Stuart and sold to the Orange Order in 1928. The original school building had a three-bay, two-storey central block (the master's and mistress's lodgings) strategically placed between the two projecting single storey wings of classrooms, one for the boys and the other for the girls. The gable fronts of these two wings, finished in ashlar stone and with basic dentilled pediments and tripartite windows over blind arched recesses, still remain. But at the back these wings, together with the centre house, were demolished in the early 1950s to make a first floor hall for the Orange Order. At the same time the colonnade linking the two side wings was built up and glazed to form the main entrance. The alterations to the windows are crude and the siting of the new fire escape on the side elevation, in full view when entering St. Mark's gates, is very unfortunate.
It should be noted how the original pedimented gables of the old school help to mask the considerable bulk of the hall. A lesson to prospective developers in the Mall.

Hartford Cottage: B. (1880s) Possibly by J.H Fullerton.
Delightful single storey dwelling of polychrome brick with two bay windows, one of which is three sided and the other rectangular. The long side elevation reveals the full charm of the brick patterning and

decorative timber roof trim.

Hartford Place
Named after a Miss Hartford, later wife of surgeon J.M. Palmer of the County Infirmary.
(Paterson (A) Vol.V)

1-4 Hartford Place: (c.1870) Architect possibly McHenry.
A red brick terrace of two-bay three-storey houses with overhanging eaves, stone quoins and cills. Now sadly denuded of their railings (except no.1 where there is a modern replacement) and most of the cresting that originally adorned the roof ridge.

5-6 Hartford Place: (1879) A pair of three-storey red brick houses linked by a central elliptical carriage arch. The building has ashlar stone quoins and cills. The canted bay windows rise through three floors to bracketed eaves and terminate in cast-iron crestings like tiaras. The doorcases are Venetian Gothic style with substantial columns painted shiny black and carved capitals and bases of entwined pugdogs, corn and shamrocks. The decorative cresting to the roof has seen better days.

7-8 Hartford Place: (1879) A pair of substantial three-storey rendered houses, the intended third house in this terrace was never built. The semi-circular bow windows rise through three floors and terminate in bracketed eaves. The ground floor render is lined out and is terminated at the left hand gable in rusticated quoins; the string course to each floor is at cill level. The semi-circular headed doorcases have panelled pilasters decorated capitals and keystones in cement.

9 Hartford Place: (c.1950) Architect G.P & R.H. Bell.
A fairly sympathetic recent bungalow of traditional design, painted white with a segmental arched doorway below a pediment gable.

GAOL SQUARE
Although Rocque's map of 1760 shows the Horse Course on the Common before the development of the Mall and depicts, at the southern end, a steep mound, there is tantalisingly no record of its purpose - was it a tumulus, a rath or a motte? It appears to have survived the building of the barracks in 1736 but to have been removed after the construction of the gaol in 1780. From the end of the eighteenth century until 1866 public executions were held in the

HARTFORD PLACE about 1910. This photograph shows gas lamps on the Mall and the Mall School as built in 1818. (Armagh County Museum).

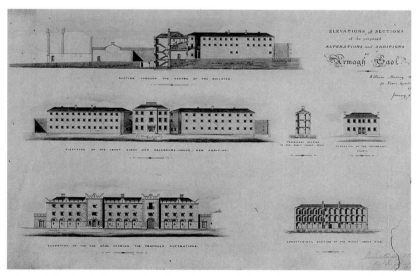

Armagh Goal elevations and sections. A proposal drawn by William Murray in 1838 and approved by the Lord Lieutenant in the following year. (Irish Architectural Archive).

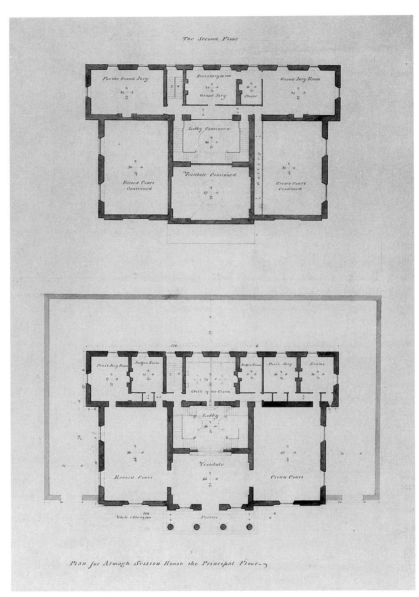

Court House; entitled "A Plan for Armagh Session House: the principal floors". This shows the original entrance before the secondary doorways were opened to give access to the courts without going through the central vestibule. (Irish Architectural Archive).

square; the earlier site was on Gallow's Hill on the main road south from the city.

The Gaol: A. (1780/1819/1840/1852) Architects Thomas Cooley, William Murray and possibly Francis Johnston.

The Gaol was built on the site of the old barracks erected in 1736. A handsome three-storey fourteen-bay building of coursed conglomerate with rusticated limestone quoins. The ground floor has two advanced entrance bays with blocked ashlar stonework. There are semi-circular windows with semi-circular recesses and springing string courses between arches stretching the full length of the front. The first and second floor windows have segmental heads with stone quoins and keystones.

The entrance doorways have semi-circular headed fanlights and side lights. Above it on the first floor there is a tripartite segmental headed window and on the second floor a triple arched window with keystone. The advanced entrance bays are pedimented - the ashlar cornice with block parapet having bare pedestals. The chimneys are an important part of the composition. The doorway to the left of the main block has a primitive pediment, on the right hand side the entrance gate has an elliptical arch. In front there is a low wall with original railings. High walls contain the prison on the three other sides.

The main block of the gaol was built in two stages. Firstly, in 1780, with Thomas Cooley as architect, the southmost entrance bay with four bays on each side (male prisoners on one side, female on the other) was built. Then in 1819 a second pedimented entrance bay (governor's house) together with a third four bay block, both identical to the original, was added to the north end. This created a new central axis between the two entrance bays and no longer in line with the central axis of the Court House. The gaol in 1819 comprised the front block as now. This was organised into three separate prisons - on the left women, in the centre debtors and on the right felons. There was a guard house at the end of the terrace in Gaol Square, other buildings included the solitary block, treadmill and engine house. Contemporary with the front block a small free-standing hip-roofed four-bay two-storey infirmary was built in excellent ashlar limestone. Francis Johnston, who was architect for the Board of Works 1805-27 was possibly the architect.

In the 1840s William Murray prepared five different schemes for further extensions, mostly on new land acquired at the back, and consisting of a series of up to five cell blocks fanning out from a central service area. In the end only one central corridor block, set on the diagonal, was built. The datestone on the rear door of 'B' wing reads 'R.C./Builder 1846' and the datestone on the front door of that wing reads 'W.M./Architect/1846'. In 1852 William George Murray was architect for a second block, a replica of the first, the builder was R. Clarke. About this time all the windows on the front were enlarged and a stone cornice and blocking course added. All the buildings described above still exist but the complex layout of segregated exercise yards behind the high perimeter walls have gone. So have the stone breaking sheds and privies which were here formerly and much of the space is taken up by temporary buildings.

G.H. Bassett visited the gaol in 1888 and commented that 'the cells in both wards are maintained in perfect condition, the most sensitive nose failing to perceive the faintest trace of that odor expected to be found associated with bolts and bars. There are two tiers of cells, one at each side of the ward. An iron gallery surrounds the upper tier, and a substantial rope netting covers the open space, as a precaution against suicide. There are good bathing facilities and the sanitary arrangements throughout are excellent. A well filled bookcase in the central hall supplies material for improving the mind. During the first month of confinement the prisoner has an opportunity to become acquainted with the 'plank bed' - a bare board. If he takes to it philosophically, he can earn two good conduct marks a day and rise triumphant from the 'plank' to a mattress in thirty days. The cells are each twelve feet by seven, and nine feet high and are heated by hot-air flues. The buildings and premises include three and a half acres. Prisoners are received from the whole of Armagh, Cavan and Monaghan, and from a portion of Down and a portion of Fermanagh.'

In 1920 the entire building became a women's prison which was closed in 1988.

(The Murray Collection, Irish Architectural Archive.
Irish Times 10th Dec. 1978.
Coote p.319.
Rogers (2) p.29.
Bassett p.115.
Black's oil painting of Armagh 1810
Stuart p.530-532)

1-6 Gaol Square and 21 Barrack St: B. (1791) A terrace of seven three-storey dwellings of random rubble limestone. The house inside the railings of the Gaol, originally the guard house, is rendered.

Extensively reconstructed in 1968 for the Northern Ireland Housing Trust, architect J. Cairncross and contractor A.C. Simpson (Partners) Ltd. Armagh, setting a pattern for all restoration to come.

THE MALL WEST

While the Mall East looks into the sun and enjoys the famous view of both cathedrals, on their respective hills, the Mall West, built at the bottom of the long gardens of English Street and Scotch Street, turns its back on this view. Nicknamed the Half-Penny Side it looks across the park and sees the Mall East as a somewhat superior residential area set apart from the old town.

From the Gaol and Gaol Square, past the muddled backyard area that is little Barrack Street, a terrace of three stone-built houses continues the scale of the stone terrace flanking the Gaol. After a long run of brick houses there is a large gap of vacant ground, now a car park but scheduled for a shopping and leisure complex with multi-storey car parking, potentially a very considerable intrusion indeed. Next a dreary government office block and a filling station, an odd pair to introduce what is to follow, an enchanting toytown Gospel Hall with a stocky campanile tower standing beside a large stern and noble Gothic Presbyterian church, its soaring tower and spire dominating the entire Mall. Then, back to earth, a fine orderly early nineteenth century classical terrace, but this time in brick, leads on to a correct classical stone Presbyterian church facade, literally cheek by jowl with a robust, five-storey stone-built warehouse that looks as if it came from Newry.

36-38 Barrack St: Tall three-storey building with flat roof. A pitched roof to the extension would greatly improve this important corner of the Mall.

Little Barrack Street has potential for small shops. The public lavatories, like a large pillbox, guard the entrance to this lane too assertively.

Armagh Old Boys Music Centre: A two-storey building with the gable entrance half turned to the Mall which does little to enhance this no-place.

Baptist Tabernacle: A modestly scaled brick frontage to an older roughcast hall behind. Jammed tightly between the tabernacle and the stone terrace there is a two-storey modern brick villa with large horizontal windows. It is an unfortunate addition, its scale relating neither to the tabernacle nor Mallview Terrace.

2-4 Mallview Terrace: B. (c.1840) A picturesque group of two-bay, three-storey terrace houses of random rubble limestone. The windows have exposed sash boxes and glazing bars except for no.4.

5 Mallview Terrace: A two-storey continuation of the terrace. Heavily restored with ugly pointing to the stonework and no glazing bars to the windows.

6-7 Mall West: (c.1870) A pair of symmetrically composed three-storey red brick houses with a central carriage arch. Yellow brick quoins and dressings to doors and windows. The dormer windows are interesting.

8-12 Mall West: (c.1870) A well proportioned two-bay, two-storey brick terrace with dormers.

14-15 Mall West: (c.1870) A detached pair of four-bay, two-storey, red brick buildings carrying on the scale of the terrace.

Nijinsky's House: (c.1918) A two storey brick villa, with virginia creeper, marooned between two car park entrances. The house was so named by the owner, Mr Stinson, after he purchased the house in 1970 the year that the famous horse, Nijinsky, won the three classic races. To be demolished for planned new development.

The entrance to the car park is marked by four squat pylon-like pillars of rubble limestone rather in the style of the entrance into a nature park of the Sixties.

Dept. of Agriculture building: A brown brick thirteen-bay, two-storey, building originally with a flat roof but now capped by a pitched and hipped roof of slate. This roof, together with a pedimented entrance porch, has improved a dull standard Sixties government building.

Garage filling station: A small two-storey gable-ended block with a single storey reception area/shop with pediment, all recently rebuilt with good use of natural stone and pleasantly repainted. The floating canopy over the service area has a hipped roof.

Gospel Hall: (originally a Masonic Hall) B+. (1884) Architect James Fullerton.
Enchanting toytown gothic extravaganza in a vaguely Venetian Gothic

Armagh Court House in 1810 from a watercolour in Armagh County Museum. Note the central doorway in No.10 Beresford Row, the Mall wall without railings and the Observatory gate lodge. The left hand wall and gates were removed when Lonsdale Street was opened. (Armagh County Museum).

145

First Armagh Presbyterian Church. A view showing the varnished pine balconies and pews of the fine interior. (M. Campbell).

style, all in polychrome brickwork. The main entrance consists of twin doors set inside pointed arches carried on short, banded columns on high pedestals and framed by a larger pointed arch supported on similar columns. Above this arch is a large, interesting plate rose window centred on the main gable of the hall which is decorated by stepped parapets and diagonal latticework patterning in the apex. On the right hand side of the centre gable there is a squat square campanile tower with high level arcading below the steep brick eaves corbelling. The tower supports the tall four-sided spire, each side pierced by a lucarne. On the left hand side of the main gable is, first a buttress, and then, at the corner, a low half round staircase tower with small pointed window openings following the line of the steps and a steep conical roof carried on steep corbelled eaves as on the campanile.

Interior:
Austerity is the keynote. Upstairs there is a long rectangular hall with the coved ceiling rising in two coves and the centre portion of the truss exposed. The pulpit is opposite the rose window. There is a sheeted, grained dado rail and fully upholstered school-type seats.

The Masonic Order moved from these premises in 1946 to no.4 Charlemont Place; in 1990 they built new premises in Charlemont Gardens, which they occupied in 1991.

(I.B. Vol.XXVI 1st April 1884
Bassett p.109)

First Presbyterian Church: A. (1878) Architects Young & McKenzie. Builder Guilder. Cost £10,000.

The congregation that later became First Armagh Presbyterian Church originally worshipped in a Meeting House off English Street close to the Shambles. In 1722 they built their own T-shaped church, off Abbey Street, which still stands and is planned to become part of the St Patrick Trian Heritage Centre.

Their present church, built in 1878, occupies a site in the Mall West at the corner of Russell Street.

The Mall elevation.
It is built of roughcut local limestone with Dungannon sandstone dressings; the style is Decorated Gothic Revival. The entrance facade consists of a steep central gable separated from a smaller gable on the left by a tall buttress rising well above the eaves and terminating in a bold crocket finial. On the right, on the corner, is the great tower and

spire. Behind the fine Gothic pattern cast-iron railings (by Riddel of Belfast) a wide flight of eleven stone steps, running the entire length of the front of the building, leads up to the four entrance doors; two in the centre, one under the small gable and one in the tower. The central paired doors (the multipanel leaves sliding open on rollers) have pointed arches on coupled columns flanked by small buttresses with tall foliated finials.

In the centre of the tympanum over each door there is a small trefoil round window of stained glass surrounded by carved stone foliage. This foliage is repeated in the side doors but, in place of the round window there are carved scrolls carrying texts. Rising up into the lofty gable above the two central doors is the great East window with reticulated tracery. Above and below the apex finial the gable is dramatically punctuated by a single circular window.

The square tower rises up in four levels with clasped buttresses and small lancet or round windows piercing the blank walls at the first two levels. At the third level there are tall paired pointed windows while at the top level only one tall pointed window, with louvres. Here the flat buttresses are slightly battered in silhouette as they change into five-sided banded buttresses topped by tall octagonal pinnacles that clasp the base of the soaring octagon spire, plain except for the delicate tall lucarnes set close in line with the top of the pinnacles.

Russell Street elevation:

The Russell Street side of the church is set back slightly from the street frontage line which is marked by the fine Gothic-style railings continued round from the main entrance side. After the great corner tower the church is five bays long with stepped buttresses rising up above eaves level and terminating in gabled finials. Each bay has a pair of lancet windows with hood moulds at ground level below a large tall pointed window with Y-tracery. A steep gabled porch projects forward between the buttresses of the third bay with a pointed arch doorway similar to the front entrance. The buttress terminating the facade is straight with a crocket finial.

Interior:

The interior of the church with its U-shaped and steeply raked balcony gathered around the pulpit and, at ground level, the pews following the curve of the centre balcony front has much of the dramatic atmosphere usually associated with an old fashioned theatre auditorium. The balconies are carried on eight cast-iron columns, with Gothic capitals, on top of which is a second tier of columns rising up to flat arches supporting the concealed nave roof trusses above the pine-sheeted heavily coved ceiling. There is a dado at both floor levels of diagonally sheeted pine boarding and the pews are also of pine. A handsome clock in a Gothic style case is fixed to the balcony front facing the pulpit.

The splendid three-seater pulpit with impressive Gothic back rest to the central seat is reached by two symmetrically placed staircases one each side of the pulpit. This assemblage is set against a magnificent three-bay mahogany arcade of Decorated Gothic arches infilled with elegantly laid out organ pipes painted in the traditional manner. This in turn is set within the frame made by the lofty pointed arch opening which probably existed as a recess before the organ was installed in 1903. Above the arch richly painted Gothic lettering on a gold leaf scroll proclaim that 'Praise waiteth for Thee Oh God in Zion'.

In the entrance vestibule there are good encaustic tiles and an original decorative cast iron radiator cover serving as a wall table under a centrally placed Gothic style memorial in marble. From the vestibule there are views of the two beautiful circular staircases dramatically lit by the little lancet windows.

It is rare to find such a fine and very substantial mid-nineteenth century church like First Armagh surviving almost intact down to the last detail. Only the introduction of the modern light oak communion table and chairs in front of the pulpit (a Second World War memorial) disturb the period completeness.

Stained Glass:

The coloured lattice-paned quarries have been replaced by Solaglas Caldermac after bomb damage, restoring the original atmosphere.

In common with buildings of similar layout the insertion of stained glass has been confined to the openings on either side of the pulpit. A First World War memorial occupies the south side. Typically the victor is shown 'in the shining armour more favoured in heavenly circles' (Marcus Patton), about to be crowned by one angel whilst offering his sword to another. Damage sustained by the inscription gave an opportunity to correct the spelling of one of the names of the fallen, McLaughlan reverted to McLauchlan. On the opposite side Heaton, Butler & Bayne provided Good Samaritan in memory of Robert Garmany McCrum of Milford.

(I.B. Vol.XX 15 Jan.1878,Vol.XXI 1 June 1879, Vol.XXI 15 Feb.1879.
Lundie.
Patton p.20.
Bassett p.95)

Gosford Place
The name pays tribute to the Second Earl of Gosford, a Governor General of Canada.

1-2 Gosford Place: (1837 rebuilt in 1960s) Two three-storey brick buildings with parapets and basements form part of the Russell Street terrace. The doorcases have half round Tuscan columns set inside elliptical headed openings with ornamental fanlight. A bay window, a replacement of an earlier feature, was crudely inserted in no.2 several years ago.
To the north side is a six-bay three-storey Sixties extension. Though considerable care was taken to carry on the proportions of the adjacent building the flat roof and general detailing, typical of the period, now look assertive and over structured.
However, the scale is good and it does continue the containment of the Mall.

On the site of what was the church school is a plain single storey building with cement-rendered gable and flat-roofed vestibule block projecting forward to the line of the church railings next door.

The Scotch Church/ The Third Presbyterian Church: B+. (1837-40)
Architect possibly William Murray.
In 1837 some members of the Presbyterian Church in Armagh petitioned the Presbytery of Armagh to form them into a separate congregation. Their request was granted and in 1839 Reverend John McAlister was installed as Minister. On arrival he had neither church, manse, nor hall; the congregation worshipped initially in the Primitive Methodist Church in Abbey Street. When they obtained a site on the Mall from Mr Matthew Robert Bell for a ground rent of £20 work started on the church. In February 1840 it opened for public worship. J.W. Lockington points out that 'along with the date of the erection of the congregation, MDCCCXXXVII, the front bears the words 'Scotch Church' - an indication of the congregation's theological orthodoxy'. He describes it as 'a plain building without a gallery and devoid of much of the decoration it has to-day. Its facade has not changed much.'
The cost of building the church was £2,500. The Reverend McAlister travelled around Ireland, and to London and Scotland, seeking financial assistance for his new congregation, the debt was cleared by 1845. Further work was undertaken in 1849 when 'John McConnell was responsible for the erection of the railings for £38-10s; Joseph

Boyd built the gallery for £116-5-7; E.J. Farrie did the painting for £33-18-6 and Joseph Gibb provided the gas fittings and outside lights for £25-5s.' In 1851 rooms beneath the church were converted for use as a school, steps gave access to the Mall. One of the Seven Houses in English Street, with six acres of land, was purchased as a Manse in 1859 for £460. A new school, built beside the church at a cost of £568-9-11, was opened in 1879.

Some time later 'in 1896 it was reported that more accommodation was needed for the choir, that draughts were a continual nuisance and lighting was far from adequate.' So, in 1900-1, 'the choir gallery was removed, the pulpit was put back to the wall and the choir were seated on a raised platform in front of the pulpit.' Lockington adds that the cost of the work would have been greater but for the fact that 'Mr Henry E. Parkinson, the architect and an Anglican, refused to take any fee for his work.' A three day bazaar was held to raise funds.

An organ was installed in the church for the first time in 1912, it was replaced by a pipe organ in 1935. In December 1915 amalgamation between the Second Armagh and the Mall congregations took place and 'the Abbey Street Church, the Greenfield Manse and the Old Burying Ground in the Lower English Street became the property of the Mall'. In the early days of the Second World War 'the railings in front of the Gosford Place Hall and the gates of Greenfield Manse were removed to be re-used for munitions'. In 1985 the warehouse building beside the church was purchased to provide additional facilities for the congregation.

An excellent three-bay ashlar limestone building. Ionic pilasters support a full cornice and frieze, the centre bay breaking forward with paired pilasters and pediment over. In the frieze there is very fine stone inscription 'Scotch Church MDCCCXXXVII'. The ground floor has rusticated stonework around the segmental headed recessed windows and first floor windows have Egyptian lugged architraves. The doorway has double scroll brackets supporting a shallow cornice and tall double doors each with twelve panels.

Good steps and low panelled walls with original railings and lamp standards, identical to those on the Mall.

Interior:

The church inside is a simple rectangle of four bays with low segmental headed windows at ground level and smaller semi-circular headed windows above and carried on moulded and bracketed cills.

The plaster ceiling is geometrically divided and the pitch pine pews follow a shallow curve. There is a balcony at the back with a curious fretwork front, supported on three thin cast-iron columns.

Stained Glass:
The original fenestration, consisting of margin-paned windows, had two stained glass lights inserted in the 1970s. On the north wall Good Shepherd, installed in 1970, is a memorial to Rev. David Graham and Mary his wife, by the Harry Clarke Studios, Dublin. A late effort, the Studios closed in 1973, in which it is difficult to see any vestiges of the hand of the master glass artist who after all died in 1931. Opposite, in memory of William Elliott, obit 1975, is a very simple Good Samaritan.

(Lockington.
Bassett p.95
Dixon (1) p.55)

Warehouse, the Mall West: B. (pre 1835)
This spectacular five-bay, five-storey warehouse is tight against the Third Presbyterian Church. It is beautifully built of coursed and squared limestone with soldier arches and ashlar quoins. The elliptically headed archway on the ground floor is not placed centrally to the building. This warehouse is more appropriate to a quayside than the Mall, nonetheless it is a building of great presence and character. Now being converted for use in conjunction with the adjoining church; the new windows are not entirely successful though it is good to see the building being refurbished.

The entrance between the warehouse and Rokeby Green was a coach entry for the buildings in College Street. They were planned like many others of this date in Armagh to have common mews service ways. Many are now blocked by all manner of rubbish and apparently unauthorised constructions of one sort or another.

Rokeby Green
Commemorates the Most Reverend Richard Robinson, Lord Rokeby, Archbishop of Armagh 1765-1794. The name Rokeby Green, although now restricted to a small group of houses on the north-west corner of the Mall, originally covered the whole area of the Mall. As the terraces on the east side took on separate names it was restricted to the west side; however, it extended the whole length until the building of Gosford Place which bi-sected it. Later Mall View Terrace and other developments were given individual names.

1-2 Rokeby Green: (c.1910) A pair of two-storey semi-detached dwellings each with a mock timber gable. Roughcast rendering to ground floor and smooth rendering above. The overhang roof detail and the bracketed hoods over the doorways have an Arts and Crafts flavour. Now shops and offices.

Rokeby Green: B. (c.1820) A dignified three-storey rendered building with a two-storey return block facing the Mall. The entrance doorway, fully cased with sidelights and elliptical radiating fanlight, together with five windows in the gable front form a strikingly strong terminating feature to this corner of the Mall, seen from College Hill. There is a fine carved stone street name plate on the gable wall.

Court House: A. (1809) Architect Francis Johnston.
The present Court House is a set piece that is the major focus of the Mall. It succeeded an earlier building in Market Street. In 1804 Coote reports 'The County Court House is deemed very inconvenient and an estimate of a new and grand edifice, to the amount of £6000 for this purpose, is now before the Grand Jury'. Francis Johnston was commissioned having been appointed architect to the Board of Works in 1806. The building was completed for use in 1809.
This controlled, symmetric, classical composition, clearly and simply proclaims order and the rule of law to all the populace. A pedimented, tetrastyle, prestyle portico in the Doric order is approached by a flight of limestone steps. The doorway leads to a central hall, also of stone, and in the same restrained architectural style. On either side are courtrooms, one inscribed 'Record Court' and the other 'Crown Court'.The plan also provided for a suite of Grand Jury Rooms. The interior has been remodelled twice, once in 1863 and again between 1965 and 1971, at which time the contractor was A.C.Simpson & Partners Ltd. Rogers writes in 1861 that the Court House 'being built on the old method, it was found to be very inconvenient. Frequent complaints having been made, Mr. Davison, County Surveyor, submitted to the Grand Jury a plan for the alteration and improvement of the house, which was approved of, and a presentment for £2,500 was passed at Summer Assizes, 1860, to carry out the proposed plan; and the work was commenced in July, 1860. The following are the contemplated alterations: A rear wing on the east side for the public offices, committee rooms, crown witnesses, police, &c. The fittings in the present courts are to be all pulled down, and the barristers' pews

placed in front of the dock so as to face the Judge;- accommodation is provided for the juries in waiting, and the public, who are to enter the gallery by a separate entrance from the outside without passing through the hall;- cells under the court for the prisoners, a room for the Grand Jury witnesses, a room for the attorneys, and considerable sanatory (sic.) improvements. Both courts are to be lighted at night by sunburners. Mr THOMAS Ross, Contractor and Builder.' In the 1965-71 restoration the plasterwork was accurately reproduced but all the joinery fittings were re-designed.

Returning to the exterior, the main front is ashlar limestone. In the central bay the stone face is smooth, on the flanking bays it is lightly tooled. The central bay contains three doorways, each within a blank arcade having semi-circular heads. Over the central door is glazing, the flanking doors are topped by stone lined niches. The two side bays each contain a semi-circular headed window set into a rectangular recess. This relationship of plains is resolved in a very strange manner at the extreme corners, where, instead of the more usual projection, the wall face in fact recedes before the composition is resolved by the staggered rusticated quoinstones. At the head of the front wall there is a full frieze and cornice, undecorated over the two side wings but, on the portico, the frieze has simple triglyths and modillions supporting the cornice projection. There is no parapet, instead the roof drains directly into a gutter cut into the top of the cornice.

The other faces of the building are roughcast rendered with stepped ashlar limestone dressings to the window and door openings. On the north side of the Court House is the gate screen of the former 'Pavilion'. Present security arrangements very much detract from the quality of the building. Hopefully the day is not too distant when they will become redundant or some alternative arrangements can be substituted as now seen at Omagh and Enniskillen.

(Rogers (2) p.31.
Coote p.321.
Brett p.37-38.
Drawings in Murray Collection, Irish Architectural Archive.
Bassett p.115.
Craig p.271.
Stuart p.529)

Old Probate Court: (c.1865) Pleasant small red brick building with sandstone dressing on rusticated base in Victorian Venetian Revival style. Presently being restored and remodelled to provide a restaurant. Rogers states that prior to the erection of this building the business of

The Mall Presbyterian Church. The church, erected in 1837, still has its contemporary iron railings and lamp standards. It bears the inscription 'Scotch Church MDCCCXXXVII'. (M. Campbell).

MARKET STREET about 1898. In the foreground are the double steps, now single, and the two storey Market House to which another storey was added in 1912. (Public Record Office (N.I.), Allison Collection).

Drelincourt School, NAVAN STREET (formerly Charter School Lane) circa 1926. Built by Dean Drelincourt's widow in 1740. The Very Rev. Peter Drlincourt was Dean from 1691 until 1722. It was maliciously burned in 1969. (Armagh County Museum).

Woodford Terrace, NEWRY ROAD. Seen through the Palace Gates in 1963, but now converted into offices. (Armagh County Museum).

the Court of Probate was transacted in the Metropolitan Registry Office on Vicar's Hill.
(Rogers (2) p.25)

MARKET STREET

The only public square in the centre of the city it occupies a pronounced hillside slope which rises up to the East end of St Patrick's Cathedral. The commercial centre of Armagh, its name is derived from its use as a market place from early times. It contained the market cross, market house, sessions house and prison and was the civic centre for many centuries. In the late eighteenth and early nineteenth centuries the prison was moved to Gaol Square, the Courthouse to the Mall and in 1908 the Market House became a Technical School. However Tuesday and Saturday markets still continue.

The down-at-heel air which used to characterize many of the buildings fronting the square is now rapidly disappearing. The successful environmental improvement scheme together with the return of the Celtic market cross (a free interpretation of the original one) augurs well for the future.

East Side

1-5 Market Street: (1978) Bland, modern eight-bay, two-storey building of dark brown brick with parapet walls raised slightly over the two centre bays and square dormers each side. Well proportioned windows to first floor with two large flattened oriel windows in the centre. The large fascia/canopy (without lettering) runs the full length of the building with a series of nine segmental 'vaults' on the underside.

7-11 Market Street: (1978) Architect W.A. Johnston. Three-bay, two-storey modern shop of brown brick with one tall pointed dormer. The bays are robustly articulated by brick piers, lined on the first floor by yellow brick inner frames, surmounted by lead lined gable shaped frames over an inner white plaster arch containing the deeply set back windows with low railings, like balconies, in front. The tall entranceway and shop windows are set behind segmental white plaster heads.

Altogether a thoughtful, well-proportioned, highly sculptural facade but over detailed.

13-15 Market Street: Architect W.A. Johnston. Four-bay, two-storey building of smooth render; moulded plaster architraves to first floor. Glazing bars to windows all removed. The absence of chimneys is noticeable.
Careful new lettering and a different colour scheme would improve the existing shop fronts.

17-21 Market Street: Ten-bay, three-storey smooth rendered building incorporating four separate frontages each with a different eaves/parapet line; last two bays beside no.15 are two-storey. There is an amalgam of late nineteenth century decorative devices around the semi-circular or segmental headed windows set between pilasters, string courses or cornices.
Below is the somewhat bleak and over deep fascia board running the length of the building. Segmental headed shop windows are fitted between piers of random rubble conglomerate.
The mutilated chimneys spoil the appearance of the building particularly when seen from the Cathedral gates at the top of Market Square.

South Side
2-4 Market Street: The present screen wall and archway were part of the building that once stood on this site. It is important that this unsightly gap is filled as soon as possible to complete the sense of enclosure of the square.

6 Market Street: Five-bay, three-storey smooth rendered building with incised blockwork. New windows with glazing bars apparently in original openings. On the ground floor are double entrance doorways each side of a central window. No chimney stacks.

8-10 Market Street: Five-bay, three-storey roughcast building with obvious signs of good coursed rubble stonework underneath. All openings except carriage arch in centre blocked up. The window openings (three bays) nearest the Cathedral appear to be original. One chimney stack missing.

12-14 Market Street: Six-bay, three-storey building; smooth render with signs of stonework underneath; carriage arch to no.14. All openings blocked; window openings on first and second floor appear to be original.

16-18 Market Street: Four-bay, three-storey roughcast building;

(entrance to no.16 at low level below no.18). All openings blocked; facade is original apart from enlarged window opening at lower level. It is welcome news that nos.8-18 are to become dwelling houses and are to be restored to their early nineteenth century appearance.

North Side
Sad remains of an Art Deco cinema, now a builder's store, to be replaced by a municipal theatre forming part of St Patrick's Trian.

25 Market Street: Eight-bay, three-storey building (the four bays nearest English Street form part of no.2 English Street); smooth render with moulded architraves around windows. Facade divided down centre by a row of coupled quoins; single quoins at each end. Bracketed eaves to roof; only one chimney stack remains. Modern sash and pivot hung windows with glazing bars.
Unsightly illuminated canopy to no.25 and long strip window at waist height detracts from the rhythm of the pleasant facade.

MARKET HOUSE: B+. (1815) C.E.B. Brett suggests that the architect may have been Thomas Duff or that the design may have originated in Francis Johnston's office. Third storey added in 1912-3, architect John Caffery, school principal; contractor for the alterations Robert Cullen.
The Market House is a square building erected where the previous sessions house and gaol once stood. It is situated on a prominent island site in the middle of the square and is intended to be seen from all sides. Each facade has five bays; it is three-storey on three sides, because of the steep slope on the east-west axis the facade facing the Cathedral is two-storey.
The front facade, facing east, breaks forward at each end bay and rises from a base of seven steps running the full length of the building. The stonework at ground floor level is rusticated and the arcade of five segmental-headed arches has a simple string course at the springing of the arches; the three centre arches have scroll keystones. Fine cast-iron gates (probably original) drawn across the archways conceal the fact that the once open market area behind has now been glazed in and serves as part of the public library. A further string course caps the rustication, then further up the cills of the first floor flat segmental-headed windows form part of another string course. At frieze level the words 'GULIELMUS ARCHIEP. ARMAGH UTILITAT. CIVIUM DEBIT. MDCCCXV' (paraphrased 'The gift of William Arch. of Armagh for the use of the citizens 1815') are carried in beautiful incised Roman letters.

Above the cornice, in the centre of the balustrade that spans the three centre bays, there is a frontispiece with a clock set in stone below a segmental pediment. Behind this is an inadequate looking square louvred cupola with pointed roof.

On the north and south facades, because of the hill, the rusticated ground floor wall drives dramatically into the slope and there is room for only one segmental headed arch and one pair of gates.

The two end bays of the west facade break forward slightly as on the east side and the three centre bays project forward to make a definite block surmounted by a pediment. Two pairs of elegant oculi, framed by architraves, are set one above the other in the side walls. The main entrance doorway in the centre bay (part of the 1912 alterations) is framed by two engaged Tuscan columns on pedestals, a cornice and pediment. The frieze below the main pediment carries the words 'MUNICIPAL TECHNICAL SCHOOL' incised in the stonework.

While the proportions of the Market House were probably better before the third storey was added in 1912-13, full marks must be given to the sensitive way the original cornice features were reproduced at the new higher level. The new entrance in the west facade is made so that all the new work is now quite indistinguishable from the original. (See article on 'The Market House Fifty Years Ago')

Armagh's other distinguished example of a vertical and seamless addition, undertaken a hundred years before the Market House, can be seen at the Primate's Palace.

(Brett p.36
Paterson (A) Vol.V. p.80 & 87
Stuart p.550
Memoirs of Wm. Blacker in Armagh Guardian 24/1/36 and 31/1/36
Rogers (2) p.29)

McCRUM'S COURT

This passage which appears on Rocque's map (1760) is entered from Market Street between new high walls of dark brown brick linked overhead by a partly built concrete bridge. Beyond this the lane widens, on the left there is a random rubble stone four-storey warehouse, with small windows with shutters and grilles on the ground floor, now well-restored as a tavern and antique shop. It is called 'The Hole in the Wall' as it was traditionally the site of an early gaol. On the right the modern building has four slate-hung square oriel windows (answering the single one at high level on the other side) which look well set against the white painted concrete block wall.

The lane then curves round through a triangular open space with new benches and trees where it divides. The path on the left leads to the Mall car park after passing a small two-storey barn with good brickwork now refurbished as the Citizens Advice Bureau. The lane leading to Scotch Street is flanked by another stone and brick building on the right, a supermarket entrance with an elongated traditional shop front and a rebuilt stone return to 43 Scotch Street with a window and two doors surmounted by good painted signs.

On the left is the new high stone wall of the car park and a recent nicely rebuilt random rubble stone warehouse with brick dressings (part of the original stone walls remain at the rear) and slated hipped roof. The alley continues, narrowing gradually, and joins Scotch Street between two brown brick buildings. These premises were rebuilt after destruction by a terrorist bomb. A more substantial arch over the entrance would look better than the present one in thin ironwork.

McCrum's Court is paved with an interesting mixture of modern square concrete pavoirs and stone square setts though the standard of workmanship in the recent upgrading of this ancient passage is disappointing. There are new traditional style tall lamp standards, set so close to the side walls that it would surely have been better (and less obtrusive) to mount them on the walls.

MELVALE VILLAS, PORTADOWN ROAD: (1887-8)

G.H.Bassett refers to these buildings as 'Mel Villas' and says that they were built by 'Mr Thomas George Peel, coroner'. A pair of elegant Victorian semi-detached two-storey villas with basement and attic. One massive shared chimney rises off the main party wall. The central bays of the main front are projected and contain the principal rooms. They are topped by pitched gabled dormers with iron finials decorating the peak of each. There is a single window in each dormer, triple windows in the room below and at ground level there is a flat canted bay decorated by an ornate iron balustrade.

The entrance doors are set back at each end in a two-storey 'lean to' bay. The door to the left hand of the pair appears to be original with four solid panels and a margin glazed fanlight over. The other door has glazing in the upper half. The main front is brickwork in flemish bond with glazed headers forming a diaper pattern, cut stone quoins frame the brickwork in. The right hand entrance bay is rendered as are all the other faces of the building.

NAVAN STREET

Original gate pillars remain at the left hand end. They are slender and square topped with a pyramid cap; the corners are chamfered back below to create an octagonal shaft.

(Bassett p.109)

NAVAN STREET

This street linked Ogle Street and Killylea Road and was the main route to the west prior to modern road developments, it is now a cul-de-sac. It was known as Belnayaleg Street until Mrs Drelincourt founded a school there in 1740, then the name was changed to Charter School Lane.

The windmill stump on the skyline is a picturesque feature when walking down Navan Street.

1-18 Navan Street: A curving terrace of two-bay, two-storey houses in red-brown brick; the slated pitched roofs step down the slope. Paired hardwood entrance doors with side panels linked by canopies.

Around the corner is a modern development, Drelincourt Close, built on the site of Drelincourt School which was maliciously burned in 1969.

A low stone wall, entrance pillars with modern gates and a stone bridge mark the line of the Armagh to Keady railway which ran beneath the road until 1957.

The street is concluded by Emania Terrace, a terrace of fourteen two-bay, two-storey dwellings.

On the opposite side of the street is a grassy slope on top of which is an impressively substantial wall in coursed rubble stone with hump-backed capping. Once the boundary of the flax market the wall now screens a large car park.

After the entrance to Culdee Street there are apartment blocks and then an open area of grass. Beyond the bridge a small blocked up terrace and a group of single storey dwellings conclude the street.

NEWRY ROAD

Described in Rocque's map of 1760 as the road from Markethill. It rises steeply from the junction of Scotch Street and Barrack Street and borders the Palace demesne. Many modern detached houses, the R.U.C. Station, the telephone exchange and the golf club are now within the Palace grounds (with spectacular views across the demesne). The entrances to these buildings individually breach the demesne wall; the higher the remaining wall the more satisfactory the general appearance from Newry Road. These buildings replace a major section of the demesne planting and form horizons from the Palace; a new belt of trees should be planted to recreate the enclosure of the Palace landscape. The R.U.C. Station is a Sixties Ministry of Finance Works Division building on an elevated site where the entrance gates to the Palace once stood (see Cathedral Close)

Coming down Newry Road the views of the city are dramatic.

Bridge House: Six-bay, five-storey modern block of flats which face Newry Road and Barrack Street. Good planting at the corner.

The best view of Scotch Street, the gable wall of Dobbin's House, the roofs of Dobbin Street and Castle Street is from here.

2 Newry Road: (c.1830) A six-bay, three-storey building of squared coursed limestone; ashlar stone to ground floor. Originally a terrace of three two-bay houses with carriage arch. The original segmental headed opening now has a very solid modern panelled double entrance door. Continuous string/cill course to first floor.

This impressively simple, attractive block is marred by modern plastic top-hung windows with implied glazing bars.

4-20 Newry Road: (1970) Architects G.P.& R.H. Bell. Contractors Collen Brothers, Portadown. A terrace of nine two-bay, two-storey houses; every house steps up the street. Concrete brick and patent white cladding to first floor. Modern windows and red pantiled roof. Small attractive gardens.

Newry Road Hall - Meeting place of the Church of God.

(re-opened 1979 following bomb damage in 1975)

A small meeting hall on an elevated site. A flight of steps leads up to the panelled doorway which breaks forward from the entrance gable facing the road. Small oculus window over door.

26 Newry Road: Three-bay, two-storey house with roughcast finish. Segmental drip mouldings over door. Bay window rises through two floors.

28 Newry Road: Three-bay, two-storey red brick house with bay window. Red brick to heads of openings.

32-34 Newry Road: Two modern brick villas with plastic windows, door and window surrounds.

36-46 Newry Road: (c.1900) A terrace of two-bay, three-storey red brick houses with modern windows and doors.

48-54 Newry Road: (1926) A terrace of four two-bay, two-storey roughcast dwellings with slated roofs, dormers and brick chimneys. Bay windows to ground floors with continuous roofs which form porches to the entrance doorways. No.48 has a single storey annexe with bay window against the gable, enlarged, slated dormer and replacement windows.

56-62 Newry Road: (c.1928) A terrace of four two-bay, two-storey roughcast dwellings with slated roofs and brick chimneys. Ground floor windows paired beneath timbered gable. Handsome heads to downpipes.

64 Newry Road: Three-bay, two-storey roughcast dwelling with garage attached. Brick chimneys; replacement doors and windows.

66 Newry Road: (1930) A three-bay, two-storey roughcast dwelling with slated roof and brick chimneys. Slated roof to porch and single storey bow windows; detached garages.

Greenfield Manse: B. (1852) Architect possibly W.J.Barre. Contemporary with the Presbyterian Lecture Hall (see College Street). An attractive three-bay, two-storey red brick building with plaster dressings and smooth rendered porch. Hipped roof with wide eaves. Shouldered architraves to first floor windows; ground floor has coupled sash windows with semi-circular heads framed by label mouldings with bossed ends and centrepiece like a keystone. Shallow porch with simple cornice and frieze supported by paired square columns. Rectangular fanlight with marginal glazing; two narrow side windows, stone plinth and steps to porch. String course above and below first floor windows. Ground floor windows to side elevation have segmental heads.
A well maintained building in a landscape setting.

90-92 Newry Road: (c.1920) Pair of semi-detached two-bay, two-storey houses. Combined single-storey bay windows with pitched roof. Entrance doors at each end with delicate plaster pilasters to semi-circular surrounds. Stained glass to front door panels, fanlights and sidelights.

Two flights of steps lead up to these well designed and unspoilt houses.

OGLE STREET

The street was named after Mr Thomas Ogle, a sovereign of the city, who owned a marble polishing mill in the vicinity. Ogle Street and Thomas Street were opened in 1759 to by-pass the steep cathedral hill. Turning the corner from Thomas Street and looking westwards up the steep hill it is still possible to catch a glimpse of an eighteenth century provincial Irish streetscape. Much of the detail has changed but form and silhouette have not.

St Malachy was reputedly born in Ogle Street in 1095, a plaque on no.21 now marks the site.

1-3 Ogle Street: A pair of two-bay, three-storey buildings, smooth rendered and lined out; flat quoins and original plaster frame for the shop sign. One chimney is missing. No.1 has original sash windows, no.3 has modern windows in original openings. The vertical illuminated hanging sign is obtrusive.

Simple shop front with good name board of black glass with gold lettering.

5 Ogle Street: Three-bay, three-storey smooth rendered building. Elliptical headed carriage arch of ashlar stone with keystone dated 1833. Fine original blacksmith made gate in need of repair. Sash windows without glazing bars.

Traditional shop front with original cornice and traditional style name board with painted lettering.

7-9 Ogle Street: A pair of two-bay, two-storey buildings without chimneys. No.7 has roughcast rendering with new hardwood windows in original openings. No.9 is smooth rendered with modern windows in original openings with moulded architraves. Good traditional style shop front.

11-17 Ogle Street: A four two-bay, two-storey well proportioned building worthy of refurbishment. No.11 has roughcast rendering, modern windows and a large sign. Nos.13 and 15 are smooth rendered with modern windows in original openings with moulded architraves (first floor windows of no.15 are boarded up). Simple shop fronts and name boards in need of repair. No.17 is smooth rendered with modern windows and a new shop front with plastic sign.

19-21 Ogle Street: A pair of three-bay, two-storey red brick buildings with moulded brick eaves cornice and sash windows with vertical glazing bars. Six-panel doors each side of shop window which is framed in hardwood sheeting.

Marble shield-shaped plaque fixed to wall between first floor windows states 'Tradition points to the site of this house as being that of the house in which St Malachy was born'.

23-25 Ogle Street: A pair of three-bay, three-storey buildings, roughcast rendering with cement surrounds to windows and original sashes with glazing bars.

Traditional plaster fascia to no.25.

Entrance to Chapel Lane

27-29 Ogle Street: Six-bay, three-storey smooth rendered building with blockwork to ground floor walls painted black with yellow joints. Modern windows in original openings and original fascia sign with good lettering. Modern hardwood sheeted doors. The hanging illuminated sign is out of keeping but the painted lettering on gable and front is good.

31-33 Ogle Street: Pair of two-bay, three-storey buildings, smooth rendering lined out. No.31 is an attractive, apparently uninhabited, dwelling house with original sash windows and some glazing bars missing. No.33 has sash windows with glazing bars to first and second floors. A basic shop front with painted lettering on the fascia to the ground floor.

35-37 Ogle Street: Six-bay, two-storey smooth rendered building with chimneys missing. First floor windows reduced in height and third floor windows removed as part of a refurbishment scheme, which includes a well designed traditional style shop front running the full length of the property.

39 Ogle Street: Two-bay, two-storey roughcast rendered dwelling with sash windows and without a chimney.

41 Ogle Street: Two-bay, three-storey building, smooth rendered and lined out. Modern windows in original openings with moulded plaster architraves. Intriguing modern 'chocolate box' shop front with a silhouette of Armagh in gilt on the fascia. A fine wrought iron bracket for a hanging sign remains.

43-47 Ogle Street: Three two-bay, two-storey dwellings, roughcast rendering to first floor, smooth to ground floor. Sash windows throughout, nos.43 and 45 have larger ground floor windows. In need of restoration.

49-51 Ogle Street: Pair of two-bay, two-storey buildings, one heavily renovated and the other still intact.

No.49 has roughcast rendering with new windows in original openings and an enlarged horizontal ground floor window.

No.51 is of coursed rubble with soldier arches to door and windows. Original sash windows with vertical glazing bars.

53-57 Ogle Street: Three two-bay, two-storey red brick buildings with moulded brick eaves cornice and brick chimneys. Modern windows in original openings.

No.53 is a dwelling house, nos.55 and 57 are shops now being refurbished. No.57, on the corner, is given prominence by a canted gable and the remains of a plaster name board and cornice.

2-4 Ogle Street: A pair of two-bay, three-storey smooth rendered buildings with modern windows in original openings.

A gap site with a passage way and an attractive rural style gate needing restoration.

8-10 Ogle Street: A pair of two-bay, three-storey smooth rendered buildings with modern windows in original openings. Basic shop front with a plethora of painted lettering at top and sides.

12-14 Ogle Street: A pair of two-bay, two-storey smooth rendered buildings. No.12 has modern windows in new horizontal openings;

no.14 has original sash windows to first floor and a large shop window with plastic sign.

Gap site converted into a pedestrian access in the most basic manner with horizontal shores between the gable walls.

18-22 Ogle Street: Three two-bay, two-storey buildings of coursed roughcut squared limestone with ugly raised pointing to nos.20 and 22. Nos.18 and 22 have modern sash windows in original openings; no.20 has plastic windows. Traditional style panelled doors.

24-30 Ogle Street: Four derelict two-bay, three-storey buildings of coursed rubble limestone with soldier arches; smooth render to ground floor of no.30. Original doors and windows, two still have glazing bars. Fine relieving arch above door and windows of no.26.

32-36 Ogle Street: Three two-bay, two-storey buildings, roughcast with smooth cement quoins. Modern windows to original openings, many blocked up. Attractive fanlight to no.32 and corrugated iron roof.

38-44 Ogle Street: Four two-bay, three-storey derelict buildings of coursed rubble limestone with soldier arches to openings. Original sash windows with glazing bars survive to top floor of nos.38 and no.42. The stonework is painted on no.40, it has a traditional painted pub sign contrasting with the standardised illuminated hanging sign.

46 Ogle Street: Fine three-bay, three-storey building of squared rubble limestone with soldier arches to openings, segmental carriage arch and tooled ashlar to ground floor. Original sash windows with glazing bars and attractive fanlight. The remains of original fascia sign and name board survive.

48-50 Ogle Street: Pair of two-bay, three-storey buildings; roughcast render to no.48 with smooth render to ground floor and quoins. No.50 is of coursed, squared limestone with soldier arches (probably originally rendered); smooth render to ground floor. Original sash windows with glazing bars to first and second floor and continuous first floor cills. Delightful miniature windows to second floor of no.50 and painted lettering to ground floor.

52-52a Ogle Street: Good five-bay, two-storey red brick building with smooth rendered ground floor; dark blue brick ornamentation and decorative brick eaves cornice. Well designed ground floor shop

No.54 OGLE STREET built about 1810. A fine shop with dwelling over, part of an incomplete pair or terrace. (M. Campbell).

Armagh Railway Station probably designed by John Godwin for the Ulster Railway Company in 1848, closed in 1957 and demolished in 1964. (Armagh County Museum).

Armagh Business Centre. Sited on RAILWAY STREET, the former office and hostel block of the Bairnswear factory built in 1950. (M. Campbell).

Stained glass from the former inner porch door of the Archbishop's Palace bearing the arms of most of the Archbishops of the See from 1562 to 1911. (Irish Architectural Archive, Lord Rossmore).

windows and entrance with segmental heads and segmental drip moulding framing the painted lettering.

No.52a has a smaller flat headed window and panelled door with hood mouldings. Well maintained and painted.

54 Ogle Street: Very fine and interesting three-bay, three-storey building of ashlar limestone. Probably the oldest existing shop/house in Armagh still all intact and a valuable asset to the street. Original sash windows with glazing bars and original elegant name board with cornice, now decayed; original sheeted half-door to shop and panelled door to dwelling. Projecting stone courses at gable indicate that this shop was to be semi-detached with a carriage arch over the laneway (now closed with a blacksmith made gate). The plastic box sign is the only intrusion.

56-58 Ogle Street: A pair of two-bay, two-storey smooth rendered buildings; first floor window blocked up. Modern shop fronts with brightly painted signs all over first floor walls.

Large illuminated sign to no.58.

60-62 Ogle Street: A two-bay, two-storey red brick gable fronted building. Large segmental headed double sash window to first floor. Basic shop front with illuminated box signs.

PALACE DEMESNE

The Primate's Palace: A. (1770) Architect Thomas Cooley. Architect for additions (1825) Francis Johnston.

(Now the offices of Armagh District Council. The Council deserves great credit for the care and attention given to the conservation of their buildings within the demesne.)

The palace is the most personal of the legacies from Archbishop Richard Robinson. The style is the restrained classicism characteristic of all his building works.

Robinson had been translated to the primacy in 1765. Unlike his immediate predecessors, he decided to be domiciled in Armagh. The old See House in English Street (which stood roughly where Russell Street now joins English Street), he considered inconvenient; it was certainly in poor repair, and so he set about planning a new building. While these were in preparation he took up residence at Richhill

Castle. By 1769 Parliament had passed an act for the enclosure of a demesne. His next move was to employ the Dublin architect Thomas Cooley to design the buildings. It is not recorded who was chosen to plan the landscape but there is no doubt of the priority given by Robinson to that element of the overall scheme.

Edward Malins and the Knight of Glin writing about the development in the design of ecclesiastical landscapes comment 'Dean Swift and Dr Delaney had modestly led the way out of formal avenues, clipped hedges and pleached alleys.' Indeed they had. The English natural landcape was, by now, all the fashion. The new Archbishop's landscape plan went beyond the enhancement of his palace to encompass the whole city. Nothing quite like this enterprise had been attempted before in Ireland and possibly in the British Isles.

Arthur Young visited Armagh in 1776 while on his tour of Ireland. Already there had been considerable progess. He writes 'He has perfectly changed the face of the neighbourhood...the view from the palace is much improved.' He goes on to describe in detail new buildings and plantations that contribute to the overall panorama. Other early commentators were George Tyner in 1794 and De Latocnaye in 1796.

Recent developments have taken away from the full appreciation of the original scheme, particularly the police station which breaks the continuity between the demesne and the Mall. Also the new houses along the Newry Road that have taken the place of the tree belt which previously formed the view. Within the demesne some of the planned vistas have been confused by additional planting in the nineteenth century. This has affected the views from the palace of the obelisk and in the opposite direction of the cathedral.

The palace building was sited on a rise in the ground at the head of a sweeping drive. Entering through the main gates, where the police station now stands, the building was seen at a distance framed by trees. The driveway then dipped into a planted hollow close to the ancient holy well of St.Bridget. The Beresford's created a picturesque walk in this hollow with a decorative gate which was moved to the grounds of the new See House. The driveway continued so that the palace was for a time hidden from view, then rose again out of the trees to present the final triumph illustrated in James Stuart's 'Historic Memoirs of the

City of Armagh' (1819). The drive in use today was originally the service entrance.

The building itself is a simple cuboid faced on all elevations with ashlar limestone. The top storey and the porch were added in 1825. External detailing is limited to the rustication of the basement storey and moulded architraves to the windows of the upper floors; those of the principal floor are emphasised by the addition of an hood. On the wall above the entrance the archbishop's arms are carved surmounted by a mitre and encircled by a wreath. The frieze and cornice are unadorned. The only expression of a classical order is the use of the Ionic on the porch where paired columns backed by pilasters of the same order, are set obliquely, flanking the doorway. A flight of five steps brings one inside the porch where the floor is of beautifully dressed limestone set in radiating rings. A further short flight leads into the entrance hall; the floor in the hall is an unfortunate modern mosaic illustrating the arms of the District Council and replacing the original stone flags. On the walls are displayed a fine collection of royal portraits previously the property of the See and by artists including Allan Ramsay, Wilheim Wissing, Nicholas Maes, Michael Dahl, William Dobson and from the schools of Kneller and Reynolds. The rooms were planned originally as a suite of state rooms and remain very much as they were with plaster work of exceptional quality, chimney pieces and joinery intact. The library and adjoining room have been stripped out to create a council chamber.

The upper floors are now used as offices. The grand staircase leads to the first floor where the archbishops had their private apartments. The service stairway was extended to the second floor which was added to accommodate visiting clergy.

(Coote p.323
Rogers (2) p.23
Stuart pp.445-6
S.A. Vol.6 No.1. 1971. pp.94-130
Dixon (3)
Drawings in the Irish Architectural Archive
Armagh District Council Leaflets)

The Chapel: A. (1781-6) Architect Thomas Cooley and later Francis Johnston.
From the ground floor a side door gives access to the archbishops' private chapel. This building fulfilled two roles in the overall scheme. The first as a chapel, the second as a classical ornament in the

landscape. In any other demesne it have been a temple, a belvedere or a gazebo.

Today its form is overpowered by the mass of the palace itself but when the chapel was built, the main building was a storey lower so that the contrast would not have been so marked as it is now. Again the designs were those of Thomas Cooley and like the palace the work was finished in 1786 after Cooley's death by Francis Johnston. It is a perfect essay in classical scholarship and ranks amongst the most outstanding of this genre in Ireland.

The building is faced on all elevations with ashlar limestone. A flight of five steps form the stylobate from which rises an Ionic prostyle, tetrastyle portico. The overall format of the building is possibly based on the little temple on the Illissus Attieus, that had been deliberately destroyed by the Turks in 1780 just as the plans for the Chapel were being conceived. The spacing of the two inner columns is slightly wider than those between the flanking columns and the body of the building is a little wider than the portico. The architrave is omitted from the entablature beyond the portico. The interior plan has been reversed with the communion table set at the west end because of the functional relationship of this building to the palace.

There are four window openings with semi-circular heads formed in both the north and south walls, two of these on the north face are blind. The sanctuary is lighted by a single similar window, the coloured glass dates from 1895. The windows are in memory of John George Beresford, Archbishop of Armagh 1822-62. It is regretted that their installation necessitated the removal of the work of Francis Eginton. His painted tracery windows survive in Hillsborough Parish Church to give an idea of the type of glass which was appropriate for buildings of the 1770s in Ireland.

The main entrance is proportioned to harmonize with the portico but the paired doors do not fill the full height of the dressed stone architrave which rises above the level of the first floor gallery. The space below forms a vestibule from which there are three doors; to the right is the room now used as a boiler room most probably designed as a sacristy, to the left is access to the stairs leading to the musicians' gallery and the door straight ahead leads into the body of the chapel. The internal bays are divided by Corinthian pilasters set on a podium of panelled wax oak approximately one and a half metres high above the floor. The stalls and throne are also of waxed oak of superb design and quality. The floor is a chequer of stone quarries alternately local limestone with smaller pieces of black Kilkenny marble. Above the entablature rises the shallow coffered barrel vaulted ceiling, each coffer containing an undercut plaster rosette. The sanctuary is closed by wrought iron communion rails and the top finished in waxed oak. The communion table is approached by the traditional three steps that represent the three times Christ fell on the road to Calvary. The present communion table and other sanctuary fittings, although in keeping, are not original to this building. The interesting pair of carved oak Corinthian columns in the gallery also originated elsewhere.

(Ulster Architect Feb. 1987)

The Obelisk

Other structures within the demesne enclosure include the obelisk erected in 1783. Its base is set just below the horizon as perceived from the south face of the palace. The siting is axial on the palace, the clear geometry is in marked contrast with the conscious informality of the rest of the landscape. The obelisk form has its origins in ancient Egypt. Here the limestone monument commemorated Archbishop Robinson's patron, the Duke of Northumberland, to whom he owed his preferment. On two sides of the pedestal are the Royal arms and the arms of Northumberland. On the other two sides are inscriptions. The shaft carries the arms of the See and those of Richard Robinson, Lord Rokeby.

Stableyard

Behind the chapel hidden in a plantation of trees is the stable yard. The buildings are a two storey range formed around a quadrangle. The construction is stone, the body of the walling is squared coursed rubble; windows and doors are dressed in ashlar work. The service drive gives access to an entrance in the centre of the north face. A second gateway in the east face leads to a service tunnel linking to the basement offices of the palace.

Conservatory

Near the yard is an early conservatory of a curvilinear type. These structures were once common features of many Irish estates but relatively few now survive. The District Council has recently saved this one from dereliction, an action for which all credit must be given. To the south-west is the Ice House.

PALACE DEMESNE

Gateway, Friary and Garden
The present entrance gateway is a copy of the original that once stood adjacent to the Newry Road roundabout and was moved to Cathedral Close when the new See House was built.

Close to the new gateway are the ruins of the Franciscan Friary founded in 1264, suppressed in 1542 and finally destroyed during fighting in 1595. What was left of the buildings became a quarry for building stone until used to create a fashionable romantic ruin for Archbishop Robinson as part of his overall planning of the demesne. The surviving remains are of the thirteenth century church. The cloisters that once stood to the north have almost entirely disappeared. The site is now a monument in state care.

The rugby pitch is situated where the kitchen garden once was. The gardener's house survives and is now in use as an office for the registrar of births, marriages and deaths.

The Palace Farm: (c.1770) Designs by Thomas Cooley.
The farm, situated at the extreme southern extent of the demesne, was also part of Richard Robinson's overall scheme for his estate. Charles Coote writing in 1804, shortly after Robinson's death, is very complimentary...'indeed his Grace's farmyard, implements of husbandry and mode of culture, afford a bright example to the gentry.' The farm is approached by a separate driveway off the Keady Road.

A pair of matching three-bay, two-storey rendered stone built dwellings of symmetrical design flank the main gate. The roofs are hipped and two stone chimneys rise off the central cross walls. The windows are small pane sashes, nine panes at first floor and twelve at ground floor level. The panelled entrance doors have shallow segmental fanlights and classical encasements. These features and the flanking ground floor windows are set into recesses, each with a segmental arched head. All the front windows have moulded stone encasements and the entrance is protected by a shallow hood supported on stone brackets. Both houses have been restored and sympathetically modernised in recent years.

In front of each dwelling is a small walled garden and behind are the farm buildings which include a pigeon-loft. The buildings, formed around a paved yard, are two-storey, slated, rendered and whitewashed.

Primate's Houses, Keady Road. (c.1840)

A range of six single storey stone cottages situated outside the demesne wall. They are built of squared limestone rubble and are symmetrically composed as wings to a single two-storied unit, over which there is a cross pitch roof that presents a stone coped gable to the main elevation. The gables of the wings are similarly coped in dressed stone and each is crowned by a stone built chimney. A tudor flavour is added by the label mouldings used only in the central bay but the underlying spirit is clearly classical. The original doors were sheeted and the windows paired casements. The building was rehabilitated after a period of neglect and the houses formally re-opened 26th March 1971.

Unfortunately an element of individuality has crept in since inappropriate alterations have taken place which spoil the architectural unity of this pleasant little group.

(Young.
Edward Malins and The Knight of Glin.
Stuart pp.446-7
Curl pp.6 & 13
Coote
Historic Monuments of N.I.
S.A. Vol.6. No.1 1971 pp.94-130
U.J.A. Vol.38 1975 pp.61-80
Dixon (3)
Specify Vol.7 No.4. Jan 1987
Murray Collection, Irish Architectural Archive
Design drawings in Armagh Public Library
Stalley pp.175-77)

RAILWAY STREET

The railway reached Armagh in 1848 and a new curving street was built to circumnavigate the steep approach over Banbrook Hill. It is still called Railway Street though the station closed in 1957.

1-17 Railway Street: A terrace of two-bay, two-storey houses in smooth render. No.5 is heavily modernised with a shop on the ground floor.

Nursery School (formerly a national school): A one and a half storey building, with a three bay single storey wing, set back from street with low stone wall in front. Bargeboards to steeply pitched gable with segmental headed window to first floor and coupled windows to ground floor. Gabled canopy on gallows brackets to entrance. Tall chimney stacks. Built of coursed rubble stone and previously rendered, now with ugly ribbon pointing.

79 Railway Street: A three-bay, two-storey building with dormers in red brick with horizontal bands of yellow brick. Entrance at right angles to street with bay windows at either side of door; wooden square columns support flat roofed entrance canopy.

81-93 Railway Street: A terrace of seven two-bay, two-storey red brick dwellings with horizontal bands of yellow brick. Dormers to roof; bay windows rise through two floors.
Nos.83,91 and 93 have retained the original fenestration.

95-151 Railway Street: The remainder of the street on this side consists of terraces of two-storey red brick and rendered shops, dwellings and a public house. The one exception, at the roundabout, is a single storey supermarket in red brick.

Large metal and mesh gates lead into the bus depot.
Railway Station: The imposing entrance gate piers are in ashlar sandstone with banded rustication. The central pair of tall piers are linked to coupled lower side piers by modern railings which carry the original flanking pedestrian gates. All four piers are decorated with small console brackets on all sides, these support a cornice and segmental pediment. This creates a cushion-like effect and the two central piers are given added importance by a frieze. The richly decorated cast-iron main and side gates with 'parasol' spikes are still in place though all badly in need of restoration.
Dr W.A.McCutcheon stated that 'the Armagh terminus was completed in 1848 to a design similar to but on a more modest scale than the Belfast terminus, opened in the same year.' He suggested that it was probably designed by John Godwin, engineer to the Ulster Railway Company, and that the station was built under the supervision of William Dargan. Alas, all that remains today are the entrance gates and the goods shed, which in spite of its corrugated asbestos roof and gutted interior is still, like the entrance, a noble monument to the Railway Age.
The goods shed is a single-storey barn of mellow red brick, eighteen bays long by four bays wide. Each bay of the long facades, except those at each end which are blank and step forward to form low towers, contains a large blind arch and keystone with smaller arches each side

in the manner of a classical triumphal arch. The springing line of the arches is marked by a stone string course which is carried around the blank walls of the corner towers. Likewise a carved dentilled cornice and blocking course of stone are carried round the building in front of the low pitched roof. Several of the large blind arches are pierced by wide doorways and there are windows in some of the smaller arched recesses.
(McCutcheon p.162)

2-90 Railway Street: Four long terraces of modern red brick Housing Executive two-bay, two-storey dwellings occupy a large section of the street on this side. They are interspersed by a monumental sculptor's premises at no.10. and several sets of steps leading to the car parking area behind. Nos. 52-66 have railings in front.

Northern Bar: A six-bay, two-storey public house in painted smooth render. Modern plastic windows; one original sliding sash window survives.

After the roundabout there is a modern service station with a large forecourt.

Railway Tavern: A four-bay, three-storey red brick public house with an explicit painted hanging sign.

110-118 Railway Street: A group of red brick buildings.

120 Railway Street: An attractive three-bay, three-storey building of painted render with quoins. Rustication to ground floor; segmental recesses and voussoirs to ground floor windows. Scroll console brackets and pediment to ground and first floor windows. Sash windows with marginal glazing to ground and first floor. Portico with blocking course, frieze, cornice and Doric columns. Rectangular fanlight with marginal glazing; four panel door, probably original.

Armagh Business Centre: (1950) Architect T.F.O. Rippingham. Engineer W.F.Bennett.
The building was constructed for Bairnswear Ltd. as an office and hostel block. Their knitwear factory workshop, now demolished, was sited behind. The construction is a ferroconcrete frame with brick cladding and precast concrete dressings to openings. The rear elevation is of roughcast render. The strong horizontal lines are balanced at the south end by the vertical expression of the stairway,

cased in a glazed apse, and a brick clad service tower at the north.
Stylistically it has much in common with Rippingham's designs for the much admired Cregagh Housing Estate (Belfast) dating from a few years earlier.
Appreciation of the building is not helped by the security arrangements, nor the signs which detract from its simple lines and assured design. The style is strongly influenced by German and Dutch architecture of the interwar period. It ranks with the best commercial architecture of its time in Ulster.
The Armagh Business Centre took possession of the building in 1985.
(Armagh Civic Week Guide p.27
Drawings in the possession of Armagh Business Centre)

RUSSELL STREET

A short, wide street cut through between 1831 and 1835 to link the Mall with English Street. It was named after Lord John Russell, a nineteenth century British Prime Minister. A section of the street, Melbourne Terrace, commemorates an Irish Secretary. It is the only brick built Regency terrace in the city.

Side of 17 English Street: An unoccupied four-bay, three-storey building of smooth render lined out; continuous first floor cill above painted fascia. Large shop window and small side door.

1 Russell Street: A four-bay, two-storey building; smooth render with brick dressings to first floor windows and entrance doorway in segmental headed recess. The bay nearest the Mall breaks forward at first floor to form a bracketed segmental arch to the entrance doorway. This is all that remains of the 'Cosy Picture House'. Paired semi-circular headed windows on first floor crowned by a rooflet with decorative cresting. Apart from the entrance bay the remainder of the building is unoccupied and awaiting demolition.

3 Russell Street: (1990) Architect Ian Donaldson.
A new four-bay, three-storey red brick and Portland stone building replacing a two-storey, flat-roofed assertively horizontal Sixties facade. The ashlar Portland stone has banded rustication with four segmental arches containing the window and door openings; three circular recesses above and between the arches contain symbols in bronzed aluminium. The first floor windows are traditionally proportioned with

eight light bronze aluminium glazing bars. Second floor windows are small and set into the ashlar stone frieze below eaves level.

A generally successful attempt to replace a Sixties facade with something more appropriate to the street.

5 Russell Street: (1883) Originally a police barracks, one of the very few purpose designed barracks erected for the R.I.C. A three-bay, three-storey smooth rendered building with basement. Segmental arched central doorway; splayed reveals with dummy arrow slits each side (decorative rather than functional!); heavy door with studs. Original ground floor windows have been replaced by large shop windows. On first floor there is a central rectangular oriel window with small pediment on corbelled brackets and two more arrow slits. All first and second floor windows have masonry mullions and transomes. The two outer gables at eaves level carry 'RIC' and '1883' in raised lettering; tall brick Tudor-style chimneys.

7 Russell Street: B. (1876) Originally the Hibernian Bank.

A fine four-bay, three-storey building with the two central bays breaking forward slightly. Basement enclosed by decorative wrought-iron railings. Smooth ashlar limestone with punched ashlar quoins. Parapet wall with plain cornice; good chimneys with moulded caps. On the ground floor there are four segmental headed openings with chamfered reveals; the two central openings are windows and the outer two are doors with fanlights and carved stone lintels. The cornice to the continuous stone frieze (with incised lettering now obscured by a modern sign) forms a cill to the first floor segmental headed windows. The second floor windows also have a continuous cill and the two central windows have stone mullions.

The building has taken on a slightly neglected appearance.

Mall Presbyterian Church: See The Mall

2 Russell Street: Six-bay, three-storey extension of building on English Street with door leading to upper floors. Modern shop fronts with simple lines and dark wall tiles; modern aluminium windows.

4 Russell Street: (c.1840) Two-bay, three-storey building with basement of smooth render lined out. New door and architrave; sash windows with original glazing bars to first and second floors.

6-8 Russell Street: (c.1840) Three bay, three-storey terrace, originally a group of three single bay houses. Red brick in Flemish bond with ashlar quoins to corner; smooth render to ground floor. Original windows with glazing bars to first and second floors.

The ground floor of no.6 is superbly embellished by an ornate entablature consisting of the original door with delicate Gothick fanlight and ground floor window with marginal glazing bars set between clustered columns with foliage capitals supporting cornice and nameboard, surmounted by extravagantly carved leaves and flowers, inside a rococo shaped frame. In the centre is a block bracket probably to take a bust or vase. This unique little structure, with two columns missing and a third crudely replaced, just survives and the building (once a post office) awaits restoration.

The first post office in Armagh was in Market Street, later it moved to Scotch Street. Robert Birch transferred his office to Russell Street in 1850 and in 1882 it was moved across the street to the site later occupied by the Cosy Cinema. It remained there until 1900 when it was transferred to English Street.

No.8 has a rectangular fanlight with marginal glazing and original door. The shop window and fascia have recently received minimal restoration - more is needed. The side elevation with three gable windows and a small attic window results from the step-back in the frontage line.

(O'Neill)

10-22 Russell Street, Melbourne Terrace: B. (1839) An attractive fifteen-bay, three-storey terrace of seven brick houses. The brickwork is in Flemish bond with flared (burnt) stretchers giving an all over chequer pattern. No.10 has a carriage arch. Carved stone doorcases with cornice breaking forward at each end over scroll brackets and fanlights all within a narrow stone architrave. Decorative semi-circular fanlights to nos.12, 14 and 16; no.10 has a plain rectangular fanlight and those to nos.18,20 and 22 are plain semi-circular; doorway of no.22 is now a window.

Nos.12-22 have paired doorways with an attractive bridge-like approach of fine Armagh conglomerate paving; all basements have original railings. Sash windows with glazing bars, some missing from no.10; plaster reveals around windows.

Nos.16 and 18 have limestone aedicules consisting of classical columns supporting an entablature decorated with carved paterae.

It is interesting to note the way the builder handled the considerable

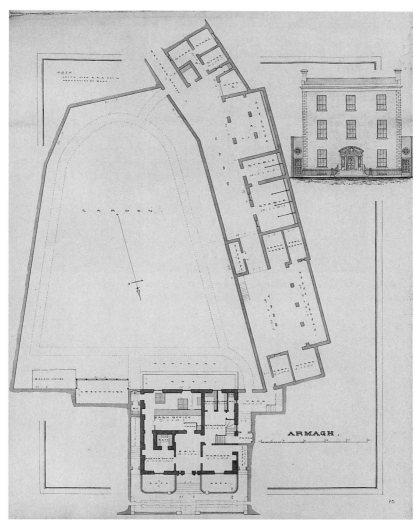

The Bank of Ireland in SCOTCH STREET; plan and front elevation; designed by Francis Johnston for Leonard Dobbin and built in 1812. (Irish Architectural Archive).

Patrick's Fold, formerly the Bank of Ireland. Designed in 1812 by Francis Johnston as part of Leonard Dobbin's commercial development. (M. Campbell).

Armagh Savings Bank. The bank was founded in 1818 and moved to this building in 1839. The architect was William Murray. (M. Campbell).

slope on which the terrace was built and how he ensured that, over the full length of the seven houses, the eaves and ridge line of the roof only steps down once.

A lot of care has been taken to conserve a length of the original Armagh limestone pavement and the coal cellar covers in front of the terrace.

SCOTCH STREET

In early rentals this street appears as Ferta Street and although Scottish Street was used in 1661 the older derivation lingered on into the early eighteenth century. Ferta derived from Tempall na Ferta, St. Patrick's first church in Armagh. Leonard Dobbin as agent of the Bank of Ireland built his house on the site; it is now known as Patrick's Fold. The name Scotch Street presumably indicates an area with a pre-eminence of Scottish settlers resident there in the seventeenth century. Earlier it may also have been known as Newry Street as it was the main route to the south-east. Now it is a street given over entirely to shops with the notable exception of Patrick's Fold.

St. Patrick's Cathedral appears high above the roof tops of Market Street and the dramatic archway beside the Northern Bank makes a view of Armagh much favoured by artists and photographers.

1 Scotch Street: Two-bay, three-storey building, pebble dash finish; black glazed tiles around modern shop front. Sash windows.

An unsightly gap site soon to be infilled by a three-storey extension to no.3.

3 Scotch Street: Three-bay three-storey painted brick building; smooth render to ground floor. Original window openings to first and second floor. Very basic pub front with modern windows; over important globe wall lights and the remains of a good ornamental bracket.
Extensive refurbishment of this dominantly sited building is now underway.

5 Scotch Street: Four-bay, three-storey smooth rendered building with aluminium shop front; fascia sign cluttered with lettering. Close set sash windows intact but without glazing bars. Moulded architraves to first and second floor windows.

7 Scotch Street: Two-bay, three-storey smooth rendered building without chimneys. Modern top hung windows with original architraves. Utilitarian shop front mainly of black polished granite.

9 Scotch Street: Three-bay, three-storey smooth rendered building with cement architraves; sash windows intact but now without glazing bars. Traditional type shop front carried across carriage arch; hanging sign in traditional manner; chimneys missing. Pleasant colour scheme.

11 Scotch Street: Three-bay, two-storey building with textured rendering; chimney missing. Top hung windows to first floor; standard aluminium shop front with assertive illuminated fascia.

13 Scotch Street: Three-bay, three-storey smooth rendered building with raised quoins and moulded architraves to first and second floor windows. Cornices and scroll brackets to first floor windows and cill string course. Sash windows but without subdivisions to the glazing; chimney missing. The modern shop front with large bland fascia and vertical sign is totally out of place and debases a handsome building.

15-17 Scotch Street: Four-bay, three-storey building of square cut coursed limestone with ugly projecting pointing; ashlar stone cills. Sash windows to first and second floor without glazing subdivisions. New black and white shop front with convenient side entrances and doors serving upper storeys. Chimneys missing.

19 Scotch Street: Four-bay, two-storey smooth rendered building without chimneys. Modern utility wood windows to original openings. Standard shop front.

21 Scotch Street: Two-bay, two-storey building with slightly textured rendering; chimney missing. Casement windows in over large openings; assertive modern illuminated sign and aluminium shop front.

23 Scotch Street: Four-bay, two-storey shop; textured rendering; smooth cement window surrounds with pediments. Sash windows to first floor without glazing subdivisions. Commendable shop front in the traditional style, well worked to a pleasant scale with a colour scheme of maroon and gold. The fascia is carried over the carriage arch and painted sheeted gate. Chimneys missing.

25 Scotch Street: Five-bay, two-storey building of coursed rubble Armagh conglomerate; raised pointing and cement edging around window openings. Chimney missing. Handsome ashlar limestone door encasement with blocked base, together with limestone cills and eaves course, suggest remains of a once fine house. The shop door is of poor modern design and the size and location of the shop fascia sign relate poorly to the other architectural elements.

27 Scotch Street: Two-bay, two-storey building of coursed rubble limestone with characteristic soldier coursed window heads; ugly raised pointing to stonework; cement surrounds to windows and painted stone cills. Modern top hung first floor windows. Basic aluminium shop front with illuminated fascia and protruding steel shutterbox.

29 Scotch Street: (1984) Architect Ian Donaldson. Three-bay, two-storey modern replacement building without chimneys in sombre dark brown brick. Well proportioned windows and recessed shop front in brown anodized aluminium. Individual letters fixed to brickwork replace the traditional fascia.

31-31a Scotch Street: (1982) Architect J.Roulston. Five-bay, two-storey brick building in same manner as no.29 but with black windows to no.35 and dark blue to no.37. No chimneys but party wall breaks the roof plane.

33-41 Scotch Street: (1982-5) Architect Ian Donaldson. Nine-bay, two-storey building in same manner as no.29 and without chimneys; all shop fronts recessed.

The pedestrian entry to McCrum's Court is marked by a little modern arch of decorative ironwork carrying a circular nameplate which is so thin and transparent that it is merely a gesture.

43-45 Scotch Street: (1985) Architect Ian Donaldson. Four-bay, two-storey replacement building in dark brown brick without chimneys. No.43 has a wide central first floor window between two smaller openings and three segmental arched openings on ground floor. Small hanging sign.
No.45 has a modern oriel window above a correctly proportioned and painted traditional shop front. Its light colour is a welcome contrast to all the dark brickwork.

47 Scotch Street: Two-bay, three-storey traditional style building of cheerful red brick. Traditional sash windows with subdivided glazing.

No chimney and timber fascia added over original brick detail. Traditional type shop front in unpainted hardwood.

49-51 Scotch Street: Five-bay, three-storey building with dormer and original chimney stack. The chamfers to the segmental-headed window openings, the pilasters, string courses and eaves cornice have all been carried out in moulded brick. More detail has been put into no.49 than no.51. The shopfronts are modern and reasonably sensitive but a little more co-ordination in the signs would have helped; the bracket stops to the original shop fascia signs remain on no.49.

53 Scotch Street: Three-bay, three-storey smooth rendered building; yellow brick detail to party walls. Moulded architraves to windows; moulded bracketed cornice and moulded brick string course. Delightful curved oriel window to first floor. Sash windows to first and second floors with undivided glazing. Good confidently detailed shop front excellently painted in brown, black and gold.

55 Scotch Street: Four-bay, three-storey red brick building with cornice and shaped parapet wall. Inset ashlar limestone string courses linking cills on first floor; intermediate string courses at window centres, together with inset stone strips, radiating from the first floor window heads and underlining the basic facade form; second floor window lintels with chamfered decoration below moulded brick cornice. Judging by the remaining traces of limestone pilasters the original shop front must have been a fine one. It is a sad loss.

57 Scotch Street: Four-bay, three-storey basic re-instatement building of smooth render. Top hung windows to first and second floor. Unfortunately a crude sign with over large lettering runs the full length of nos.55 and 57.

59 Scotch Street: Architects Ernest Knox (1990 restoration). Very important two-bay, four-storey building; smooth render with rough dash to gable. Entire facade is all in one piece with the original robust shop front still intact. Fascia and heavy cornice have terminating blocks on console brackets and are topped by miniature pediments. First floor has a wide elliptical headed window with blocked out voussoirs framed by blocked out pilasters and an intermediate cornice. Second floor windows have segmental heads; third floor has a single window with blocked out architrave and keystone. Well restored and painted.

61-65 Scotch Street: (1990) Architects Ernest Knox. Six-bay, three-storey replacement building with faced render and recessed courses. Taking the cue from the gable of no.59 the first and second floor windows are united to form tall strips, these are terminated by diamond shaped small gables. The main shop entrance, opposite Thomas Street, is recessed below a broad canopy which forms a balcony to wide first floor windows. A further recessed balcony on the second floor is sheltered by a pointed glazed roof. The entrance to the upper floors is in Market Street under a small Post-Modern pediment. The building 'turns' the corner very well and shop windows and signs are suitably integrated.

Generally the effect is Thirtyish, jolly and bright, with a strong whiff of the sea. Appropriate enough close up in commercial Scotch Street and pleasant from Thomas Street but not quite so successful when seen from the relative distance of the top of Market Street.

(Ulster Architect Feb/Mar.1990)

24-34 Scotch Street: Six shops (in total twelve-bays), partly two and partly three storeys. Eaves line carries right through but first floor steps up at end of first four bays and last two bays. Punched ashlar limestone with segmental headed soldier arches to all windows. All sash windows have intermediate glazing bars.

Shop front of no.24 has a rather too emphatic timber fascia board running from end to end and round corner for two bays. Other shop fronts maintain a reasonable scale but the illuminated sign to no.28 is out of scale, as is the affixed sign to first floor and illuminated sign over entrance to no.32. Cornice and blocking course to side of no.34, with corner urn, forms part of Dobbin House frontage.

36 Scotch Street: A (1811-12 datestone at rear) Architect probably Francis Johnson. Architects for conversion and extensions in 1979-81 G.P.and R.H. Bell.

Built for Leonard Dobbin (M.P.1833-38) as part of a planned commercial development. At the time he was Sovereign of the city and also agent for the Bank of Ireland.

An extremely handsome three-bay, three-storey building with basement. Ashlar stonework with blocked chamfered quoins; fine cornice and blocking course. At either side are screen walls with doorways and oculus window over. Sash windows with glazing bars. Stone chimney stacks gabled.

Splendid doorway with sidelights, four engaged Tuscan columns, cornice and segmental fanlight with integral lantern and approached by a flight of steps fanning out each side with railings to basement areas.

The house is set back from the street to provide a front garden with two lawns. Good contemporary railings with stone retaining wall to street; fine railing lanterns each side of front entrance. The side walls of the adjoining houses form part of the composition; finely carved urns adorn the gables.

The building is now sheltered accommodation and is well maintained. The only intrusive feature is the clumsy central guard rail from front gates to top of entrance steps and the multiple bell/call box at the entrance.

The courtyard of new buildings created at the rear relates sympathetically to the original building.

(J.I.A. IV 1987/88 p.68-9
Specify Vol.5 no.10 Aug 1985 p.29
Drawings in Irish Architectural Archive
Paterson (A) Vol. IV p.71-72)

38 Scotch Street: Three-bay, three-storey building, (except first bay adjacent to No.36 which is two-storey) with cornice, blocking course and corner urn of ashlar limestone. Fine stone chimney with moulded coping.

Impressive central doorway with engaged Ionic columns; pole moulding to edge, cornice and decorative wheel pattern fanlight; panelled reveals and soffit to door opening; stone step. Wooden painted shop fronts in traditional style served by a central doorway. Good hanging sign.

40-42 Scotch Street: Four-bay, three-storey building in coursed squared limestone with heavy pointing. Segmental soldier arches to sash windows; glazing bars thoughout. Two new shop fronts in traditional style. Chimneys missing. Two good hanging signs.

46-48 Scotch Street: (1987) Architect John McCarter. Five-bay, two-storey replacement building with one chimney. Random rubble stone in crazy paving pattern with cement quoins. Sash windows throughout without glazing bars. The shop front lacks vertical subdivision though Trueform did modify their 'house' fascia to be in sympathy with the conservation area.

50-52 Scotch Street: (1986) Architect Ian Donaldson. Four-bay, three-storey replacement building of random rubble stone without chimneys. Segmental soldier arches to sash windows. New shop front in traditional manner links both buildings.

54 Scotch Street: (1984) Architect J.G. O'Neill. Two-bay, three-storey replacement building of random rubble stonework with raised ribbon pointing and without a chimney. Segmental headed soldier arches to sash windows. New shop front in traditional style. The illuminated sign is out of place.

56 Scotch Street: Five-bay, three-storey building largely rebuilt in 1986 (Consultant D.J. Dreaning); smooth render with great black and white horizontal painted stripes across the entire facade from top to bottom. Above the windows are painted voussoirs and in several areas the black stripes merge to form black panels carrying white letters. Sash windows with one vertical glazing bar. Simple ground floor shop fronts in black and white. Unobtrusive entrance to shopping arcade with wall lanterns.
This unique, imaginative and very brash painted decoration has been so well worked out and is there so long that it can now be deemed a success.

58-60 Scotch Street: Prior to demolition this four-bay, three-storey building was of coursed limestone and conglomerate with soldier arches to windows and stone cills. Now being rebuilt.

62 Scotch Street: Prior to demolition this single-bay, two-storey building was smooth rendered with modern horizontal windows on first floor. Now being rebuilt.

64 Scotch street: One-bay, three-storey smooth rendered building framed with raised bands and an hood mould over the window; three-quarters of the facade is window. Shop front rises through ground and first floor with second floor window blocked out. This unusual treatment of the shop as a portal has a Thirties feel, almost suggesting a cinema entrance.

66-68 Scotch Street: Five-bay, three-storey building; smooth plaster rendering with incised joints; quoins at one end. Two bays towards Thomas St. have retained moulded architraves, sash windows and combined cill and string courses.
Utility aluminium shop fronts, one with illuminated fascia.

70-72 Scotch Street: Six-bay, three-storey smooth rendered building with incised joints and quoins. Three bays have retained sash windows; three have utility modern windows. Modern aluminium shop front and plastic sign to no.70. Small pub window with traditional style glazing bars in blank wall under well painted fascia with cornice.

The corner of Scotch Street/Thomas Street has a double pitched roof and a chamfered corner entrance with a supporting column on the apex. The painted lettering above is a pleasant feature. The corner is strengthened by plaster quoins and the gables are surmounted by rendered chimneys.

76 Scotch Street: Impressive three-bay, three-storey building of red brick with two tiers of brick pilasters; the four pilasters on the first floor with moulded brick Ionic capitals and four pilasters on the second floor with Corinthian. Between the pilasters are three large windows with painted plaster surrounds and keystones on the first floor and semi-circular headed windows above. The heavy cornice is decorated with moulded brick swags and above there is a parapet balustrade with a semi-circular headed upstand, once containing a clock, like the Market House nearby. The shop front is modern and basic.

This building is to be demolished and rebuilt.

78 Scotch Street (Northern Bank): B+. (1869) Architect and contractor Mr.Conner of Belfast.

Fine smooth rendered, four-bay, three-storey bank building with two-storey wing. A symmetrical entrance (facing Market Square) with semi-circular fanlight. Windows have semi-circular heads and are set in semi-circular recesses embellished with ornamental banding and keystones. Intermediate cornice cill with fascia and discreet modern lettering. First floor windows have pilasters, scroll brackets and segmental pediments, all highly decorated.

Second floor has segmental headed windows with lugged architraves and keystones. The low pitched roof has a splendid bracketed cornice with console brackets and paterae between.

In the two-storey single bay wing the blank wall is enlivened by a semi-circular recess with a keystone and blind window above, the intermediate cornice is carried through.

The elevation to Scotch Street is virtually an exact repeat of the Market Street facade except for the doorway. The attached screen wall has a splendid carriage arch.

This noble nineteenth century public building, in the Italianate palazzo style, is truly worthy of its important position right in the centre of Armagh.

(Armagh Guardian 19th March 1869)

ST LUKE'S HOSPITAL: B+. (1820, 1841, 1875, 1901)
Architects Francis Johnston, John Boyd.

The legislative base for this venture was the parliamentary enactment of 1817 to provide asylums for the lunatic poor. At this time the Richmond Asylum in Dublin was the only purpose built asylum building in Ireland.

A programme for providing nine District Lunatic Asylums was prepared in Dublin Castle under Robert Peel, then Chief Secretary. The Commissioners for Directing Lunatic Asylums were appointed to realise the scheme. They chose Francis Johnston to design and supervise the building operations. Johnston was already well known in Armagh and had achieved preferment, with the help of the Primate, to the appointment as Superintendent to the Board of Works.

Work commenced on the first of these nine asylums, Armagh, on 14th October 1820, the formal laying of the foundation stone took place in May 1821. The building was designed to accommodate one hundred and twenty-two patients in separate cells. The building contractors, McCartney and Ballintine, were supervised by Johnston's nephew, William Murray, and the total cost of the project was £20,900-4-6d.

St. Luke's first patients were admitted on 14th July 1825 and from the start treatment was enlightened. The first superintendent was Thomas Jackson who was not a member of the medical profession. Staff were instructed to use 'moral management' rather than the simple physical restraint which was the norm at the time. The policy was to select patients for whom a degree of cure was possible and so the ultimate aim was always discharge back into the community. In 1841 a school was opened for the use of patients. After the Famine the Commissioners were ordered to extend the building to accommodate one hundred and forty four lunatics, the work was completed in 1863. Sanitary annexes and day rooms were added to designs by John Boyd in 1875 and a separate block was added on the hill in 1901.

Due to changes in therapy and the availability of new drugs a less custodial and more domestic arrangement was required. Consequently a major scheme of modification and repair was entrusted to architects G.P. & R.H. Bell. Work commenced in 1979 to replace the cells by 'domestic' rooms, to modernise and increase the sanitary arrangements and to equip new kitchens. The original cast iron custodial windows were replaced by sliding timber sashes in keeping with the architecture of the building and more domestic in appearance than the original windows.

It is to the credit of all those who, through time, have been given the responsibility to alter or add to this fine building that, in almost every case, they respected the work of Francis Johnston. The result is that today the building presents a satisfying unity overall.

The main building is two storeys over a basement and is symmetrical with the superintendent's lodging and administrative accommodation set centrally with the main entrance. The cell blocks radiate from this hub and at the far end of each wing are the added dayrooms etc. The kitchens and associated offices are set axially on the main entrance with a service road along the back giving access to a range of workshops, laundries, stores and the boiler house.

The whole construction is in limestone; the central section is all ashlar work, the remainder is squared rubble brought to courses with smooth ashlar used for the dressings. Architectural embellishments are used sparingly to articulate the careful massing and proportions of the overall design. The main entrance is emphasised by a full height canted bay containing a glazed lobby. Above, on the roof, is a copper roofed cupola housing a clock. Flanking the entrance and separated from it by two window bays are projecting pedimented wings. The dominance of these projections is strengthened by a full height recessed panel approximately three-fifths of the total width of the wing. Unifying the whole of this section is a block parapet and projecting cornice. The present windows are sliding timber sashes with a single vertical division, they possibly date from renovations in 1901 when the Hill Building was under construction.

The cell blocks have a simple corbelled eaves course but are otherwise unadorned. The windows of these blocks are now small paned timber sliding sashes but, before the renovations ten years ago, they were cast iron with much smaller panes. Some of the windows were enlarged at the same time but the proportions were carefully regulated so that they fit happily into the original design. Each dayroom has a hipped roof and a projecting full height canted bay. At the left hand end of the main front is a three stage water tower added in 1875. It is also built of limestone but in Lombardic Italianate style and fits into the overall composition well. The pyramid roof is supported from deep, corbelled ashlar brackets and in the stage below the roof there are pairs of windows with semi-circular heads.

In the grounds there are a number of small ancillary buildings. The gate lodges and mortuary were part of the original design, the Protestant and Catholic chapels were added later. The Hill Building is a very imposing addition to the group. It is sited at the top of a rise overlooking the main asylum but, by being set at right angles, does not attempt to compete visually with it. The symmetrical design is in the French Renaissance style and has steeply pitched and mansarded roofs. The silhouette is enlivened by decorative iron crestings, copper clad ventilating cupolas and massive stone chimneys; the central unit has two storeys and an attic decorated by a tower. There is a block parapet, mainly rock-faced but panelled in smooth ashlar, over a cornice that is supported by massive stone dentils. The advanced central bay is topped by a decorative stone built gabled dormer. The whole composition is rock faced with smooth dressings. The windows in the central block and the canted pavilions at each end are distinctly French in style with heavy stone mullions and transoms. At ground floor, in the central section, they are decorated by pedimented hood mouldings, the detailing is unusual in that the sashes are made to slide past the stone transoms. The other windows are small paned sliding timber sashes. The wings that link the advanced central section to the canted pavilions have iron framed pergolas.

(Public Works p.15-16.
S.A. Vol.8 No.1 1975/6.
Specify Vol.7 No.7 April 1987.
Rogers (2) p.28.
Drawings in the Armagh County Museum.
Irish Architectural Archive documents including 'specifications of the works' dated Nov. 1820 and signed. Drawings in I.A.A. dated Dec. 1820, Apr. 1825, July 1826 and March 1827)

THOMAS STREET

Thomas Street and Ogle Street, opened in 1759 to by-pass the steep Cathedral Hill, are an early example of a ring road development. The streets were named after Mr Thomas Ogle, an important citizen in the mid eighteenth-century, who had a marble polishing mill nearby. Thomas Street runs southwards from the top of Scotch Street, it is more or less parallel to Castle Street on the higher ground above. After the junction with Dobbin Street it continues west as Ogle Street. Like Scotch Street it is a street of shops.

1 Thomas Street: Two-bay, four-storey building of smooth render with plaster quoins; brick chimney and slate hanging to gable. Sash windows without glazing bars; moulded architraves and keystones to first floor windows. Basic aluminium shop front.

3 Thomas Street: Three-bay, three-storey smooth rendered building; sash windows without glazing bars. Cluttered shop front with mosaic tiles.

5 Thomas Street: Two-bay, three-storey building. New long horizontal window to first floor; new casement window to second floor. Aluminium shop front with assertive plastic sign.

7 Thomas Street: Three-bay, three-storey smooth rendered building with brick chimney; sash windows without glazing bars. Projecting fascia in textured plaster.

9-11 Thomas Street: Four-bay, two-storey building; first two bays in roughcast render. Ornamental parapet with stepped profile, half round centrepiece and balls at each end. Modern horizontal windows. The end bay extends upwards to form a third storey with window. Ground floor faced with terrazzo tiles.

13-15 Thomas Street: Three-bay, three-storey building in roughcast rendering with smooth cement architraves; brick chimney. Remains of original shop front cornice and end pieces behind new fascia. Good hand painted lettering.

17 Thomas Street: Two-bay, three-storey smooth rendered building. Moulded architraves to first floor windows; frames of original windows remain on second floor. Simple wooden shop front.

19 Thomas Street: Two-bay, two-storey building in smooth render. Wide front window opening; very large illuminated wall mounted sign. Aluminium and terrazzo shop front.

23 Thomas Street: Three-bay, two-storey rendered building with parapet wall to single pitch roof. Modern windows in original openings (second floor windows have disappeared). Interesting shop front with small window; recessed entrance with bold lettering above.

25 Thomas Street: Two-bay, three-storey building. Sash windows with hood moulding to first floor; semi-circular headed casement windows with moulded architraves and decorated cills to second floor. Stylish glossy black shop front with incised gold lettering.

35-37 Thomas Street: Five-bay, three-storey building with carriage arch. Modern windows with moulded architraves. First floor cills form cornice for the new 'clip on' fascia. One large chimney remains.

39 Thomas Street: Two-bay, two-storey rendered house (the only one in the street) with modern windows on the ground floor and original sash windows above.

41 Thomas Street: Two-bay, three-storey smooth rendered building. Modern windows in original openings. Modern tiled shop front with canopy fascia.

43 Thomas Street: Two-bay, three-storey smooth rendered building with brown brick facings to ground floor. Sash windows without glazing bars. Heavily moulded window architraves. Assertive illuminated and wall mounted signs.

45-47 Thomas Street: Four-bay, two-storey dark brick building with chimneys. Horizontal modern windows and front doors with sidelights create a domestic air in the middle of the assertive shop signs.

49 Thomas Street: Three-bay, two-storey smooth rendered building with elliptical carriage arch. Modern windows and illuminated shop sign; chimneys missing.

53-55 Thomas Street: Five-bay, two-storey building with dormers. Sash windows to no.53; modern windows to no.55. No.53 has a well painted fascia and attractive simple shop front with side door. No.55 has ugly mock random rubble stone surround to entrance and shop window; illuminated sign above.

There is a gap site facing Dobbin Street at this point.

61-65 Thomas Street: Ten-bay, two-storey red brick replacement building. Well proportioned aluminium windows to no.63; timber windows with glazing bars to no.61.

2-4 Thomas Street: Seven-bay, two-storey building in smooth render. Sash windows without glazing bars and moulded architraves to last three bays. Side doorway with elliptical shaped sidelight. Simple aluminium shop front with oversized and lettering running almost the full length of building.

6 Thomas Street: Imposing three-bay, three-storey building in smooth render with plaster quoins. Moulded architraves to all the sash windows with cornices to those on first floor; large bracketed eaves cornice. A small portion of the original shop front survives in the truncated clustered columns. Assertive illuminated plastic sign.

8 Thomas Street: Three-bay, two-storey red brick building. The two first floor horizontal steel windows with glazing bars each side of a vertical semi-circular headed window make a sort of elongated Venetian window. New traditional style shop front with good colour scheme.

10-14 Thomas Street: Ten-bay, two-storey replacement building in rustic brickwork with corbelled eaves course; traditionally proportioned first floor windows. Simple shop fronts recessed into brick facade with service entrance treated likewise. No fascia but lettering and signs mounted directly on to the brickwork.

16-20 Thomas Street: Eight-bay, three-storey building with one chimney stack; smooth render with moulded plaster surrounds to the sash windows, no glazing bars. Much of the original shop front survives with traditional painted sign boards spoiled by an illuminated box sign.

22 Thomas Street: Interesting two-bay, two-storey replacement building faced with hand made rustic bricks with uneven, jagged edged quoins of random conglomerate limestone. Tall, narrow first floor windows project in the form of pointed oriels supported on brick corbel brackets. Hardwood shop front with deeply recessed entrance doors.

24 Thomas Street: Three-bay, two-storey smooth rendered building with one chimney stack. Modern windows in original openings. Simple shop front with illuminated box sign.

Entrance to Abbey Lane.

26 Thomas Street: Five-bay, two-storey smooth rendered building. Sash windows without glazing bars, moulded plaster architraves and cill course forms cornice to very basic shop front with plastic sign board and illuminated box sign.

28 Thomas Street: Two-bay, two-storey building with painted roughcast walls. Modern horizontal timber windows. Large horizontal shop window with separate door. Illuminated box sign.

30 Thomas Street: Four-bay, three-storey smooth rendered building with incised blockwork and one chimney stack. Modern windows in original openings with moulded plaster architraves. First floor window cills form cornice of original shop front. Projecting painted fascia with painted lettering above simple colour coated metal shop front.

32 Thomas Street: One-bay, three-storey smooth rendered building with sash windows. Painted wood shop front in the traditional style with lively fairground lettering even on the large 'stick on' price tags.

34 Thomas Street: Three-bay, three-storey replacement building with modern dark red brick walls and chimney. Coupled windows to first and second floors of first bay; gable above smooth rendered and painted. Long fascia, still unpainted, above simple aluminium shop front and service entrance.

36-40 Thomas Street: Seven-bay, three-storey smooth rendered building with one chimney stack. Traditional sash windows without glazing bars. Full length plaster cornice and string course at first floor level is part of original painted fascia. Illuminated box sign to shop and small pub window near corner.
The diagonal corner entrance, shared with Dobbin Street, is lovingly celebrated by a small pediment perched above the fascia and a thin pair of pilasters each side of the door. Above the pediment is an elaborately framed blind window and above this a decorated panel reading 'M.J. 1901'. This is crowned by a hefty cornice on brackets, set above the eaves line and holding aloft another pediment, this time segmental. A fine example of some unknown Armagh plasterers' artistry which should not be swept away.

42-48 Thomas Street: At the other corner with Dobbin Street is a large modern supermarket building of dark brown brick with a diagonal entrance under a tower. The Dobbin Street frontage is a three-bay, two-storey flat-roofed building with the 'frame' expressed by lines of red brick and devoid of windows except for a few high level lancets. The three-storey tower has a conical slated roof and a large oval 'house' sign in place of the usual clock face and paired semi-circular windows at first floor level. Flanking the tower is the main shop; two-bays, two-storeys to Dobbin Street, four-bays to Ogle Street, all with shop windows, a long white profiled plastic fascia and segmental headed windows above. There are pitched roofs on the street side of the building. The materials and scale are alien to the street, the opportunity to put a good building on an important site was lost.

TOWER HILL

This short road connects College Hill and Victoria Road. It appears to have been created when the work house was built in 1841.

On the right, when approached from College Hill, a low stone wall with a substantial area of tree planting behind forms the boundary to the Royal School and in part to St. Mark's burial ground.

On the left is a low stone wall, well built and pointed recently, with a discreet entrance to a new development of red brick two-storey dwellings.

Charles Sheil's Institute: B. (1866-8) Architects Lanyon and Lynn.

A range of one and a half storey buildings, providing living accommodation in the form of individual compact maisonette units, each with its own entrance door. The composition is articulated by a tower forming part of the warden's accommodation.

The style of the building is Gothic Revival in the Lombardic form made popular through the writings of Ruskin. It is constructed entirely of stone, the main mass of the walling is squared rubble honey-coloured sandstone, probably from quarries in the Dungannon district. This work is quarry faced while the window and door openings are dressed in ashlar sandstone.

The roof line is dominated by elegant stone chimneys and the three stage tower. The roof of the tower pitches in from each of the four faces to form a short ridge. In each face of the roof is a decorative lucarne. There is a wide eaves overhang, which is formed by a stone corbel projecting over a decorative course of bracketting, taking the form of a modified billet moulding. The upper stage of the tower has an oculus on each face. The one on the main front is filled by a clock, the others with windows divided both horizontally and vertically through the centre; each corner is modulated by a single engaged column. There is a plain ashlar string course at mid height to this stage

Sheils Houses, TOWER HILL. Almshouses built by the Charles Sheils Trust in 1868 and still occupied. The Superintendent's house is beneath the clock tower. (M. Campbell).

in red Dumfries sandstone with carved bosses at the corners. This course divides the upper stage from the one below; this has a pair of ventilators on each face. They have pointed Gothic heads with recessed trefoils, each pair divided by a single column. The bottom stage is defined by a simple projecting moulded string course and is otherwise detailed in a similar manner to the bulk of the building. The tower marks a change in angle and the free corner is strengthened by a two staged buttress in smooth ashlar work.

The entrance to the warden's house is a grander doorway than the rest being cased by a smooth ashlar Gothic arch bearing the inscription 'CHARLES SHEILS INSTITUTE'. All external doors are sheeted with plain rectangular fanlights over. All the windows are double hung sashes, the larger ones are subdivided by one vertical glazing bar. The joinery is painted in a dark reddish brown paint which is very probably the original colour. The roof line is varied by a series of small dormers and large stone gables. The entrance gate screen is in the same style as the main building.

About 1912 a smaller detached wing was added. This time the architects were Young and Mackenzie who faithfully followed the form of the parent building.

The whole range was orientated to enjoy views of the pleasure garden. It is very sad that this land had to be sold to a developer quite recently in order to raise funds for the Institute and is now covered by new 'luxury' homes.

Charles Sheils was born in Killough, County Down, and made his money in trade after moving to Liverpool. In 1851 he returned to Killough and founded a charity to provide accommodation for 'Those who in their former lives are entitled to a better provision in old age than the workhouse'. He died in December 1861 before his dream was realised. As a result of his endeavours an Act of Parliament was passed in 1864 that established the legal foundation from which building could proceed. As well as in Armagh similar building groups were erected in Killough, Carrickfergus, Dublin and Dungannon.

(Act of Parliament 1864 (PRONI)
I.B. Vol.IX 15 Oct. 1867
Bassett p.111).

Tower Hill Hospital: B. (1841) Architect George Wilkinson. Builder Mr.S.Carroll.

The building was commissioned for the Poor Law Union of Armagh, to accommodate a thousand inmates and as such was one of the largest workhouses to be built in Ulster. It was commissioned under the 1838

Poor Law Act. According to E. McCourt the guardians of the workhouse
(Gould pp.7,14,19 and 27
McCourt)

The stone wall continues down the hill to Victoria Road; behind the wall is a well-screened new development of single storey red brick dwellings.

VICTORIA ROAD

Victoria Road, formerly known as Belfast Road, runs eastwards from the top of Victoria Street at the back gate of St. Mark's Church and then turns northwards in a wide curve. Here it becomes known as Drumadd and skirts the wooded grounds of Tower Hill Hospital and the Ballynahone River, to meet the Portadown Road at its junction with College Hill.

On the south side of the road, after the massive stone wall of Gough Barracks, there are two pebble-dashed bungalows, probably dating from the Twenties, with half-timbered gables and decorated bargeboards. After this, following the wide curved corner of the road, there are three pairs of two-storey, two-bay, pebble-dashed, semi-detached houses with hipped roofs, two-storey canted bays and canopies on console brackets over the front doors. Nos. 47, 49 and 57 have retained their original sash fenestration.

At the Drumadd Road corner is a modern bungalow with a steep roof, this building replaces a former gatelodge to a mill. On the riverside are two roughcast rendered houses with a lower two-storey extension and garage to the southern end. Originally this was a terrace of three two-bay, two-storey houses; rear access was by a verandah overhanging the Ballinahone river; it now serves only the two end portions. The group occupies the site of a mill destroyed at the end of the last century. Opposite, there is a long terrace of Sixties N.I.Housing Trust two-bay, two-storey brick houses. Between the end of this terrace and the Portadown Road junction are several large modern villas stepping up into the hill, also a garage and workshop and a dry-dashed two-storey modern house with a flat-roofed shop extension.

On the northside of the road there is a stone wall around the grounds of Tower Hill Hospital. This area is soon to be developed by the Housing Executive as sheltered dwellings.

VICTORIA ROAD

Further along, where the river flows close to the road, there is a garage car park with mesh fencing and a small workshop. Then a group of mid-nineteenth century houses sited well below the level of the road. Meredith Cottage is a three-bay, two-storey slated dwelling with modern windows, porch and conservatory; its hipped gable faces the road. The next two dwellings are semi-detached, two-storey, two-bay and built of coursed and squared roughcut stone with an inset datestone in raised lettering 'M.A. 1842'. On the gable of no.1 is a fine stone name plaque inscribed 'Meredith Place'. The fourth house is two-storey, three-bay and rendered with two canted bays rising with pointed roofs to eaves height. In the centre is a gabled oriel over the entrance door carried on two slim cast-iron columns. There is a wing of outhouses terminating in a loft.

VICTORIA STREET

As the town spread out from its hilltop nucleus it had, by the second half of the nineteenth century, expanded eastwards beyond the Mall. Victoria Street commemorates such development during the reign of that monarch, though nos.11-41 were erected in the Inter-War period. From the important bank at the corner of the street it ascends to become Victoria Road at the top of the hill. Polite red brick terraces with lively decorations predominate.

1 Victoria Street: A. (1837) Architect William Murray.
The Savings Bank functioned in the Tontine Rooms, English Street, from 1818 until it moved to this site in 1839.
A handsome bank building on a commanding site with elevations to Gaol Square, Victoria Street and Barrack Hill. It is two storeys in height and beautifully built of ashlar stone with deeply recessed blockwork to the ground floor. The building originally provided for a banking hall, offices and a manager's residence.
The main elevation is to Gaol Square and is of three bays symmetrically designed with the centre bay advanced. This central bay houses the main entrance; the doorway opening has a semi-circular head containing a modern radiating fanlight, below is a modern multi-panelled glazed varnished door. Flanking the door are narrow margin glazed lights. This grouping is contained beneath an Ionic portico, prostyle, tetrastyle and approached by a full width flight of three dressed stone steps. Beyond these are two more narrow steps leading

up from the iron gate at the back of the footpath. The gate and the flanking railings are modern, sympathetically designed, replacements and enclose the Gaol Square and Victoria Street elevations. Between the railings and the main front is a free standing sign, well designed but it confuses the classical symmetry of the building and should be removed. Finely incised in the frieze of the portico are the words 'Savings Bank'. The portico is completed by a full moulded cornice and a blocked parapet divided by raised blocks with semi-circular heads.

The stonework to the ground floor is rusticated; in the bays flanking the entrance are single windows having flat heads formed of radiating voussoirs. A fine moulded string course divides the ground from the first floor, above which the stonework is dressed flush.

At first floor the corners are defined by panelled pilasters. The three windows, one in each bay, have moulded stone architraves. The central opening is pedimented, while the flanking openings have hoods. Above, the frieze is unadorned, the cornice is complete and the parapet is similar to the porch below, but at a different scale. In the bay above the entrance the words 'Savings Bank' are raised in bold Roman type.

The Barrack Street frontage is not symmetrical but its treatment is similar to the main front. The first bay, at ground floor, contains the Banking Hall lit by a pair of windows. These are replacement frames into original openings. Above is the original tripartite sash window with moulded stone architrave and hood mould supported by decorated consoles. The two bays beyond have minimal detailing and beyond these again are offices built of rubble limestone.

The Victoria Street elevation is four bays. The two front windows at ground floor have been truncated to provide for a night safe and cash dispenser, with modern steps and ramps added as part of the development. Immediately above the string course at the corner the street name is beautifully incised into the stone. A special feature of this elevation is the pendant wreaths carved above each of the first floor windows. As at the front the parapet is decorated with the words, in raised Roman type 'Savings Bank'. The stone chimneys have been raised at some time, the upper stage is rendered.

(Armagh Guardian 1968.
Lock p.1
Royal Hibernian Academy 1838 no.192.
Paterson (A) Vol.1V, p.99.
Rogers (2) p.45.
Basssett p.113)

3-9 Victoria Street: (c.1860) Four handsome, well-proportioned two-bay, three-storey red brick terrace houses with bracketed eaves cornice. Rusticated quoins and base in punched ashlar stone. Tripartite windows to ground floor; traditional sash windows with horizontal glazing bars.
Everything appears to be original in this attractive terrace.

11-13 Victoria Street: Pair of two-bay, two-storey semi-detached houses in painted roughcast with dormers. The hipped roof of the bay window and porch roof are combined.

15-17 Victoria Street: Pair of semi-detached two-bay, two-storey roughcast buildings. Bay windows rise through two floors to half timbered gable containing small casement window. Porch roof covers both entrance doors. Plastic windows replace the original.

19-21 Victoria Street: Pair of semi-detached two-bay, two-storey houses with hipped roofs. Flat segmental bay window to ground floor; flat bracketed canopy over door. Stained glass to lights in bay windows.
23-33 Victoria Street: Three pairs of semi-detached two-bay, two-storey houses. Bay windows rise through two floors and have conical roofs (nos.27-29 have flat roofs). Nos.31-33 have original sash windows and doors; original doors on nos.23-29 have been replaced by modern ones with integral fanlight.

35-37 Victoria Street: Pair of semi-detached two-bay, two-storey houses. Centre bay breaks forward; two small porches; hipped roof; casement windows. Frontage set back from street with sloping grass bank.

39-41 Victoria Street: Pair of bungalows set at an angle to each other with steeply sloping grass banks in front and high barracks wall behind. Steep hipped roofs with central dormer windows; deep eaves with exposed rafters. Segmental arched brick entrance with front door panelled in an Arts and Crafts manner; no.39 has a modern glazed protruding porch. Mullioned and transomed windows.
Nos.15-41 show the influence of 1930s Ideal Home Exhibitions.

The street line is continued by the high barracks wall of coursed limestone with flush ashlar quoins containing outshots and slits. All topped with rusty barbed wire, corrugated sheeting and half round concrete coping.

2-10 Victoria Street (Winder Terrace): (1877) Built by Mr Joseph Atkinson Anderson.

A terrace of five substantial three-bay, two-storey houses with attic and basement. Smooth render; bracketed cornice with fretted eaves board to nos.6-10; fine chimney stacks. Entrance doors reached by flights of steps. Original four panelled doors with fanlight and sidelights. Good cast iron railings. Moulded architraves to windows with hood moulds on console brackets; continuous moulded string course. Canted bay windows rise through basement and ground floor to flat roof. No.4 has a projecting portico. No.10 is painted and has a modern continuous dormer in place of the original small segmental headed dormers which still survive on the other houses.

(Bassett p.109)

Good screen wall of squared and coursed limestone with flush quoins and two flat topped buttresses.

12 Victoria Street: (c.1850) Three-bay, two-storey house in stone with brick dressing and red brick facade. Stone doorway surround with attached Doric columns, simple cornice and empty fanlight. Deep stone cill course to first floor window; large chimney stack; original sash windows.

14-24 Victoria Street (Richmond Terrace): (1880) Six two-bay, three-storey red brick houses with yellow brick dressings; basement to no.14 made possible by the lower ground level. Canted bay windows with shallow pitched lead roofs except no.14 which has a flat roof. Broad bracketed eaves cornice; sash windows; stone cills; monumental chimney stacks. Coupled entrance doorways, four panelled doors; arches supported on floriated capitals and clustered columns on bases. The terrace is set back from building line with low brick walls enclosing the front gardens.

No.24 has strange Thirties style two-storey flat-roofed curved extension to side gable with stained glass to upper lights of windows.

The whole terrace is generally unaltered.

(Bassett p.109)

26-36 Victoria Street (Grantham Villas): (1887-8) A terrace of six two-bay, two-storey houses with attics. Red brick with yellow brick dressings and horizontal string courses. Canted bay windows rise through two floors below gables with original fretted bargeboards, nearly all intact. Coupled semi-circular windows in gables; decorative brickwork below eaves. Segmental headed doorways with fanlight. Windows and doors have not been altered except in no.26.

(Bassett p.109)

36a Victoria Street: (1978) Modern bungalow set back from street with stone wall in front.

38-42 Victoria Street: Three three-bay bungalows with dormers. Central segmental arches with doorways and side panels; mullion and transom windows. Flights of steps to entrance doors; raised gardens.

The street is concluded by the coursed and squared stone wall which surrounds St. Mark's on this side. There is a fine entrance with gates, ashlar stone gate piers and railings.

(See St. Mark's, The Mall)

WINDMILL HILL

The name is derived from a windmill which stood here in the early seventeenth century. The large tower windmill stump which can be seen today was erected on the same site in the nineteenth century.
The stone walls and good landscaping give the road an attractive rural aspect

A good coursed roughcut stone wall lines the hill on the St. Catherine's School side. It is well maintained and unbroken except for entrances. At the crest of the hill there is a short section in modern concrete brick.

St. Catherine's Primary School: (1938) This eleven-bay, well proportioned and detailed, brick and faience building is an excellent example of its period. Originally an E-shaped structure but later flat roofed extensions to the rear now link the wings. The entrance doorway is the main feature of the front elevation. It has double doors and a semi-circular fanlight set between pilasters at two levels carrying a pedimented cornice that rises above the roof line.
Large windows are a dominating feature of the building with mullions and transoms and plastic windows with implied glazing bars. The elegant steeply pitched and slated roof is hipped and has a bell cast and ridge finials.

The four-bay wings are linked to the main building by well detailed side entrances.

An extension, at right angles to the front facade, is a simple essay in modernism and not too obtrusive.

Callan Bridge: (possibly as early as 17th century)
Though not located on Windmill Hill the bridge is a striking feature from the end of the road.

A most picturesque hump-backed bridge located on a former main road to the west; stone built with four main semi-circular headed arches and one subsidiary segmental arch. In the parapet wall are six deeply angled recesses for travellers on foot to escape coaches. A modern bridge, built parallel to the north face of Callan Bridge, now serves those on foot.

The best view of the bridge, the south side, is 'interrupted' by modern flat roofed school buildings behind and a bungalow.

The bridge has been immortalised in a painting by the artist John Luke who lived for a time near Killylea.

(McCutcheon p.34.
Weatherup (1) p.44.
"The Old Callan Bridge" by John Luke A.C.M. 2-45)

2-10 Windmill Hill: Five two-bay, two-storey roughcast dwellings with timber windows and pantiled roofs. Each house steps forward as well as upwards to take account of the slope.

Windmill House: (c.1960) A two-bay, two-storey modern brick villa with hipped pantiled roof set back from the road.

Windmill (1810): Historically this structure is of interest as it was erected as a flour-grinding windmill at the time of the Napoleonic Wars. It was one of several other similarly large windmills built in Ulster in the late eighteenth and early nineteenth centuries. In terms of size it is impressive as, with the exception of the windmill at Ballyloughry, Co.Londonderry, it is the tallest in the Province.

The tower stands to its full height of over fifty feet and is built of tapered rubble-stone construction. The openings and cills all appear to be complete and the stonework in reasonable order. The date is engraved in the first floor window cill above the north facing door. Internally, wall markings indicate that the tower accommodated eight floors. External socket holes indicate that once it had a stage at third floor level from where the sails were adjusted.

A four-sailed tower is shown in a view of Armagh of 1842, although this does not necessarily mean that the mill was working at the time. It was not noted in the Second Valuation so was certainly defunct by the late 1850s; in the 1860 6" map it is marked as 'Old Windmill'.

It is an important landmark of Armagh that deserves to be well maintained and respected.

(McCutcheon p.231.
Jas. Black 'View of Armagh' 1810.
OS 6/2/12/1. OS 6/2/12/2.
Griffiths' 1864.
Hall Vol.2: 454.)

St.Brigid's Boys Secondary School: (1971) Architects McLean & Forte. An U-shaped modern block in light brown brick stepping down an undulating site. A typically Sixties building with a factory roof to the technical section. The building and its grounds, with large areas of grass and tarmac surrounded by long stretches of standard security fencing, are bleak and in need of humanising.

LISTED BUILDINGS/STRUCTURES IN ARMAGH CITY AS AT 1/1/91

ABBEY STREET
Armagh City Hospital, Front Block	Ref. 15/20/9
Diocesan Office & Hall, 46 Abbey St	Ref. 15/20/7
Methodist Church	Ref. 15/20/13
Public Library	Ref. 15/20/8
Rehabilitation & Training Centre (formerly Presbyterian Church)	Ref. 15/20/14
Unionist Hall	Ref. 15/20/34

BARRACK HILL
7,9,11,11A, 15-31 & 33 Barrack Hill	Ref. 15/17/40
Victoria House, 109 Barrack Hill	Ref. 15/17/41

CALLAN BRIDGE ROAD
Callan bridge	Ref. 15/20/32

CASTLE STREET
14,16-36 Castle St	Ref. 15/19/3
48 & 50 Castle St	Ref. 15/19/4
52, 52a, 54, 56 & 58 Castle St	Ref. 15/19/5

CATHEDRAL CLOSE
Cathedral Church of St Patrick	Ref. 15/20/1
Boundary Wall & Railings	Ref. 15/20/2
Vicar's Houses	Ref. 15/20/3
1 & 2-11 Vicar's Hill	Ref. 15/20/5

CATHEDRAL ROAD
St Patrick's	Ref. 15/20/20
Synod Hall & Sacristy	Ref. 15/20/21
Sexton's Lodge & Gates	Ref. 15/20/23

COLLEGE HILL
Armagh Observatory	Ref. 15/16/3
Dean's Hill	Ref. 15/17/39
Romney Robinson Memorial Dome at Observatory	Ref. 15/16/4
Royal School	Ref. 15/17/38

COLLEGE STREET
1 College St	Ref. 15/17/27A
3 College St (Elim Church)	Ref. 15/17/27
5-7 College Street	Ref. 15/17/26

9-19, 21, 23 & 25 College St   Ref. 15/17/25
First Presbyterian Church Lecture Hall   Ref. 15/16/15

CONVENT ROAD
Convent of the Sacred Heart   Ref. 15/20/30

DAWSON STREET
Market House   Ref. 15/20/19
17 Dawson Street   Ref. 15/20/35

DOBBIN STREET
8,10-44 Dobbin   Ref. 15/18/6
21 Dobbin St   Ref. 15/18/10a
23 Dobbin St   Ref. 15/18/11
Gate House, Old Butter Market   Ref. 15/18/8
Gateway Arch, Old Butter Market   Ref. 15/18/9

ENGLISH STREET
LOWER ENGLISH STREET
15 Lower English St   Ref. 15/16/16

UPPER ENGLISH STREET
Beresford Arms Hotel, 11 Up. English   Ref. 15/17/30
45-55 Upper English Street   Ref. 15/16/5
Northern Bank   Ref. 15/20/15
Northern Bank House   Ref. 15/20/16

HAMILTONSBAWN ROAD
Ballinahone House   Ref. 15/18/23

UPPER IRISH STREET
2,4,6,8,10 & 12 Upper Irish   Ref. 15/19/6

LISANALLY LANE
Stone Cottage   Ref. 15/16/6

LOUGHGALL ROAD
St. Luke's Hospital (Main   Ref. 15/16/9
St. Luke's Hospital (The Hill Block)   Ref. 15/16/10

THE MALL
Armagh Prison, Front Block   Ref. 15/17/16
1 Beresford Row/Sovereign's House   Ref. 15/17/5
2-4 Beresford Row   Ref. 15/17/6

5 Beresford Row	Ref. 15/17/7
6-9 Beresford Row	Ref. 15/17/8
10-11 Beresford Row	Ref. 15/17/9
Boundary Wall enclosing Inner Mall	Ref. 15/17/1
1-5 Charlemont Place	Ref. 15/17/10
Court House	Ref. 15/16/1
1-6 Gaol Square & 21 Barrack Street	Ref. 15/17/17
Glendara, The Mall East	Ref. 15/17/51
1-2 Gosford Place, The Mall West	Ref. 15/17/21
Gospel Hall, The Mall West	Ref. 15/17/19
1-4 Hartford Place, The Mall East	Ref. 15/17/52
5 & 6 Hartford Place	Ref. 15/17/53
7 & 8 Hartford Place	Ref. 15/17/34
2-4 Mallview Terrace, The Mall West	Ref. 15/17/18
Portico Front, County Museum	Ref. 15/17/11
First Presbyterian Church, The Mall West,	Ref. 15/17/20
also steps, gates, walls & railings	Ref. 15/17/20B
The Mall Presbyterian Church (Scotch Church)	Ref. 15/17/22
3 Rokeby Green	Ref. 15/17/24
St Mark's Church	Ref. 15/17/13
1-5 St. Mark's Place	Ref. 15/17/12
Warehouse, The Mall West	Ref. 15/17/23

MARKET STREET

| Armagh Technical Institution | Ref. 15/20/4 |

MONAGHAN ROAD

| Umgola House & conservatory & front gates, | |
| side gate & | Ref. 15/19/14 |

NEWRY ROAD

| Greenfield | Ref. 15/18/22 |

OGLE STREET

| 18,20 & 22 Ogle St | Ref. 15/19/8a-c |

PALACE & GROUNDS

The Bishop's Palace	Ref. 15/18/16
Private Chapel	Ref. 15/18/17
Coach Yard and Stables	Ref. 15/18/18
Gardener's House	Ref. 15/18/14
Glass House	Ref. 15/18/20

| Palace Farm, off Keady Road | Ref. 15/19/13 |
| The Rokeby Obelisk | Ref. 15/18/21 |

PORTADOWN ROAD

Avon Lodge, Dean's	Ref. 15/17/47
16 Portadown Rd.	Ref. 15/1/23
'Sunnymead' & conservatory & gates	Ref. 15/17/59

RUSSELL STREET

4 Russell	Ref. 15/17/49
5 Russell St	Ref. 15/17/50
7 Russell St	Ref. 15/17/34
6 & 8 Russell St	Ref. 15/17/32
10 & 12-22 Russell St	Ref. 15/17/33

SCOTCH STREET

22-30 Scotch Street	Ref. 15/18/1
32 & 34 Scotch St	Ref. 15/18/2
36 Scotch St	Ref. 15/18/3
38 Scotch St	Ref. 15/18/4
40 & 42 Scotch St	Ref. 15/18/5
78 Scotch Street (Northern Bank)	Ref. 15/19/1

TOWER HILL

Charles Shiel's Institution	Ref. 15/17/46
East Administration Block, Tower Hill Hosp.	Ref. 15/17/45
West Administration Block, Tower Hill Hosp.	Ref. 15/17/44

VICTORIA STREET

Armagh Savings Bank, 1 Victoria	Ref. 15/17/42
3,5,7 & 9 Victoria St	Ref. 15/17/61a-d
12 Victoria St	Ref. 15/17/43
14 & 16-24 Victoria St & front boundary wall	Ref. 15/17/55
26 & 28-36 Victoria St	Ref. 15/17/56

Classical

1	Parapet	26	Balcony	51	Panel		
2	Coping	27	Quoins (stepped)	52	Jamb		
3	Blocking Course	28	String course	53	Dado panel		
4	Cornice	29	Aedicule	54	Stile		
5	Corona	30	Cornice	55	Threshold		
6	Modillions	31	Patera	56	Weather vane		
7	Dentils	32	Frieze	57	Cupola		
8	Diocletian (blind window)	33	Architrave	58	Bellcast		
9	Oculus	34	Cap (ionic)	59	Belvedere or lantern		
10	Lunette (blind)	35	Shaft	60	Cap		
11	Venetian window	36	Base	61	Corbel		
12	Pediment (open/scrolled)	37	Carriage arch	62	Shaft		
13	Pediment (segmental)	38	Keystone	63	Balustrade		
14	Pediment (open)	39	Extrados (stepped)	64	Hip		
15	Swag	40	Voussoirs (cabled)	65	Pediment (broken)		
16	Vertically sliding box sash	41	Abutment	66	Cartouche (in tympanum)		
17	Crown mould	42	Intrados	67	Dormer (segmental head)		
18	Console	43	Inpost	68	Acroterlon		
19	Bed mould	44	Jambs (stepped)	69	Chimney stack		
20	Reveal	45	Rustication	70	Attic		
21	Meeting rail	46	Hood/canopy	71	Second floor		
22	Glazing bars	47	Fanlight	72	First floor		
23	Pane	48	Head	73	Piano nobile		
24	Sill	49	Sidelights	74	Basement		
25	Apron panel	50	Muntin				

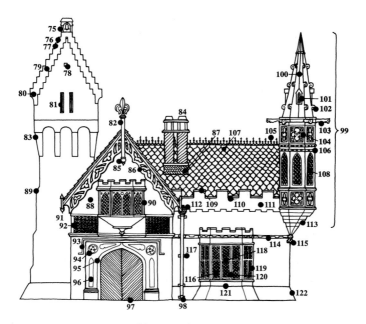

Gothic

75	Bellcote	99	Turret
76	Crow step	100	Fleche
77	Skew gable	101	Lucame
78	Vent	102	Crocket
79	Kneeler	103	Gargoyle
80	Skew corbel	104	Tablet mould quatrefoil
81	Loop	105	Ridge (crested)
82	Finial	106	Cable mould
83	Machiolations	107	Slating (fishtail)
84	Tudor chimneys	108	Lancet
85	Pendant with boss	109	Merlon
86	Bargeboard (fretted)	110	Crenelle
87	Herringbone brickwork	111	Parapet (embattled)
88	Crossgable	112	Hopper/head
89	Buttress (stepped)	113	Corbel
90	Oriel window	114	Billet mould
91	Soffit (eaves)	115	Boss
92	Diaper panel	116	Quarry glazing
93	Label mould	117	Ears
94	Spandrel with trefoil	118	Transom
95	Ogee arch	119	Casement
96	Niche	120	Mullion
97	Doors- diagonally sheeted	121	Bay window (canted)
98	Rainwater shoe	122	Plinth (battered)

217

NOTES

NOTES

NOTES

NOTES

NOTES

222